THE SQUEEZE

A Novel Approach to Business Sustainability

By Gary Langenwalter

with Foreword by Robert W. "Doc" Hall

Society of Manufacturing Engineers
Dearborn, Michigan

Library of Congress Catalog Card Number: 2006932796
International Standard Book Number: 0-87263-850-2

Additional copies may be obtained by contacting:
Society of Manufacturing Engineers
Customer Service
One SME Drive, P.O. Box 930
Dearborn, Michigan 48121
1-800-733-4763
www.sme.org

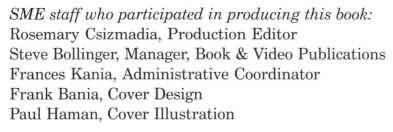

SME staff who participated in producing this book:
Rosemary Csizmadia, Production Editor
Steve Bollinger, Manager, Book & Video Publications
Frances Kania, Administrative Coordinator
Frank Bania, Cover Design
Paul Haman, Cover Illustration

Printed in the United States of America on recycled paper

Contents

Foreword

Business novels are written to explain a major change in a setting that executives can relate to—illustrating how it might actually work in a real company, and how an executive, beset by many diverse concerns and distractions, might lead such a change. By making abstract ideas come alive, they serve a real purpose. Pontificating about them is almost always useless. Few of us can easily picture how an abstract idea will work in practice.

Several dry abstractions play out in this novel. First, the ecological challenge to us all is serious, and seriously underestimated. Brookings Manufacturing, after much pawing and snorting, gets off to a great start.

Second, properly approached, becoming environmentally sustainable does not harm the financial bottom line. If waste and pollution are eliminated at the source, costs are sure to decrease, and if customers prefer a green company, sales may rise. That's always a nifty financial combination.

Third, lean manufacturing and lean process thinking are really ways to eliminate waste in operations, business processes, marketing, and everywhere else—a change in business strategy, not just a set of tools. Eliminating waste is almost always accompanied by use of less material and less energy. Using less of everything and simplifying the processes in which they are used has an important collateral effect. It creates fewer opportunities to proliferate waste, including the environmental kind. Improvements begin to reinforce one another. The benefits begin slowly, but accumulate into a very big overall effect.

Fourth, the heart of any organization is its people. The most pressing problem for 30% of executives is recruiting good people; an additional 28% of executives say that it is motivating people. When an organization starts reflecting the deepest values of its employees, which is the well-being of their families, it unleashes motivation and creativity that have lain untapped for years. The employees treat their customers and suppliers with the same respect that the company shows for them, which fundamentally shifts those relationships for the better. Finally, the employees take these new values into other aspects of their lives (for example to other companies whose products they use), again multiplying their effect.

Thinking managers easily see the connection between lean and green. For example, almost 20 years ago the president of an industrial chemical company asked me to speak to his management team and sales force about returnable containers and small lot sizes. The company adopted the policy of shipping small lots in returnable containers as a condition of purchase, refusing customers that did not agree. Distribution and logistics had to be substantially overhauled at modest cost, but they did it to prevent their hazmat barrels from going to landfills where they would present future site clean up liabilities. The policy turned out to save money for the company and most of its customers too, by cutting the amount of working capital tied up in inventory and reducing the expense of treating hazardous materials.

That's the bare facts, but unembellished with drama. The president, a rabid football fan, proclaimed the need for this policy in a meeting held on a football Saturday afternoon, to employees who would have preferred to be watching a game. One could have heard a pin drop. "He has to be serious," they thought.

That episode was a cultural jolt to the working culture of the company. Learning to think lean, and learning to think green, requires changing lifelong instincts and habits. Many of our learning experiences include significant emotional trauma. Old ways and old temptations lurk about, waiting to emerge from hiding every time we are tested. That too, is part of Adam Brookings' story. It's an adventure into a different kind of business counterculture—learning to lead a very different kind of company in a different kind of way. Only Adam is a rebel with a cause, much larger than himself.

Because of this, no novel about sustainability would be complete without personal drama and ethical issues. Business ethics (an oxymoron?) and personal responsibility are the behavioral underpinnings of both lean operations and sustainability. Ethics comes down to nobility of purpose, consequences of real processes, and integrity of real people. But presented in the abstract, this is tedious. We need stories that make it come alive.

Projecting yourself into the role of the protagonist undergoing personal crisis, you wonder whether he will face down his demons, yield to temptation, erupt in anger, or sneakily retaliate against those trying to undermine his environmental and social initiatives, and his company besides. Those working toward sustainability have to put aside petty commercial rivalry and collaborate with those who will join in. That becomes obvious to those who are into it, but it's a bland description of an emotional roller coaster. It's much livelier to illustrate how a real leader on this journey deflects malicious attacks, whether they are brazen or subtle.

And finally, *The Squeeze* illustrates leadership—taking people into the unknown, toward a level and type of performance where many fear to venture. As a leader, Adam Brookings seems mature beyond his years, but he demonstrates "the right stuff." So buckle up to read a tale that is partly an adventure story, and partly a 21st-century adult version of old morality fables.

—Robert W. "Doc" Hall
Professor Emeritus, Indiana University

Preface

Why would an otherwise sane person, one who has written several business reference texts and professional development courses, write a business novel? Because it seemed to be the best way to help the most people understand the true essence of sustainability—the way it touches people's deepest and most powerful places. And why choose a manufacturing company as the setting? That's where I have spent my professional career. I deliberately left the company's location and product line vague, so readers can project more easily how sustainability can fit to any industry—including non-profit and government entities.

It is my hope that you, the reader, will extrapolate this story and apply it to your own company, your own community, and begin your sustainability journey as quickly as possible.

Almost all authors thank their editors and publishers. I also wish to, because Steve Bollinger and Rosemary Csizmadia have been really wonderful people to work with. Thanks, Steve and Rosemary. Thanks also go to Mark Tomlinson and Bruce MacKender for inspiring me to write this novel.

Thanks go to Jim Newcomer, who insisted that we create the characters first, and to Jill Sughrue and Hal Busch for helping flesh out the original character set. For her editing, thanks go again to Jill, and to Jim for spending hours helping me refine and streamline sections and chapters so they worked together.

The greatest fear of most people is speaking in public. But unless the speech is recorded, it is soon forgotten. Writing is much worse because once in print, the life of the written word goes on indefinitely. What has been this author's biggest fear is saying something foolish or wrong in print. Therefore, I am grateful to the people who read earlier versions of this novel and made countless suggestions for improvement (or cheered me on, which was equally important). The "tough love" award for constructive criticism goes to Darcy Hitchcock; it took me three days to re-read her suggestions for improvement. But once I could look at them objectively, I incorporated 90% of them. Thanks, Darcy! And thanks to Dick Pedersen, Jim Warren, Al Lapierre, Jenni Cawein, Charles Martin, Steve Bell, Kent Moorehead, and Jeanne Longley, for your feedback and suggestions.

I hope you will tell me about your sustainability journey. It's your gift to future generations and yourself. You can contact me at glangenwalter@confluencepoint.com.

About the Author

Gary Langenwalter is a founding partner of ConfluencePoint, a sustainability consulting firm based in Portland, Oregon. With a client list that includes the U.S. Navy, Hasbro, and R. R. Donnelley, as well as several smaller companies, he has led numerous workshops on sustainability, Lean, and enterprise information systems. He is completing an MTS at Boston University and is chair of the Oregon Interfaith Global Warming Campaign.

Gary has taught classes at eight universities and created professional development courses for the American Management Association and the American Institute of Certified Public Accountants. He is also the author of two professional books. He is an experienced manager, consultant, and entrepreneur, and has held executive and management positions with Manufacturing Consulting Partners,

Pricewaterhouse Coopers, KPMG Peat Marwick, Faultless Caster Corporation, and Unisys.

Possessing an M.B.A. in Organization Behavior from Michigan State University, Gary Langenwalter also has a B.A. in Industrial Management from the University of Oregon and a diploma in International Business from the Nederlands Opleidings Instituut voor het Buitenland, Breukelen, The Netherlands. He is a member of the Oregon Natural Step Network, the Zero Waste Alliance, Organization Development Network, the Association for Manufacturing Excellence, APICS—the Association for Operations Management, and the Society of Manufacturing Engineers.

CHAPTER 1
Desperation

We were only three-quarters of the way through the Monday morning staff meeting and my headache had already started. I get headaches every Monday now, but this week's was the earliest and the worst. After the routine updating of new quotations (one), new customer orders (none), shipments (two), new products (none), and financial status (abysmal), we were still talking about the same problems as last week, and the week before, and the week before that. There seemed to be no way out, and each week the problems were getting just a little worse. Now I know why Dad had been so tired when he came home from work. It sounds almost unfeeling, but in a perverse way I almost envy him—gone now from the daily pressure of having to do the impossible in a ridiculously short timeframe with insufficient resources. Luckily, he did not suffer; he just collapsed from a heart attack Monday afternoon eight weeks ago. When Mom called to tell me, she begged me, "Adam, please come home and keep the company running." How could I say no?

To be honest, when I said "Yes," my only intention had been to tidy up the company and sell it so Mom could retire without worrying about financial matters. That is what I had told Dad he should do. So that is what I came back to do. Unfortunately, what I found was a company that no intelligent person would want to buy—too many problems and no way out. If the company tried to continue to keep the plant open, it would whimper itself away, slowly but surely, until it closed its doors.

Back at the staff meeting there were seven of us in the executive conference room. We call it that to give it a little more cachet, but it really is nothing special. The carpet has seen better days; the table has a couple of permanent coffee stains; the chairs were really nice 15 years ago—you get the picture. Since I am now the CEO, I sit at the head of the table, with a large oil painting of my dad hanging right behind me. It sounds weird, but I am convinced I can sense his presence as I am sitting here, in "his" chair.

Wayne Doernbacher, the plant manager, began, "We're making our shipments on time—no late shipments again last week. Our quality is excellent—no customer returns or credits, and everything is falling well into the green range. Our plant is clean and safe—no injuries for more than two years. People are cross-trained and very flexible; the Lean effort has paid off big time. On the surface everything looks pretty good. But our union knows we're having trouble."

I asked, "What are they saying?".

Wayne replied, "Well, they know that Electronic Products and Industrial Electronics (they are our major competitors) have closed their plants here and outsourced manufacturing to China. And they're scared stiff because they can tell that we're not as busy as we once were. I've told them we want to keep going, but they can see the trend. They smell another layoff coming in a few months. I can't BS them and tell them everything is wonderful, because it isn't. And it seems like the workers don't have the energy, the spark they had when we started our Lean journey five years ago. They're still working hard, but they don't have the new ideas like they used to." (*Lean* is a way of improving performance by focusing on what customers want, what adds value to them, and then viewing all other processes and materials that do *not* add value as waste. It uses teams to create and implement ideas for continuously improving a company's performance.)

I sensed some personal desperation behind Wayne's statements. He was 52 and had come to work for my dad 30 years ago. If our plant closed, he probably could not find another job as a plant manager anywhere in the area because most of the manufacturing plants had closed. But he was too young to retire. His workers were not the only ones who were scared—he was, too. He and his wife Julie had been almost like second parents to me while I was growing up. Back then, he was "Uncle Wayne."

Wayne concluded softly, "So how do I motivate my work force and bring back the spark?" This was not really a rhetorical question, just one that nobody, including me, could answer.

Tom McCarthy, the chief financial officer, spoke next. "Our profits keep slipping. Right now we're down to a 1.5% return on assets, making a lower return on our investment than if we sold everything and put the money into government bonds! Our variances are killing us. Purchase price variance is going through the roof. Overhead absorption is dangerously low. We're really in trouble, and it keeps getting worse. We have to get those variances back in line!" There was silence in the room. Each week Tom complained about the variances. Sometimes Wayne would challenge him, "Tom, how do the variances help my foremen make better decisions?" And Tom would give some sort of answer, but whatever he said did not seem to make sense to anyone else, and it sure did not make any sense to me.

Tom was 52, a certified public accountant who had left the rat race of public accounting 20 years ago and settled down to raise his young family. He was honest, hard-working, and personally as generous as a human being could get. But when he put on his controller's green eyeshade, he was brutal. He had been described as someone who could squeeze a nickel so hard that a dollar's worth of change would fall out, and then he would squeeze it again for what was left! He was convinced that if he let our costs slip just 2%, the company would go out of business. Given our current financial situation, he was probably right.

Mary Pulaski, the VP of materials and logistics, responded, "Our purchase price variance is out of control because our raw materials costs are going through the roof. Have you gassed up your car recently? Have you paid your natural gas bill at home? We mold the plastic housings for our product—they use oil from the same barrel as your car. We heat the plant and the ovens with natural gas. We pay truckers to bring all our raw materials in, and to take our finished products out, and their cost for diesel fuel just keeps rising. So tell me, Tom, how are we supposed to keep those costs down?!" and she glared at him.

Mary was one tough lady—she had succeeded in a profession that was dominated by men when she entered it. At 43, she still had half her career in front of her, and with her M.B.A. from the University of Michigan, she got occasional calls from headhunters. I was worried that she might give them permission to start presenting her paperwork to another company. With her knowledge of suppliers, her analytical mind, and her connections in the industry, she would be a big loss.

I interceded, "I know we're all frustrated, but yelling at each other isn't going to help. Let's get another cup of coffee before we continue." That is when the headache started to throb.

After the break, Mary continued, "You all know I was 100% behind the Lean journey we started five years ago. I still am, but now I'm starting to think we might want to examine some of its unwritten assumptions—like cheap energy. Maybe we need to go to less frequent deliveries of some items to minimize fuel costs, which would increase our inventories. I'm not saying we *should*, I'm just saying I'm open to discussion at this point. But the rest of Lean—like minimizing waste, and listening to the customer, and quality, and flow . . . I'm still all for that."

"You guys are all missing the point!" burst out Jeff Holland, VP sales and marketing, who had been fidgeting in his chair. "Our product line is old and getting older. The main reason sales are down is our competitors are starting to bring out new products with lower prices. We keep trying to sell 'Made in the U.S.A.' and all that, but it only goes so far. When are we going to get some new products? When are they going to be price-competitive with the ones our competitors are importing from China? My salesmen used to be proud to represent Brookings Manufacturing; now they're embarrassed. And I spend more than half my time doing damage control; that's a lot higher than it was when I hired in here. We gotta do something, and do it NOW, dammit!" He slammed his hand down on the table.

At age 38, Jeff did not have the same level of personal investment in the company as the rest of the executive staff. After getting his M.B.A. at night, he thought he knew more about how to run a company than all the rest of us combined. Actually, he knew less about running a company than anyone else in the room, except me. All he focused on was his bonus and what he could buy with it. He lived in a house that he could barely afford, drove a flashy new Escalade® with all the trimmings, and golfed twice a week at the best country club in town. If confidence and bluster alone could sell products, he would have been rolling in dough. I was not sure how much longer he would be with us, even if we could turn the company around. This was his second marriage; his first had ended five years ago when his wife caught him with her best friend. His new wife was also in sales—very sharp, and very professional. I almost wished we could have her on our staff rather than him, but that was not possible.

Our young VP of engineering, Walter Chen, spoke next. "We haven't had any time for new product development. Those new European Union standards that required us to eliminate all lead, cadmium, and other toxics from all our products have really drained us. My engineers have spent so much time redesigning and re-sourcing to insure that we can keep selling in Europe that we haven't made any real progress on our new products. If I push my guys any harder, they'll quit. They haven't had a raise for awhile—I know, nobody else has had one either—but I can feel the discontent rising. If a recruiter calls them, I'm not sure what they'll say. And right now, we can't afford to lose any of them. We're already using the best 3D program around for mechanical design. I don't know how to get more done, and we're falling behind."

Walter was the resident genius—a master's degree in electrical engineering from Massachusetts Institute of Technology and three patents to his name. Why he chose to come here was simple—he had married Katherine Gutmacher, whom he met while they were both in school in Boston, and she insisted on living here because her parents' health was declining. He had come to the U.S. on a student visa. It was not like they married just so he could stay in the country, contrary to some of the gossip in the redneck bars at the edge of town. Anyone who watched them together would see that they were very much in love. And now with two children, he seemed truly happy. But he was clearly very worried. Yes, he could get a job elsewhere in a New York minute, but that would mean moving the family, which would be very hard on Katherine, their children, and her parents.

Tom, ever the CFO, added, "I almost hesitate to say this, but our bank's senior VP was showing me some ratios from Robert Morris Associates last week, and our numbers look pretty weak compared to industry averages. He was asking, just asking mind you, if we were thinking about moving manufacturing overseas. Otherwise, we need to show them how we can honestly forecast that we'll remain profitable, so they can continue our loans."

There was a period of silence. This discussion had surfaced at more than one staff meeting since I joined the company, and from what I could gather, at many, many staff meetings prior. But this was the most open acknowledgement of what we were all thinking. It was the tentative voice of the collective fear that our company was in the beginning stages of its death spiral, and nobody knew how to stop it.

Barbara Joiner, VP of human resources, finally spoke, very softly. "We've been through these issues so many times I could almost say each person's statement for them. There has to be something that we're not seeing here. Otherwise, I don't hold much hope for the company to still be in business in five years, or maybe even three. I can't put my finger on it, but I think there's something we're not seeing."

Barbara was our resident bleeding-heart liberal. She started with the company as a factory records clerk right out of high school, then kept working as she got her bachelor's degree. Her parents, who thought a woman's place was in the home, would not help her with her education. My dad recognized Barbara's potential and encouraged her by allowing flexibility in her hours and schedule. He and Mom were both cheering when she received her degree six years later (in English literature, of all subjects). She transferred into personnel, as we called it then, and then went on to earn her M.A. from Antioch in organizational development. At 49, she may have been soft-spoken, but she had a deep understanding of people, which we really appreciated.

I felt an overwhelming amount of pressure to say or do something wise, something that would start moving us out of the box we were in. Here I was, completely ill-prepared for running a company, with the jobs of 300 people riding on my woefully small shoulders! Life is just not fair! I suddenly remembered my boss in Massachusetts talking about the off-site meetings for planning that their executives had attended. He said the off-sites helped them find creative solutions to difficult problems. So in desperation I said, "These topics are too much for us to cover in a Monday morning staff meeting. Let's plan to spend a day on them, all day, off-site. Can you all make it two weeks from this coming Saturday?"

I received several quizzical looks, five heads nodding, and one "I'll have to reschedule something." So I continued, "Fine, let's plan to start at 9:00 a.m.; we should be finished by 5:00."

The meeting was over; we all filed out. And all I could think was, "Where am I going to get the rabbit to pull out of a hat in two weeks?"

When I got back to my office, I asked Marie, my secretary, to book us at a good off-site conference center that was reasonably priced. She had been my dad's secretary for years. Marie knew how things really worked and kept me out of a lot of potholes, quicksand, and bad places. I probably did not have to add the "reasonably priced," because we operated that way automatically. What other people considered "frugal" we thought of as reckless squandering of resources.

The rest of the day was thankfully busy; it kept my conscious mind off my dilemma. I was reviewing new quotations, signing forms for the bank and the government, meeting with our shop steward to try to assure him we were not planning to cut jobs, answering the phone, and talking with our lawyer. But my subconscious was working on the underlying problem all afternoon. By the time I left the office at 6:00, I was completely whipped.

I staggered into my mom's house and collapsed on the couch in the living room with a weak, "Hi, Mom." I had been staying there ever since Dad died, sleeping in my old room, because I did not have the time or energy to go look for a place to live yet (and hadn't even cleaned out my condo in Boston). Besides, Mom enjoyed having me around—she kept telling me the house would be way too empty if I weren't living there. So I stayed. And she was pretty cool, too, giving me my personal space and respecting me as an adult.

As we sat down to dinner, Mom asked, "Adam, what's wrong?"

"Mom, we're in trouble. Wayne, Tom and everybody else are really concerned about how we're going to keep the company going. Forget 'concerned'—we're scared stiff. We've been having the same discussion for weeks, and the despair underneath the words just keeps building. Nobody has any answers; it just keeps slowly getting worse. I didn't know what to do, and I *still* don't. But at the end of today's staff meeting, I said we'd have a full-day, off-site planning meeting two weeks from Saturday. I don't know what an off-site meeting *looks* like, let alone how to run one! But I felt like I had to do *something!* And I don't have a clue what we'll do at that off-site besides talking through the same stuff we've talked through before. And I don't even know where to turn for any ideas. I have never felt so hopeless . . ."

Somehow I kept control of my emotions. I continued, "I don't know what we'd do if one of our key people left. We can't afford to lose any of them right now. But they can see we're in trouble, and I'm afraid that they're starting to update their resumes and contact their friends."

"The worst part of it, Mom, is not what will happen to you. The company wouldn't have to actually close; most likely, we would just outsource manufacturing overseas like everyone else and keep marketing and engineering here. So you'll do fine. But if we have to lay off our plant—that's 60% of our people—they will have no decent choices left. There are no other high-paying jobs; all the other manufacturers have left town. Wayne would have no options at all—who else would hire him at 52, when all he's ever done is manufacturing? Where will Annie get a job that pays enough—she's barely making it from paycheck to paycheck right now."

Annie was my first love as a junior in high school. She married right out of high school and had divorced her husband a year after their baby was born. Now she was a single mom with a young son and not many marketable job skills other than experience on our assembly line and with leading Lean team meetings.

There. I had finally told Mom the worst. She reached across the dinner table, gently covered each of my hands with hers, and looked directly into my eyes. "I know, Adam, I know. I've known for months. I think this is what caused Chris' heart attack. Lord, I miss him!" she said with a small sniff, and a single tear slowly descended down the right side of her face. "But Adam, we'll do the best we can with what we've got. That's all anyone can ask, right? And deep in my heart, I truly believe we'll make it. Chris and I went through times like this before, and somehow we always made it. Funny thing, though, the *way* we made it always looked and turned out different than what we were expecting. So let's just let it go for now. And Adam, please don't take this so seriously. I can't afford to lose you, too. Now let's eat dinner before it gets any colder."

So we did. And somehow, the meatloaf tasted better than it had a few minutes before, the sauce on the green beans seemed a little more piquant, and even the coffee afterward had more flavor than usual. It was probably all psychological, but when you're desperate you cling to every little sign.

After dinner I didn't feel much like going out or even watching TV. What I felt like instead was calling Kelly, my best friend from college. During our sophomore year at Clark, I had shared a dorm suite with her and four others. And while the six of us remained friends, Kelly had become my best friend. She was the sister I never had. Funny, irreverent, compassionate, unpredictable, highly intelligent . . . yeah, that was Kelly. And she had the best listening ear—the absolute best! When I got so stuck that I didn't know which end was up, she would help me get through it somehow. We both were psych majors when we met. She finally majored in geography with a minor in psych. Somehow I had the sense she understood people better than I did. Maybe that's why I majored in psych—to find out if there really was a way to understand people.

But I would have to wait for a while to call her due to the three-hour time difference. Kelly had taken a job in the marketing department of an insurance company in Portland, Oregon after we graduated, because she loved the mountains and the ocean. "Come visit me," she had asked, then almost begged. So I had. And she was right—it was beautiful out there! We had driven up to Timberline Lodge on a drop-dead gorgeous day in July—85° F and sunny—and taken the chair lift, then walked back down in the snow fields wearing t-shirts and shorts! And the view—oh, what a view! She entreated me to move out to Oregon. But I did not want to move that far from my parents, so I stayed in Boston. Yes, it is still a long way from the upper Midwest to Boston, but at least we were both in the same time zone. And I liked Boston—it was a great place for college students and young professionals. Harvard Square on a Friday night is an experience like nothing else—a combination of a zoo, a graduate course in Marxism and Capitalism, a night club with live entertainment, and an artists' bazaar. Ethnic food? Try Harvard Square or almost any place in the Boston area.

I spent a couple of hours checking out my latest e-mails and instant messaging some friends. Finally, the grandfather clock in the living room (which my grandfather had actually built with his own hands) chimed 9 p.m. and I called. I caught Kelly on her way home from work, in what Portlanders complained was rush hour. They have no idea how good they have it—they have never seen a *real* rush hour! They should try Boston in November during a snow storm.

"Adam, what's up? Have you found your next girlfriend yet?" she asked.

"Hi, Kels. I'll find her about the same time you find your one and only true love. But that's not what I'm calling about. Could you fly out here this weekend?"

"You're kidding me, right?" But her voice said that she knew I was not joking. She had always been able to read me like an open book.

"No. I'm not kidding at all. I really need a day or two with my best friend, face to face. In the staff meeting this morning, we basically all admitted out loud that the company is dying, and we don't have any idea how to keep it alive. So I, like an idiot, scheduled us to have a one-day, off-site planning meeting two weeks from this weekend. And I don't know where to start. But what I *do* know is if we walk out of it feeling the way we do now, the company probably *won't* survive. And I'm suddenly responsible for creating a miracle. So, can you come out for the weekend? I'll pay for your ticket and you can stay here with us."

"Adam, I think I can come. I'll have to back out of a couple of promises I made here, but it's no biggie. I'll be giving up a weekend of some primo skiing, so you'll owe me big time." (I could hear her grinning as she said that.)

"Thanks, Kels," I said, at once relieved. "You don't know how much this means to me."

"I'll find out how much it really means to you when I collect on what you owe me." I could hear her grin again, and it made me smile. That felt so good—I hadn't smiled much ever since that initial phone call from Mom. She continued, "And it's the least I can do for my best friend."

So we chatted a bit more, then she had to hang up. Why was it that I always felt better after talking with Kelly? I was pretty sure she felt the same way about me; she would call me when she needed a listening ear too. I had even flown out to Portland for the weekend to comfort her after a nasty breakup last fall.

When I went downstairs to find Mom, she was just getting off a phone call with a friend. "Mom, I just got off the phone with Kelly. She'll be here this weekend."

"I'm glad, Adam. You seem more relaxed now." Mom knew me better than I knew myself. I did not even notice I was nervous, but she was right.

"Yeah, I guess I am. I hadn't even noticed it. I hope some of this 'new relaxed Adam' goes to work with me tomorrow. The rest of the staff is pretty uptight at this point."

"It will, Adam. Trust me," she assured me.

Surprisingly enough, when I got to work the next day, I was still calm. It seemed to rub off on my staff. Marie even commented, "You seem more confident today." Well, I guess I was more confident. Maybe it came from Mom's assurance that she and Dad had weathered times like this before. But I think it mostly came from knowing Kelly would be here for the weekend. The rest of the week was nothing special, just day-to-day high-pressure routine. I noticed I was starting to look forward to picking Kelly up on Friday afternoon. She was going to have to miss a day of work due to the time change flying east; she would be arriving at 5:15 p.m. It was really going to be good to see her; it had been way too long. Phone calls are not the same as being in the same room with your best friend.

Optimist that I am, I was at the airport at 5:00 Friday evening. Her flight was actually early, just like the computer said. When I first saw her walking down the concourse toward security, I was almost breathless. Her dark brown hair was longer, tied back in a pony tail. Her eyes sparkled with life and joy. She was wearing a long-sleeved sweater in various shades of blue, green, and white, and designer jeans, which fit her very nicely. When had my gangly, self-conscious friend Kelly become the stunning, confident woman in the prime of her life who was walking toward me? Then she saw me and ran the last few yards into my hug. It was so good to see her again! I have hugged lots of people in my life, but only one person hugs like Kelly. When she hugs me, it seems like our bodies sort of meld together. This hug was a Kelly Special! Then she leaned back, with our arms still around each other, and said, "Hi, Adam. I've missed you." I could have stayed there, looking at her slightly freckled face and her expressive brown eyes, for the next hour or two. The last time I had seen her was at Dad's funeral. But I was not able to really "see" her then; I was too numb from grief, and there were too many other distractions. I just knew she was at my side most of the time.

"Hi, Kelly. I'm so glad you came. I've really missed you, too." The words sounded trite, but she knew that I meant every one of them with every fiber of my being. As we walked toward baggage claim, I asked, "How's your family?"

Her father is a professor of history at Notre Dame; her mother teaches middle school in South Bend. Kelly is the oldest of four children. She surprised everyone in her family by deciding to go to Clark University in Worcester, Massachusetts, rather than Notre Dame. She wanted to attend a small liberal arts college in New England that had a strong psychology program.

"My parents are great, thanks, and so are Kaitlin, Danny, and Michael. Kaitlin and George are expecting a baby this summer—isn't that exciting? And Danny's talking about going on for his Ph.D. in English after he graduates from Notre Dame this spring. Michael is in his second year at Purdue, still majoring in engineering and girls, but not necessarily in that order," she chuckled. "How's your mom?"

"She's doing better than I would have expected. I guess having me living with her has kept some of the loneliness away. I wouldn't feel right moving back to Boston yet. Besides, the company really needs me right now, not that I can do anything to help."

"I never thought I would hear you say those words about your dad's company 'needing you.' You always seemed like you didn't want any part of it."

"You're right, as usual. But things change, I guess. The first week or two, I was just trying to get it ready for sale. I started to realize that if we sold it, the new owner would probably ship the manufacturing overseas, followed by the engineering, causing most of the jobs to disappear. I have friends who work there, who depend on those jobs, and they would be hurt really badly if the manufacturing went to China. I'll tell you more about it in the car."

"Okay," she said. We stood beside each other in comfortable silence while we waited for the horn to announce the arrival of the luggage from her flight. After collecting her bag, we headed for short-term parking and the Chrysler 300m my father had owned.

She looked at the car questioningly, so I remarked, "It's an excellent car. You know my dad; he would never buy an import. He did everything he could to keep jobs here. Funny, he never thought of this as an import, even though he bought it after Daimler bought Chrysler."

I called Mom to let her know we were on our way home and pulled onto the highway. "Do you remember when we were sophomores in the suite, the evening all of us told about our first true love?" I asked Kelly.

"Yes," she said.

"Well, mine was Annie Zabransky. I was a junior, she was a sophomore. I bumped into her in the cafeteria when I was watching a cheerleader walk by; I spilled my tray all over her. Anyhow, we started talking, then I asked her to a movie and just like that we were each other's first true love. When I left for Clark, she hooked up with Jake Miller. They got married right out of high school and had a son a year later. Unfortunately, Jake wasn't ready for marriage and was even less ready for fatherhood. So they got divorced a year or so after the baby was born.

"Annie works on the assembly line at the plant now. She's really good at what she does, but she has no skills that would get her a job anywhere else in town at anything close to the pay she earns with us. And she does really earn it. So if the plant shuts down, I have just condemned Annie to moving back home with her mom for the rest of her life, because she couldn't afford to keep her own apartment. And there is something else. She's been taking advantage of the company's tuition reimbursement program and attending night school at the local community college. She still has a year to go to get her associate's degree. She's been kicked in the teeth by life once already and is doing everything she can to build a new life for herself. I just can't be the person who kicks her in the teeth again."

It was silent for a little while, and then Kelly replied, "Yeah, it isn't just about the numbers, is it? It's really about the people."

"During Dad's wake and funeral, so many people came up to me and told me they hoped I would keep the business going. I was like their hero, the cowboy riding into town to make things right. *Me*, of all people! I'm only 27, I have a degree in psychology and five years' experience working in sales for a distribution company in Boston, and suddenly I'm supposed to be more brilliant than my dad? I feel so under-qualified and unprepared. And it's not like there's anybody else who can do it any better. Even Dad, with all his skills and wisdom, couldn't turn the company around. We're dying, Kelly, slowly but surely, we're dying. And it hurts . . . it hurts almost as bad as losing Dad!"

Her hand reached over to rest on my shoulder. She was too smart to try and fix anything; she knew it was enough to listen and understand. And it was. How grateful I was that she didn't try to tell me what to do without knowing any more than I had told her. We rode the rest of the way home in silence. As we pulled in the driveway, I turned to look at her face. Her eyes were slightly moist. She had never looked more beautiful, more vulnerable, more real.

"Kelly, sorry I just dumped on you during the drive home. I was planning to wait until after dinner, but I just couldn't keep it in any longer. I am so glad you're here. I needed you more than I was willing to admit to myself."

"I understand, Adam. We can keep talking after dinner when we're alone again. For now, let's go in so I can tell your mom hello." And with that, she stepped out of the car and said in a bad parody of a spoiled rock star, "And when will that lazy bellhop bring my luggage (pronounce with fake French accent, "luh gazh") to my suite?" I cracked up. She knew just how to break the tension.

Ignoring the raw March weather, Mom opened the door with a big smile on her face. "Kelly, it's so good to see you again. Thanks for coming."

"It's good to see you again, Mrs. Brookings." And they hugged while the bellhop shivered patiently behind them holding the luggage safely above the wet steps.

I put her bag in the guest room, then rejoined them in the kitchen. I noticed the dining table was set with the crystal and good china. "Nice," I thought. As we sat down to eat, Mom asked me to say grace. I was a little surprised, but didn't want to decline, because her faith had kept her going since Dad's death. So I sort of fumbled through it, feeling rather self-conscious. I realized it was Mom's way of saying publicly that I was now the man of the house, at least for the time being. My feelings of inadequacy resurfaced for a bit. But Mom and Kelly apparently didn't notice; they were busy talking about all sorts of things, ranging from how Kelly liked Portland, to how Mom was coping with Dad being gone, and everything in between.

After dinner, Kelly helped Mom clean up the kitchen while I checked my e-mails. One from Wayne was a bit unsettling—an Environmental Protection Agency (EPA) auditor was going to be coming by the plant at 9:00 a.m. Monday. So I called Wayne at home. He suspected that one of the people who had bought an upscale house in the new neighborhood near our plant was trying to harass us a bit to encourage us to move our manufacturing operation elsewhere. So they had tipped the EPA about some sort of odor coming from our stacks. Most of the new neighbors are decent people, but some have been a real pain. I mean, our plant has been in the same place for 25 years and their houses were built two years ago. So if they didn't want to live next to us, they shouldn't have bought there, right? But that's not the way it works, not here in the real world. Homeowners have a lot more clout than us dirty manufacturing companies. This *is* the real world in our town.

I headed back downstairs to the family room where Mom and Kelly were still talking. The last time they had been able to chat was five years ago, at Thanksgiving our senior year of college. I had brought Kelly home with me (again) and Mom and Dad had thought maybe we were getting serious. It took a long time for us to convince them we were just best friends.

At 9:30 that night Mom excused herself and headed upstairs to give us some time together. Kelly got a chair from the kitchen, put it about two feet in front of my knees, then sat down in it, eye to eye with me. We just looked at each other, and then she quietly invited, "Adam, you can tell me. I can handle it."

Her invitation somehow created a safe place, and all the control I had managed to keep tightly in place for the last nine weeks evaporated. I sat there quietly, saying nothing, with tears slowly forming in my eyes. Kelly got up and sat beside me, pulling me to her. I lost it. I had needed to be strong for Mom; I had needed to be strong for the company. I had not had the chance to really, truly grieve Dad's death. And I had not squarely faced my own fears— the fear of failing and causing Dad's company to also die; the fear of letting my classmates, friends, and neighbors down; the fear of . . .

Then I started talking, in semi-coherent phrases, telling her of those fears, of the loneliness, and of how I could never measure up to Dad, all the time looking into her compassionate eyes. She just kept holding me, comforting me. And after I had gotten it all out of my system, she leaned down and kissed me gently on my forehead. "Adam, I don't know how yet, but I really believe things will somehow work out. I've got faith in you."

"I want to believe you, Kelly. And Mom said the same thing, that it would all work out somehow. But I sure can't see how."

"I know, Adam. My family has been in some very difficult situations too, where we couldn't see any way out. And somehow things worked out, often better than we ever could have imagined. I have a feeling this will too."

After I sat back up, she snuggled against me so I could put my right arm around her shoulder. We just sat there for a long time, watching the fire slowly burn down in the fireplace until it was just a few glowing embers. And as we went upstairs to our bedrooms, I felt better than I had felt in the last nine weeks . . . maybe even longer.

Saturday morning I was awake at 8:00, feeling more relaxed than I had felt in years. I got up about 8:30, showered and dressed in a flannel shirt, jeans, and my favorite hiking boots. Smelling coffee, I wandered into the kitchen. Mom was already dressed for the day in jeans and a sweatshirt and fixing breakfast—eggs, bacon, toast, orange juice, and coffee—our traditional Saturday morning breakfast ever since I could remember. As we sat down to eat, Mom guessed that Kelly would be a little later because of the three-hour time difference. Then she asked how the evening had gone. I knew she was interested in my welfare and not prying.

"I finally got to the bottom of some of my grief. Last night was the first time I felt like I could really let go, that I didn't have to be strong."

"Oh, Adam, I'm so sorry that you couldn't do that before."

"Mom, it's okay. You needed me to be here with you, and I needed to keep the company going. Kelly is my best friend, so it's only logical that I should feel comfortable enough with her to finally let go."

"Any plans for this morning?" she asked.

"Yeah, any plans for this morning?" sounded an echo as Kelly walked into the breakfast nook, wearing jeans, her favorite red Clark University sweatshirt, and sneakers. "And any coffee? It's only 6:30 a.m. back in God's country," she continued, smiling a sleepy smile.

"God's country?" asked Mom.

Kelly replied, "That's what a lot of the natives and transplants call the Pacific Northwest. Funny—it's the most non-religious part of the U.S., and they call it 'God's country.' I can see why, though. It's a wonderful place to live."

I said, "To answer your earlier question, Mom, I thought I'd take Kelly over to the plant to show her the place. There won't be anybody working there today, but I'd still like her to see it."

"Sounds good," replied Kelly.

CHAPTER 2
Help from an Unlikely Source

After finishing breakfast on Saturday, Kelly and I headed for the plant. The air was still brisk, with the temperature hovering just about the freezing mark, but the sun shone brightly in the brilliant blue sky. Kelly remarked, "That's more sun than I've seen in three weeks in Portland. I'd forgotten what it looked like."

I unlocked the front door, and then relocked it after we were both inside. Kelly looked around the reception area, "I'm glad you have plants in your reception area. It makes it homier, less sterile."

"Thanks," I replied. "We try to help the place feel less institutional any way we can."

Down the corridor I unlocked a door and then showed her into my office, trying to sound enthusiastic. Kelly had been friends with me far too long; she saw past my outward exuberance. Somehow she knew that, to me, this was still my father's office, and that every time I entered it I compared myself to my father, with Dad always finishing first. I could tell an idea was forming in the back of her mind, but she chose to file it away for later.

Obviously distracted, Kelly had missed a sentence or two of what I had been saying. She asked, "My mind was wandering for a bit; would you repeat what you just said? And before I forget, could we come back here to your office again on the way to the airport tomorrow?"

I replied, "Sure, we can stop by. And it's not like what I was saying was very important, anyway."

"Adam, what you're going through right now is *very* important."

"Thanks, Kelly. That means a lot to me. So anyhow, can I show you the plant, or is this enough?" I was hoping she would want to see the entire facility, but if she didn't want to, I wouldn't insist.

She enthusiastically replied, "Sure, I'd love to see it all."

I took her through the offices first—sales and marketing and customer service, then accounting, engineering, HR, purchasing, and finally scheduling and materials management. When we walked through the cafeteria onto the factory floor, it was lit only by the emergency/off-hours lighting. I walked directly over to the main switches and flipped them on. The area blazed with so much light that our eyes hurt for a moment before they adjusted. "Sorry, I should have told you to close your eyes, and then open them slowly," I said as we both winced.

We started at the receiving dock, then made our way through raw materials storage where barrels of resin are kept for the plastic injection molding machines, on to the electronic subassembly cells with their pick-and-place robots, through the final assembly cells, then rounded out our tour in shipping.

"You know, Adam, I've never been inside a manufacturing company like this before, especially out here where products actually get made. It's exciting and a little like seeing an alien universe, especially those robots—any relation between them and the Star Wars® movies?"

I said with a half grin, "You should see the shop floor when we're actually working—it's like it's alive, its own version of an alien from outer space."

Kelly smiled, "I'd really like that . . . maybe on my next visit?"

"You know," I mused, "these robots may look state-of-the-art, but they are actually anything but that. Dad bought them used about 20 years ago. The newer machines look more like an ink jet printer. These are slow, complex, and less precise. But we haven't had the cash flow to replace them. They're almost a symptom of our company."

"So let's go back to your office and you can tell me what's happening," she said.

On the way back, we stopped in the cafeteria and bought a couple of sodas from the vending machine. When we got back to my office, she sat down in a guest chair. I started to sit behind my desk, then got up and sat in the guest chair beside hers. "I didn't want so much distance between us," I nervously explained.

"So," she said, looking me dead in the eye, "why are you doing this in the first place?"

"Well," I drew a long breath, "here's the deal. Dad had a rare combination—he was a top-flight electrical engineer who also knew how to bring out the best in people. He started his career working for another company in town. The company stayed with older technology, and it is closed now. When he had his idea for his first product, he couldn't get the bank to lend him enough money to start. So Grandpa mortgaged the family farm to the hilt—the farm that had been in the family for four generations. Dad paid Grandpa back as quickly as he could. My aunt Janet took over the family farm and my cousin Vince is following in her footsteps."

"So it's rooted deep in the whole family's history," Kelly said tentatively. "But why you? You never seemed to talk about the company when we were in school."

"Nobody in the family, especially me," I grinned ruefully, "ever expected me to be CEO of Brookings Manufacturing. You know Dad groomed my older brother, Jim, for that position almost from the day he was born. Jim had both the talent and the desire to make the company prosper. He joined the company three years ago after he got his M.B.A. Then just a year later, while driving home from vacation he swerved to avoid hitting a deer and his car hit a tree. You were such a comfort to me all those times I called you on the phone after his death. We were all devastated. Dad had been trying to persuade me to join the company ever since, but I was just not interested.

"My older sister Jillian is married, living in southern California and pregnant with her second child. She's completely focused on her 2-year-old and her next baby, and has no interest in leading the company. There's only one family member left—*me*. And nobody, including me, ever expected it to happen this way."

"But do you know anything about it? You never studied engineering, that's for sure," Kelly said with a concerned look on her face.

"I know," I answered. "But I worked in the factory during summer vacations starting when I was 16, so I know the products and many of the people. I've got a first-hand understanding of what really happens out on the plant floor, in shipping, and in quality, because I was a 'gofer' in all those places for four summers. And after my junior year in college,

Dad made me a customer service assistant, which helped me substantially when I applied for the industrial sales job in Boston. It also gave me a sense of who our customers are and what they need, and maybe that's the most important thing."

"Okay," she said, "and now?"

"As best I can tell, we're slowly dying," I said with a sigh. "Our costs and selling prices are higher than our competitors' who've outsourced their manufacturing to China, and now they're starting to outsource their engineering. We haven't had any real technological breakthroughs in the last decade or so, so we don't have an advantage there anymore. During the staff meeting last Monday morning, each person reported a chronic problem, and I keep getting the feeling they're somehow connected. But even worse, the feeling of despair is starting to permeate our staff. It will kill the company, even if the other problems are solvable. People will become indifferent, lose their creative edge, and look for jobs in other companies. So we need to find some way to create hope again, or this building will be for sale in a year or two, like so many others around here."

Then I explained the problems in each department, one by one. "When Dad started this business 25 years ago, there was just one other company competing with him, Industrial Electronics of America. Five years ago, a high-flying investor with deep pockets lured our best design engineer and our best salesman away to start a new competitor, Electronic Products, out in Silicon Valley where most electronics firms are headquartered now. They've been aggressively increasing their market share. Our market share has dropped from over 50% to under 30%, and our volumes have dropped too. This effectively raises the price on our custom-manufactured components like ASICs." Noticing her frown, I explained, "That means application-specific integrated circuits.

We have to buy a minimum quantity, and when we have a design change before the minimum quantity is used up, we have to throw the rest away.

"There are three basic competitive strategies: innovation, lower price, and being close to the customer. Innovation is where you are always the leader in new stuff, like 3M. And any time a potential customer wants something new, they come to you, because you've got the reputation and the ability to deliver. Lower price is the Wal-Mart approach—its advertising has the public believing it has the lowest prices. Being close to your customers means living with them, knowing what they want and need even before they do. Nordstrom's is a good example of that, with their personal shoppers. Amazon.com does a pretty good job on that, too. We were always price competitive, but our strengths were in knowing the customer and being innovative. That's why losing our best design engineer and our best salesman really hurt. Our new VP of engineering is a better designer than the one who left, but he has a different style, and it's taking a while for the market to catch on to his ideas."

After a pause I added, "Our margins are being viciously squeezed by the two competitors who have outsourced to China. They are now selling for 20–25% less than us. My CFO told us last Monday that if we sold the company at book value, we could make a higher return by investing in government bonds!

"But that's just the start. New product development has been delayed while we scramble to meet new environmental standards for the EU. We had to get written assurance from all our suppliers that all the products they sell us are lead-free, cadmium-free, and who-knows-what-else-free. The union is starting to get worried about our ability to survive; they see the sales volume slowly shrinking. And our bank is getting nervous too.

"And now I have to pull some sort of rabbit out of the hat two weeks from today at an off-site planning meeting. I just don't know where I'm going to get one. Hell, I don't even know what a rabbit looks like!"

Kelly just sat there listening the whole time. When I was finally finished, she got up, came over, sat down gently on my lap, and put her arms around my neck. She looked up into my eyes, and said, "This will all work out okay. Trust me." In spite of everything that was going on, I did. I couldn't help but draw the parallel between her doing this for me, and what Mom said she and Dad had done for each other over the years.

Then she got up and started walking around my office, thinking. She came back, sat down in her chair, and asked, "Adam, have you ever heard of sustainability?"

"Sort of—the tree-huggers, right?" I continued, "Like, spotted-owl-loving environmental radicals?"

"Not at all—no more than you'd be a thieving capitalist," Kelly said with a hint of a grin.

"Okay, you got me." I looked at her inquisitively, "So why are you bringing it up now?"

She began, "Well, sustainability is a new movement, just starting in America and around the world. It seems to be a much better way to run a company, *any* company, including manufacturing. The basic belief is that if a company honors its people and its community, and treats the environment with respect, it will make more money for its owners and gain long-term competitive advantage."

I interrupted, "Huh? How can that be? That would cost more, not less. Adding that pollution control equipment a couple of years ago cost a bundle. I don't think we'll *ever* get that back."

Kelly persisted, and said with a sideways glance, "Let me guess—that was required by the EPA, right?" I nodded.

"So you had to do it, as did other companies?" she said, looking straight at me. I nodded again.

"That's why people think sustainability is too expensive and can't be a viable strategy. But I remember, Adam, how you were all gung-ho for Earth Day back when we were at Clark. You like the outdoors. I hike or ski almost every weekend. That's why I moved to Portland." Kelly paused to organize her thoughts. Then she quietly asked, "Have you ever felt like you are leading two separate lives—the 'work' Adam and the 'real' Adam?"

I gazed into her eyes as I nodded. It was almost scary how she could tell me things about myself that I could not even verbalize, but as soon as she said them, I knew they were true.

Kelly continued, "The biggest reason that sustainability is so powerful is that it not only allows, but it actually *requires* a person to integrate these two parts. You can finally bring the real Adam to work here at Brookings, and use your deepest values when you make your decisions. The other employees can do that too."

Almost stunned, I just sat there for a while. Finally I mused softly, "I never would have believed that would be possible."

"Would you be willing to talk with someone who knows a lot more about it than I do? On the phone?" she asked.

"I guess, why?"

"You know that I'm in this mountain climbing club in Portland, the Mazamas. Almost every weekend some members are going up one mountain or another. I met a guy there a year ago—he led my basic climbing school, actually. He's a great guy, about 55. His name is Dennis LeBlanc. He's a consultant with a small firm in Portland. He used to be CEO of a manufacturing company, and from the way he told his story, about five years ago his company was facing the same problems you're facing. He was desperate enough, or wise enough, to try implementing sustainability, even though it was pretty much untried and unproven. He was a real pioneer. And there's something else. He's like you; he also majored in psych.

"Anyway, his plant had already done the lean thing a few years earlier. He started putting this sustainability stuff in, and somehow his company turned itself around. In fact, they've been included in the top 10 of Oregon's '100 Best Companies to Work For' the last three years. Their sales have increased, profits are up, and when they needed a zoning variance from the city's planning board, it sailed through the approval process like it had wings. He retired from the company last year and started a consulting firm with a couple other senior executives from other companies. I think you should call him Monday and talk with him. And if you like what you hear, you can invite him out to help you lead that off-site in two weeks."

I just sat there and looked at her. It seemed so weird, like such a long shot. But then, the more I thought about it, the more I knew I had to at least call the guy. I trusted Kelly; I would trust her with my life, actually. And what could it hurt to talk with the guy—it was only a phone call. Besides, my list of brilliant ideas was, at that moment, completely unpopulated. She waited patiently, studying my face as I thought. She had been able to read me like a book since our sophomore year. I was glad, too; I had nothing to hide from her.

"Okay, Kels, I'll call him at 10:00 Monday morning, his time. That's 5 p.m. my time, right?" I enjoyed tweaking her about the time difference.

"Nahh, only 4:45," she countered with a grin. She knew I knew about the time difference; we had talked on the phone far too often for me to forget it. Suddenly it hit me that tomorrow evening she would be leaving again. And I started to feel a void that I didn't want to face.

True to form, Kelly asked as she studied my face, "Whatcha thinking about, Adam? You look so serious and unhappy." See what I mean? I can't hide *anything* from her!

I replied in a serious tone, "Well, I could try to BS you and say 'nothing,' but it wouldn't be true. You caught me. I was just realizing that you'll be leaving on the plane tomorrow evening, and I'll miss you . . . a lot. There . . . I said it."

Her eyes softened, into even deeper brown, as she softly replied, "I'll miss you, too."

Just then my stomach growled. Talk about the world's worst timing!

"Perhaps we should take your stomach to a place where they serve lunch," and she laughed infectiously. And in less than five minutes we were in the car, with the plant locked up tightly.

Ten minutes later we were at the local sandwich shop. Kelly ordered a salad, while I had a cheesesteak. Afterward, she asked me to show her around town. I showed her the somewhat frumpy town center, not unlike many small cities (two malls and the Wal-Mart had sucked much of the business from the city center). Then we drove through the industrial section and some of the residential areas. After an hour or so, we headed for the nicest mall in the area so she could check it out. Once we were through in the mall, we headed home.

One thing happened on the way home that was much more important in hindsight than it seemed at the time. We stopped to get a bottle of wine and as we were waiting to pay the cashier, we bumped into Annie. I felt a little awkward, but greeted her warmly, "Hello, Annie. This is my best friend from college, Kelly Donovan. Kelly, this is Annie Zabransky, my good friend from high school. She's one of the sparkplugs in our company." Even though Annie was dressed in jeans and a sweatshirt, she still looked nice. The two smiled and shook hands politely, but the looks they gave each other as we parted were not as friendly as I expected.

When we got home, I checked my e-mails while Kelly went to her room to check hers and do whatever she needed to do before dinner. The intensity of the last 24 hours was starting to tell on me and, I suspected, on her too.

Dinner was somewhat quiet; we were all lost in our own thoughts. I kept thinking about Kelly and how lonely I would be as I watched her plane take off tomorrow afternoon. After dinner we gravitated toward the family room and the warm fire. Mom excused herself at 9:00 this time to retire for the evening; she was obviously trying to leave us some time together. Kelly was sitting next to me on the couch, with both of us facing the fire. She had started with a little distance between us, but after Mom left, she moved over to snuggle against my right side, putting her head on my shoulder. Responding naturally, my arm went around her shoulder, holding her close. "Mmmmm," she said, as she snuggled even closer, as if that were possible. We must have stayed like that for 10–15 minutes. Then she sat up, twisted a bit, and leaned across me so that I was holding her in my arms, with her face looking up to me.

"Adam," she said. "We've been best friends for years. And I don't want to lose that. But I can't keep pretending that's all I want us to be . . . it isn't fair to me, or to you. Do you think we could be more than best friends?"

She looked so beautiful. I responded from my heart, "Kelly, I've been thinking the same thing. I was afraid to risk what we have, but I want us to be much more than best friends." And with that, we each leaned forward and our lips met in confirmation. I had never experienced a kiss like that in my entire life. We finally leaned back, and looked into each other's eyes for a long time. I don't know what she saw in mine, but what I saw in hers was much more than friendship. Did I dare to admit that I might be in love with my best friend? Did I dare to hope that she might feel the same way about me?

She broke the silence, "Adam, that was incredible. I've never been kissed like that. I need some time to think."

"Me too," I said.

So with one more kiss, we went to our respective rooms. Part of me was hoping Kelly would visit me during the night; part of me was petrified at what was happening to our relationship. I had never felt this way about any of my other girlfriends, and I had come very close to proposing to one of them. I went to bed hoping she felt the same way too, and thinking that being scared was a good development. But not knowing, I slept fitfully.

Sunday morning Kelly said nothing about the night before. We had coffee, cinnamon rolls, and grapefruit for breakfast. Then we went to church with Mom. Kelly looked great—dressed in a shimmering light blue silk blouse, a liquid silver choker, and stylish navy blue pantsuit. I was in my grey sports coat, blue dress shirt (no tie), and black slacks. Mom was elegant as always, wearing a wine-colored dress with her favorite necklace.

Since I came home I had started going back to church with Mom. The new pastor, John Franklin, had an interesting background—an M.B.A. and 30 years in sales, then back to get his Master's of Divinity at Boston University, then into the pulpit at our church. Not surprisingly, his sermons connected directly with the world I lived in. He preached that morning on the text, "All things work together for good for those who love God" (Romans 8:28), illustrating it with his own background.

Pastor Franklin was drafted in 1969 and spent a year in administrative duties at Fort Campbell, Kentucky. Then he got his orders for Viet Nam. When he arrived at Fort Lewis for his shots and jungle fatigues, his orders somehow got changed; he spent the remaining months of his army career at Ft. Shafter in Honolulu. He met his future wife at the base where she was working as a civilian. Her parents introduced him to the Dole pineapple people. Since he was getting out of the Army soon, they offered him a job, and he stayed there another 10 years before moving back to the mainland.

Today Pastor Franklin kept looking at Mom and me when he repeated his text—"All things work together for good." I was seated between Mom and Kelly; when we first heard the text of the morning, Kelly took my hand in hers and squeezed it gently to reinforce the message. She didn't let go until the end of the service.

After church, we went out to Sunday brunch at one of the better local restaurants.

When we got home, Kelly asked, "Would you like to read the sustainability book I brought with me—*Mid-Course Correction**?" She told me the author, Ray Anderson, the CEO

---

* Anderson, Ray C. 1998. *Mid-Course Correction, Toward a Sustainable Enterprise: The Interface Model*. Atlanta, GA: Peregrinzilla Press.

of Interface Carpets, learned about sustainability by reading Paul Hawken's *The Ecology of Commerce*[†]. Anderson wrote about how he changed his company from the inside out. He was now in great demand as a speaker across the country and around the world.

I replied, "Sure, loan me your copy."

"Okay," she said. "I'm also reading an excerpt from a book called *Teaching Business Sustainability*. One chapter by Molly Brown and Joanna Macy[‡] is profound. They talk about work that reconnects—about people finding meaning in their lives at work. I'll leave that with you too; I can print another copy when I get home." She started for her bedroom to get the materials and I followed her.

As we entered the room, she turned to face me and said, "Adam, remember we're going to stop by your office for 15 minutes on the way to the airport."

"Yes . . ." She could tell I was perplexed at her reminder and smiled enigmatically. She proceeded to a nearby table where she had left the book and printed article. She handed them to me and then asked me to step out for a bit while she changed into her jeans and sweater to be comfortable on the plane. When she gave the all clear, I came back in and sat on the bed to watch her pack, which only took about 10 minutes. I carried her bag downstairs. She said good-bye to Mom and we headed for my office.

[†] Hawken, Paul. 2005. *The Ecology of Commerce: A Declaration of Sustainability*, First Collins Business Ed. NY: Collins Business.

[‡] Brown, Molly, and Joanna Macy. 2004. "Teaching Sustainability: Whole Systems Learning," chapter excerpt from *Teaching Business Sustainability*. Sheffield, United Kingdom: Greenleaf Publishing.

The drive was quiet. We were both lost in our own thoughts.

When we entered my office, she turned to me, held out both her hands to take mine, and said, "Adam, I sensed yesterday that part of you still thinks of this as your father's office. Was I right?"

"Yes, my more-than-friend," I replied and squeezed her hands softly.

"And you keep comparing yourself to your dad, and you feel like you don't measure up?"

"Yes, you are right once again," I admitted.

"Adam, I want to try something to help you get past those ghosts. Are you willing to try it?"

"Of course, Kels," I said, wondering what she had in mind.

"Then please sit down in your chair." I followed her direction, and she came over, sat on my lap, and started kissing my face, tenderly, passionately. And then she changed our relationship forever.

"Adam Brookings, I love you. I love you with all my heart. That's why I have never married or even gotten very serious with anyone else since we graduated. When you are in this office, when you are in this building, remember this: there is one woman who loves you completely. You cannot fail in my eyes. If things don't work out the way you want, that's okay. You have not failed. You have tried with everything you have. You, my love, are the CEO of this company. This has happened for a reason. Your dad, in spite of his experience and wisdom, did not have the same gifts and insight as you. Remember that. You are unique, special, and gifted. And remember that I am yours, and I love you with all of my heart."

And with that, she leaned into me and kissed me again, slowly and tenderly.

"Kelly Donovan, I love you too. I couldn't admit it till last night. But I've just realized that's why I couldn't get serious with anyone else I've dated. You've always been special to me; I just didn't recognize that it was love. These last five years I have missed you more than I could ever say. And I've been afraid to admit that I love you because I didn't want to risk losing you as a friend."

We had to leave for the airport. But this time as we parted, we knew we would see each other again soon. We knew we were in this together, whatever the future held. As she left me at the security check-in, she mused aloud, "As sorry as I am for your father's death and your company's current condition, I'm so glad we got together this weekend. You have been missing from my life for far too long. And now that's changed."

I discovered in the coming weeks she had very effectively banished the ghosts of my father's image and expectations from my office. It was now truly my office, not his.

When I got home, Mom took one look at me and said, "I hope this means what I think it means."

"Mom, we finally admitted that we love each other."

She was not at all surprised. With a broad smile, she said, "You two are so good for each other. You belong together."

I started reading Ray Anderson's book as soon as I finished talking with Mom. I felt closer to Kelly while I was reading the book she loaned me, about a subject to which she had introduced me. I could see her curled up in a chair, twirling her hair around the index finger of her right hand, reading those same pages and grabbing her favorite green highlighter for an important thought. I also started gaining a better understanding about sustainability, and what and why and how to implement it. And I felt more relaxed and ready for tomorrow morning's staff meeting. Something deep inside my belief system was shifting, and I knew it was for the better. I now had hope, whereas before Kelly arrived I had almost none. It had been an *excellent* weekend.

CHAPTER 3
Rearranging the Mental Furniture

Well, the good news was I slept better last night than I had ever since I got the call about Dad's heart attack. The bad news—it was Monday morning again, and this time the EPA wanted to extract some of our flesh, on top of all the other problems. But underneath it all, I was much calmer; somehow, Kelly's confidence had rubbed off. I knew that things would indeed work out. As I was thinking that, I made a mental note to make an appointment with Rev. Franklin. He seemed like the kind of person I wanted to get to know better. I felt I could trust him to keep a confidence. He would understand the pressures I was under and provide the wisdom of experience and a longer viewpoint.

I had really enjoyed reading both the chapter by Brown and Macy, and the first five chapters of Ray Anderson's book. They were making a lot of sense to me.

At the staff meeting, I said, "I've come up with some ideas for what we could do at the off-site, but I'm not yet clear enough on them to share them. I want to talk to you, Barbara, after this meeting and the EPA visit today. What I can say is: I hope that we can come out of this in good shape, and that we won't be moving any jobs to China or laying anyone off." There were lots of questions, but I gently refused to answer them, saying, "I don't know enough about this yet, and it's something you've never heard of, so just trust me, okay?" That was the first time I had asked for their trust. Somewhat skeptically, they agreed.

Sure enough, the EPA had received a complaint from an unnamed neighbor about supposedly illegal discharges into the air. So Wayne and our maintenance chief, Sam, spent a couple hours of their precious time showing the EPA lady our records and controls. She finally left. It's so frustrating. On one hand, I want our country to have clean air. On the other, sometimes I feel like we're a target, and the EPA inspectors are the arrows.

At 10:30 that morning, I called Kelly; she would be up by then and getting ready for work. I just wanted to hear her voice and tell her how much the weekend meant to me. She said she would let Dennis LeBlanc know I'd be calling him as soon as she got to work. Then I called Barbara and asked if we could meet for 15 minutes; she said she would stop by in half an hour.

I routinely walked the plant floor every morning just to keep in touch with whatever was going on. As I walked by the final assembly area, Annie motioned me over. "Could I talk with you for a moment?" she asked.

"Sure," I said.

A forklift came roaring by, so she said, "Let's get a cup of coffee in the cafeteria; it's a little quieter in there."

After getting our coffee, I followed her to a table in the corner. I was curious as to what this was all about. Annie took a sip of her coffee and began, "You introduced me to Kelly on Saturday evening. And I know it's none of my business, but she was sending out possessive vibes pretty strongly. And sometimes guys don't have a clue what a woman is thinking. So do you have any idea how she feels about you?"

"Yes," I replied, with a huge grin on my face. "We talked that over yesterday afternoon before she left on the plane. We've both been hiding our feelings for each other for years, but not anymore."

"I'm so happy for you! That was all I wanted to say," she said abruptly, looking down into her cup. But she didn't seem to look happy.

"Annie, thanks for telling me. I really appreciate this."

"Gotta get back to work," she said quietly as she got up and left without looking at me again.

Barbara arrived in my office just after I did. I briefed her on my conversation with Kelly about sustainability and the consultant she recommended, Dennis LeBlanc. I asked Barbara to join me when I called him. She rearranged her schedule so we could call right after lunch.

At 1:00 p.m. I called Dennis. "Hi, Dennis. I'm Adam Brookings, Kelly Donovan's friend. She was out here last weekend and got me interested in sustainability. I've got Barbara Joiner, my VP of HR with me. Is this a good time to talk? And can I put you on speakerphone?"

"Hi, Adam. Yes, Kelly let me know you'd be calling. This is a good time, thanks for asking. Can you tell me a little about your current situation?" I proceeded to brief Dennis, with Barbara adding her perspective; I could hear him jotting notes about each major topic. When I was apparently finished, he asked, "Is that all?"

"I think so, at least for the major problems."

"Well, let me tell you my story," Dennis began. "My company had problems similar to yours, although we were in a different industry. Like you, we had started our Lean journey several years earlier and it had lost energy. Our sales were starting to slip, the workers were demoralized, competitors were outsourcing to China and selling below our production cost, and our best engineers were leaving. We didn't know how we were going to survive. I was having trouble sleeping at night; our staff was getting just plain uptight, like a balloon being filled too full and just waiting for some reason to burst. Hey, I didn't want to stay with the company either, but I was the second generation owner, so I couldn't just walk away. And I couldn't figure out how to sell the mess to anyone else—by the time the buyers would have finished due diligence, they would have been asking me how much I wanted to pay *them* to take the company off my hands!"

Boy, did *that* sound familiar! He had indeed walked not just one, but several miles in my shoes.

"But I happened to read an article by Paul Hawken, where he quoted the philosophy, 'First, do no harm.' And I looked around in my own company and was appalled and ashamed when I realized the harm we were doing—to our employees, to our community, to our environment. We were a truly harmful company. And we were one of the better ones in the Portland area!

"So I told my staff we were going on a strategic planning retreat, and I had them read *Ecology of Commerce** and *Leadership and the New Science*† beforehand. They gave me some weird looks, let me tell you, when I passed out the books.

---

* Hawken, Paul. 2005. *The Ecology of Commerce: A Declaration of Sustainability*, First Collins Business Ed. NY: Collins Business.

† Wheatley, Margaret. 1999. *Leadership and the New Science: Discovering Order in a Chaotic World*, 2nd ed. San Francisco, CA: Berrett-Koehler Publishers.

They gave me even weirder looks when they started reading them. But they humored me, because they knew me well enough to trust me even though this was very unorthodox, and because nobody else had any ideas at all about how to survive.

"Unlike your staff, nobody had said out loud, publicly, that our company was dying. So I started by asking the group for a show of hands as to how many thought our company would still exist in 10 years. That drew some gasps—I was saying the unthinkable. Not surprisingly, there were no hands.

"So I had them brainstorm the type of company that *would* be around in 10 years in terms of how it would operate, and not from a production process standpoint. I told them to forget assembly lines and new products with bells and whistles and supply chains and special financial incentives to customers. I wanted them to describe 'who' we would have to become. They came up with a pretty good list, and it surprised us in that it united our personal values with our work. We suddenly realized we had a choice about how our company operated; it could be what we wanted it to be, and we could be who we wanted to be at work.

"Then I threw the second bomb at them. Could we design a company that would 'do no harm?' That was difficult, very, very difficult. But we came close. And that became our blueprint for future decisions. We created a whole new operating model. It was really different in several ways. One tenet was to respect all people—employees, customers, suppliers, and the community. Another was to tell the truth, the whole truth, always. The third was to truly listen to each other and honor that others were telling the truth, as they best understood it. When it comes down to it, a company is all about relationships, not about products. So we renamed our HR department, Human Relationships.

"From a practical standpoint, we started making as many decisions as possible, at all levels of the company, based on the Triple Bottom Line. Did Kelly tell you about that?"

"I don't think she did."

"The single bottom line that most companies use for decision making is financial. Profitability—that's all there is. But sustainable decisions consider two other bottom lines: social and environmental. That gives us a Triple Bottom Line. Sometimes people call it the three Ps—profit, people, and planet. Sometimes it's the three Es—environment, social equity, and economics. What you call it doesn't matter. What matters is that people consider all three as they make a decision. And that's how our company started to operate."

Barbara asked, "So how did your company do after that?"

Dennis replied, "If I said it was easy, I'd be lying. And I won't do that, to you or to anyone else. It was difficult. Our salespeople risked sales by telling the truth about delivery dates. Like most salespeople in most industries, they were used to telling a customer whatever the customer needed to hear to close the deal. When they started to tell whole truth to customers, they lost a few sales. But then when the word got around about the integrity of our salespeople, we started gaining business, including most of the customers we'd lost, and more business from other customers, plus a few new ones.

"We tackled the environmental side by phasing out the worst chemicals and replacing them with more benign ones. Some of the replacement chemicals cost more, and some of them were less efficient and effective. But we did it. And the results were like the experience with sales. At first, it hurt our financial bottom line. But then, somehow, our commitment to our people caused them to get much more creative, and they started finding and reducing waste in all sorts of places. They really became part of the company team. They knew that we needed to save money, so they helped us reduce our energy usage, both electricity and gas. That's another thing—we started telling our people where we were and what was going on, good news and bad. And they responded by supporting us better than ever before.

"We started supporting our community—opening up our cafeteria for after-hours meetings, for example. This drove our security folks crazy, let me tell you. And our CFO had a fit—'what about the legal liability if somebody gets hurt on our property?' But I insisted, and we did it anyway. It worked out fine.

"Slowly but surely, our fortunes started improving, though it was hard to see where the improvements were coming from. I'm pretty sure the root cause was that our customers and suppliers responded to being treated with respect, as if they were important just because they were human beings. We started treating each and every worker, from executive to line worker, as if they were special, gifted, and talented. And almost all of them lived up to that vision. In the first year about 5% of the workforce left the company, not all of them voluntarily, because they were uncomfortable with the new way of doing business.

"Our long-term results were excellent: our workforce now has palpably higher morale than just about any other company in the area. Once again, we were included in the top 10 of Oregon's '100 Best Companies to Work For.' Workers at all levels keep thinking up new ways to improve the company. They come up with things that amaze us, and even themselves. Our customers are a lot happier, our suppliers are a lot happier, and our workers—well, they're off the charts. We have discovered that if we focus on growing our people, everything else falls in place. Two years ago we went public with our pledge to be in the human development business, like Toyota. So now we deliberately help each person develop not only their work skills, but also other ancillary skills. We offer parenting classes for new parents, after hours, at no cost to the participants. We have a multilingual workforce, so we offer English improvement courses. Our boldest statement was that if a person was ready to be promoted and we had no foreseeable places to promote them, we would help them find a job in another company if they wanted us to do that! So far, we have only had one person take us up on that—it worked well; he is now plant manager at another company. He's starting to change their culture for the better. And the publicity we've gotten from that has caused other good things to happen.

"Our customers discovered that they like doing business with us better than the competition, so our sales volumes have increased. Our costs have decreased—we couldn't believe the amount of cost and waste still in our products and processes even after we had been doing Lean for five years!

"The company was successful enough that I decided to devote the rest of my career to helping other companies go through the same transition. I left two years ago and sold my shares to an ESOP (employee stock ownership plan), so the company is now completely employee-owned. When I left, profitability was very healthy. And it has continued to improve; the employees are doing *very* well financially. In terms of the Triple Bottom Line, when we improved the social dimension by giving company ownership to employees, we improved the financial dimension too. The EPA has showcased our company regionally. When they call us, it's to ask if they can bring someone by for a plant tour. This free publicity has helped our financial bottom line as well. Who would have thought being environmentally friendly would help us financially?

"But the most important realization about sustainability is that I finally got to feel whole. And others in my company, at all levels, have told me the same. Until we started implementing sustainability, I had separated the business part of me, and the values part of me. And they never connected—it was like I was two different people. I had gotten used to it, become numb over time. But when I could actually bring my deepest values to work, when I could look someone in the eye and ask how a decision was going to affect their grandchildren's lives. *That's* when I discovered the importance of sustainability. Not just to our businesses, but to our lives, and our sense of well-being. That is the power of sustainability—it harnesses the deepest beliefs of the people who work in the company. Likely for the same reason, we now have fewer job openings—because no one is leaving. And ironically, we have lots more applications to work for us. We get the brightest young people we have ever seen, while other companies are complaining about the quality of young workers and engineers. People really, really want to come to work for us, even on a rainy Tuesday morning in February, because work brings meaning to their lives.

"So, is that what you wanted to know?" Dennis asked.

"Wow," I responded. "I'm so glad Kelly told me about you. That is even more powerful than she said, and I was skeptical when she was telling me. Give us a minute to absorb what you just said, okay?"

We just sat there for I don't know how long—10 seconds, 20 seconds, 30 seconds. I couldn't have told you how long; it didn't matter. My mind was awhirl with conflicting thoughts. Could this work at Brookings? Would it matter to our customers, our employees? Here was maybe the only hope the company had of surviving. But could I ask this stranger to help us? If I didn't, where else could I find someone or something for the off-site? I looked over to Barbara. She whispered, "Can we call him back?"

I asked, "Dennis, I have an idea that I want to talk to Barbara about. Can I call you back in 10 minutes?"

"Sure, Adam," he replied.

"Thanks. I'll call you in 10," I said.

When we hung up, I turned to Barbara and said, "I know I'm being completely impetuous, but I'd like to invite him to lead our off-site."

"Adam, I have the skills and experience to lead an off-site like that myself. And we're so tight for cash that I can't logically justify inviting him out." I started to protest, but she raised her hand to stop me. "But," she said, "I think we should, and here's why. The off-site needs a person who has new ideas, who can convince our staff to try moving forward. As skilled as I am, I can't present his ideas in a way that our staff would buy. I don't have the track record of having put sustainability in. You don't either."

"What do you think the rest of them will say?" I asked seriously.

"I'd be careful what I tell them about sustainability, so they don't decide it can't work here before they give it a fair shot. And for sure they'll dislike spending the money. But when it comes down to the decision, all of us can only advise. It's you and your mom who have to decide if it's worth the money."

"Then I want to call him back and invite him to lead our off-site. Can you stay here for this next call, too?"

Barbara replied, "Sure. This is more important for the company than the stuff sitting on my desk."

So I called Dennis back. As soon as we said hello, I asked, "Dennis, could you come lead our off-site a week from Saturday?"

"I appreciate the invitation, Adam. Let me tell you how we work. The intention is to provide the best possible service and the best possible value to our clients. For something like this, you want two of us—we have complementary skills, so if one of us misses something, the other person will catch it. And we would need to spend the Friday beforehand meeting with your management staff and a few people from your workforce, one on one, so we can be more effective during the meeting."

"Sounds reasonable," I said in agreement.

"At the risk of alienating somebody I've only met by phone, may I suggest a change to your meeting design?" Dennis asked.

"Go ahead," I responded, starting to feel a little defensive and unsure of myself.

"For something of this magnitude, one day alone is just plain not sufficient. We should start Friday evening, then let the ideas soak for a while Friday night. Then we meet again Saturday, from 9:00 to 4:00, then again let the ideas soak. Then we meet Sunday morning for three hours, four maximum. We'll achieve a lot better results that way."

I looked at Barbara. She nodded, and said, "Dennis, that makes sense."

I interjected, "I think so, too, but I only asked the staff for Saturday. I'll have to talk with them tomorrow and ask them to free up the rest of the weekend. Also, this is the Midwest—many of my people go to church on Sunday mornings. Could the Sunday session start at 2:00 in the afternoon instead?"

Dennis responded, "I think we could do that. It would be a really long weekend for us, but we could do that. Can you wait just a minute while I check our calendars? . . . Yes,

Karen Hoshibata and I will be delighted to help you. We were going to be leading a climb up Mt. Hood that Saturday. But we can get somebody else to lead it so we can do this. We'll be honored to assist you. We'd like you to help us determine the approach we should take. What results do you want by the end of the off-site, and afterward? And, how will you measure those results?

I responded, "Good questions! Let's talk this through. Our goal is to have each person understand the underlying causes of why we're stuck right now, and create a way to move forward. There needs to be buy-in during the off-site, and energy and enthusiasm as we complete it."

Barbara nodded to me, and then said to Dennis, "In addition, and this will be more difficult, the energy and enthusiasm need to continue after we get back to work. I've seen too much 'workshop euphoria'—I realize that enthusiasm during the workshop is necessary, but it is not enough."

I continued, "I want the two of you to basically lead the off-site. While I might be the CEO, I've only been here nine weeks. And I'm enough younger than the rest of the staff that it would be better if you led most of it. Barbara and I talked, and we think an outsider would be seen as less biased. I want to lead off, though."

Dennis replied, "Sounds fair to me. Here's one idea to think about. While you've only been there nine weeks, you have authority as the owner of the company. Don't underestimate the power this provides you. And we'll make sure this off-site helps you build respect and cooperation from your staff."

I continued, "I've got a couple more questions, and they're not easy. First, how does this really work? How does it help our profitability? Since we started Lean five years ago, we've reduced setup times to a fraction of what they were before. So we make what our customers want, when they want it. Our inventories have dropped to less than 20% of where they were. Our quality, which was high to begin with, is now the best in the industry. Our first-pass yields through the entire process are now in the low 90% range and climbing. So, where will the increased profits come from?"

Dennis replied eagerly, "My turn to say 'good question' now! You know why a speaker says 'good question' when answering questions from the audience, don't you?"

"No. Why?" I asked.

"Because, what is being asked *is* a good question and drawing attention to it acknowledges that. And in saying so, the speaker also buys a little time to pause and formulate an answer. So now that I've bought a little time, let me try to answer your question. There are two answers—quantitative and qualitative. Which do you want first?"

"Quantitative," I said.

"Okay," Dennis replied. "When a company's staff starts using sustainability to make their decisions, they move their focus from the financial bottom line to something broader— the Triple Bottom Line. That means profits, of course, *and* people *and* planet. Once they do that, they make decisions differently. In Lean terms, they can now identify two additional groups of waste—or non-value-added activities—which they couldn't see before. Then they start reducing those wastes. You might check out an article in *Target* magazine, the first issue in 2006, entitled, 'Life is Our Ultimate Customer[‡].' Does that make sense so far?"

[‡] Langenwalter, Gary A. "Life is Our Ultimate Customer: From Lean to Sustainability." *Target*, first issue, 2006. Available on-line from the Association for Manufacturing Excellence. http://ww.ame.org/MagazineOnlinePDF.aspx?artid=3301.

"Basically, but it's not as tangible as inventory reduction," I replied uneasily.

Dennis replied, "Yes, and that's precisely why sustainability has not yet been embraced by most companies. However, there is now plenty of data to show that it produces superior financial results, but most company executives won't even consider the possibility, because they can't get beyond their own assumptions."

I countered, "Yes, but do you have any numbers for the companies that have done this? I can understand the 'how,' but does this really work?"

"Here are a few," Dennis responded. "Timberland's profits are up almost 10% per year over the last five years; and its ROI to shareholders is up 20% per year. Wal-Mart has saved $26 million per year on fuel for its truck fleet, and another $28 million per year by recycling and selling plastic—stuff that used to be thrown in the dumpster. GE is doubling its R&D in clean technologies, and expects to double its revenues in those products in five years. Jeff Immelt, GE's CEO, announced, 'Green is green,' in his 2006 speech to top employees. And DuPont produces 30% more product with 9% less energy; the company has saved $2 billion in energy costs since it started reducing greenhouse gas emissions several years ago. Does this help?"

"Yes, thanks," I replied.

"But now the qualitative answer," Dennis added. "When people inside your company really start believing that you and the company care about them, as individuals, and about their children and their community, there is a huge shift in attitude. They start thinking like partners, like fellow entrepreneurs, and not like employees. This unleashes creativity they didn't even know they had, even more so than when you first started the Lean teams. And this creativity will produce results. We just can't predict exactly where the improvements will be; we only know that they will occur."

"Okay, I think I understand. Let me rephrase that. I *do* understand from an intuitive standpoint. It still sounds a little California 'woo-woo' to me, but I'm willing to try it. After all, what do I have to lose except my pride?"

"Thank you for trusting me this far," Dennis said. "It takes courage to openly question conventional wisdom. Your first question was a really good one. You said you have 'questions'—plural. Are there more?"

"Just two more that I can think of right now. I'm sure I'll have plenty of others."

Dennis answered, "Yeah, you probably will. So what's number two?"

"What about the rising cost of oil and how it will affect our raw stock and transportation costs?"

"You do know how to ask the *tough* questions!" Dennis replied. "That's the mark of a good CEO, you know, the ability to discern underlying patterns and ask penetrating questions, and be willing to hear the answers. This is a hot topic right now, as you can probably guess. It's basically a demonstration of the law of supply and demand stemming from a classic case of denial. You know how we talk about oil production, right?"

"Right," I agreed.

"Well, that implies we can produce more if we want to— that the raw materials are unlimited. Unfortunately, the amount of conventional oil in the world is, indeed, limited. And we're currently hitting two limits simultaneously."

"*Two* limits? What are they?" I asked.

"The first is the supply of conventional oil. There have been no new major finds, or elephant fields as they're called in the industry, for about 40 years now, in spite of all the money the oil companies have spent worldwide prospecting on land and in the oceans. So it's pretty safe to assume we have already discovered all the conventional oil there is."

"What do you mean by conventional oil?"

Dennis explained, "Liquid crude oil that we pump out of the ground in places like Texas and Saudi Arabia."

"So there is such as thing as unconventional oil?" I inquired.

"Yes—the oil sands in Canada and Venezuela, and oil shale in the Rockies," Dennis replied. He went on to explain, "But it is much more difficult and costly to extract. For example, in the 1950s we could extract 10 barrels of conventional oil from the ground for the energy cost of one barrel of oil. Now, at best, we only get four barrels of oil for every barrel used. And the oil sands in Canada are even worse—it takes two barrels of oil, in energy, to get three barrels out. And that process creates some major environmental issues, like pools of naphthalene, which don't go away."

"That doesn't sound too good," I sighed.

"It's not. But what this means is that we, as a society, need to quit assuming oil is unlimited, and therefore cheap. That's a huge culture shift. But there's even more bad news, the second limit," Dennis said, baiting my curiosity.

"The first was bad enough," I said.

"Yes, but the second is kicking in even more quickly."

"Oh?" I said.

"The second is simply this—the world's capacity to extract and process oil is limited, at about 85 million barrels of oil per day, although with additional technology that might be increased a bit. This is because the maximum rate at which oil can be pumped from a field declines as the field matures.

Trying to pump faster ultimately ruins the field, and means that less oil will be recovered from that field in total. All the major oil fields worldwide are in decline now; oil fields in the U.S. have been declining for decades. So we can't just pump faster. At the same time, the rapidly growing economies in China and India are causing their oil consumption to rise. In March, 2005, the *Wall Street Journal* estimated that there was only about a million barrels of oil per day in unused capacity in the Middle East, and that virtually all other oil-producing countries were already maxed out.[§] This means that demand, which keeps increasing, will soon exceed supply. This is without any major disruptions caused by hurricanes in the Gulf of Mexico, or supply difficulties in the Middle East. So, when you look at the fact that the supply of oil is basically maxed out and may be even starting to slowly decrease, and demand is exceeding supply, there is no way to avoid rising prices. The only question is how far and how fast. This is one topic that we need to include in the off-site."

"Yeah," I said, followed by a long, deep sigh. We were quiet for a few moments while I absorbed what I had just heard.

Dennis continued, "So sustainability produces long-term advantage by unleashing the creativity of people inside the company, partnering more closely with customers and suppliers, and honoring the environment. The environmental issues are bigger than you think; addressing them reduces risk in ways that are not immediately obvious, like reducing the possibility of lawsuits by employees or the community, and reducing the risk of unexpected price increases of raw materials."

---

§ Bahree, Bhusha. "Saudi Oil Minister Urges OPEC to Increase Output Limit by 2%." *Wall Street Journal,* March 15, 2005, p. A2.

"I think I understand that," I said. "Final question for now—actually two questions."

"Hey, you only get one more!" Dennis laughed.

"Sorry, I renewed my license to ask as many questions as I can think of," I joked.

"Okay, go ahead," he said.

"So after the off-site, what do we do next? What will we need your help with? What can we do on our own? That was the first part. The second part, how much will this cost us?" I was apprehensive about his reply.

"During the off-site, we'll create a vision, then a strategy, then some ideas for moving forward. Your challenge after the off-site will be that you'll have too many projects and not enough people, so you'll need to prioritize, using the Triple Bottom Line. How much you want to use us after the off-site depends completely on the two of you and your staff. But, for planning purposes, one possibility is for us to come out one day a month. And, as for how much this will cost—that depends completely on how much you use our services. We'll work our fees for this first visit by asking for half when we finish the off-site, and half one month later. If you don't think the off-site provided value, you don't have to pay the second half. Oh, and we'll bill you for our actual travel expenses."

"I like that; it puts some of your skin in the game, too," I commented.

"Thanks, we think so, too," Dennis said. "In fact, the first time we accepted a deferred payment schedule it was because a client suggested it, almost as a joke. But then we realized it was a great idea, so we've done it ever since. And clients like it."

"Dennis, you've given me a lot to think about. I want to do this."

Barbara interjected, "Oh, one more final question."

Dennis started laughing, and so did I. "Is this your 'final' final question?" he asked.

"Well, probably not. But it's a good one," Barbara replied.

"They've all been good ones. So what is this final question?" Dennis asked.

Barbara replied, "Are there any books or articles the staff should read before the off-site? Oh, and that brings up another one," and we started laughing again, including Barbara this time. "I think I won't use the word 'final' anymore."

"Good idea," replied Dennis. I could actually hear him smiling.

She continued, "Who do we include? Just the executive staff, or others? If we have reading to do before the off-site and we decide to include another person after you talk with people on Friday, how does that person get up to speed?"

Dennis replied, "Let me suggest this. I think you'll get the best results if you include more than your executive staff. So why don't you think about it for a day or so and talk with some of your staff to see who they'd recommend. Some companies have included middle management and key professionals, like materials managers or key customer service representatives. Others have gone even further and included hourly workers from the shop floor or front line. We're looking for the informal leaders, the people who create the opinions, no matter their title. You should invite them as soon as possible to show respect for their prior plans for the weekend."

I replied, "I hadn't thought about the respect angle. I guess that really will shape lots of our decisions, won't it?"

"More than you realize, Adam," Dennis assured.

I asked him, "Can you e-mail me the suggested reading list? I'll have the participants selected by tomorrow night."

"Will do—I'll get that out today."

"Dennis, I am amazed at how much I've learned in this one phone call. I'm really looking forward to your visit and to the off-site," I said.

"Me too," added Barbara.

"Adam, I'm really looking forward to it, too. See you a week from Friday. Do either of you have any more 'final' questions?" asked Dennis.

"Not right now. Thanks," I said. "Good-bye."

"Good-bye," Dennis said and hung up the phone.

Barbara and I just looked at each other for a moment. "This is really a creative step," she finally said when she'd gathered her thoughts. "I've read about this kind of off-site at other companies, and we studied it at Antioch. It can enable us to create miracles. I am absolutely excited to be a part of it. I'll help Dennis and Karen in any way they want. And you'll be surprised by how effective this can be.

"When you're ready, I'd like to talk with Dennis and Karen and see what they're planning and where I can be of help. Would that be okay with you?"

"Yes." I didn't have to think twice as I answered her. I knew I could trust Barbara.

These conversations had given me a lot to think about! Even though I felt like I had been drinking from a fire hose, I was feeling much better than before. My gut was telling me that we might actually be able to turn the company around, and that sustainability looked like a really good way to do it.

I hadn't been this excited about any company ever before in my life. I am more intuitive than many of my friends, and I have learned that my gut generally reaches conclusions that I can verify later with numbers. But I also knew that this could be a disaster if we didn't do it right. I sensed that the two secrets to success would lie in the list of participants and the design of the discussions. I could hardly wait to talk with Mom over dinner and Kelly later in the evening to get their perspectives.

When I got home, Mom could tell I was excited. I had just finished hanging up my coat when she took a long look at me and asked, "Adam, what happened today? I haven't seen you this way since you took over the company."

So I told her what Kelly had told me about sustainability yesterday afternoon, then about my conversation with Dennis today. I was clearly on a high, with no chemicals required.

She thought for a while, and replied, "This sounds like an awfully big change. But I can see what a huge difference it has made to you already. I'm not sure what to say. Are there any big risks?"

"Mom, I can't see any big risks at this point, other than having me look like a complete idiot to everyone at the company. I know that cash is tight, but the money for the consultant is pocket change compared to what's at stake here. I guess the biggest risk is betting on sustainability and having it not work, which would cost us time that we should have spent elsewhere. Barbara likes the idea too. I really don't have any other alternative that can keep our plant open, and nobody else seems to either. So even though sustainability is a long shot, I think it's worth trying."

"Adam, it is so good to see you have hope again. I've been worried about you, you know. I hadn't told you because you had enough worries, but I was starting to be afraid I was going to lose my son as well as my husband, and the business just wasn't worth it. I was getting ready to tell you to just sell it for whatever we could get so you could walk away from it."

I replied, "For the first time I think the company has a fighting chance to not only survive, but really thrive. I feel like the weight of the world has been taken off my shoulders."

"You look like it, too," she said. "Get washed up and come into the kitchen. I need to get back to the stove to make sure the vegetables don't burn." Mom told me several months later that she was worried I was getting my hopes up too high, and that they would crash and burn later, leaving me, and the company, in even worse shape. But she hid that from me successfully during those next few weeks.

As I expected, Kelly was just as excited as I was when I called her later. She said, "I know it sounds too good to be true, but I've known Dennis ever since I moved out here. From everything I know about him, it will work. I've met some of the people from the company where he was the CEO. They all say the same things that he has said about the company. It's real, Adam, it's real."

"Thanks, Kelly; I really needed to hear that. I just hope I'm not getting my hopes up too high, too fast. This is a huge risk, you know. Not just from a monetary standpoint, but something much more important. If we try this and it doesn't work, I won't have enough credibility left to try anything else that's really bold. And I don't see how any of the conventional choices can keep the company going for the long run, except moving jobs to China. So this is our only real chance to keep the jobs here. As much as I hope it will work, I'm scared. And I know I'm going to have to start addressing doubts, direct and unspoken, starting tomorrow."

"Adam, when that happens, remember what I told you in your office when we were on our way to the airport. I have complete faith in you. You are the right person to lead the company through this—you, Adam, and nobody else. And remember that I love you."

"Kelly, you're my anchor right now. I kept thinking of your kiss, your words, your eyes all day today.

"Oh, hey," I continued. "I almost forgot. You met Annie Saturday evening. She talked with me today. She told me she could see that you had some really strong feelings for me, and she wasn't sure if I knew it. I really admired her courage for doing that. When she asked the question, I think my huge grin gave it away, even before I told her that I knew. She's really good people, Kelly. She's one of the reasons I want to save the plant here. And you don't have to worry about her and me. The only woman I want in my life is you."

"I knew that, but it sounded good to hear you say it," Kelly said softly.

"I love you, Adam."

"I love you too. Goodnight. And sleep well."

"You too," Kelly said, her voice trailing off as she hung up the phone.

CHAPTER 4
Setup and Pushback

First thing Tuesday morning I received an e-mail from Dennis with his reading list for participants at the off-site. It included:

- *Natural Capitalism*, by Paul Hawken, Amory Lovins, and Hunter Lovins.*

  - Chapter 1, "The Next Industrial Revolution."
  - Chapter 6, "Tunneling Through the Cost Barrier."
  - Chapter 7, "*Muda,* Service, and Flow." (*Muda* means waste.)

- "Life is Our Ultimate Customer: From Lean to Sustainability," by Gary Langenwalter.†

---

* Hawken, Paul, Amory Lovins, and L. Hunter Lovins. 1999. *Natural Capitalism.* New York: Little Brown.

† Langenwalter, Gary A. "Life is Our Ultimate Customer: From Lean to Sustainability." *Target*, first issue, 2006. Available on-line from the Association for Manufacturing Excellence. http://ww.ame.org/MagazineOnlinePDF.aspx?artid=3301.

- Chapter 1, "A Question of Design," in *Cradle to Cradle: Remaking the Way We Make Things,* by William McDonough and Michael Braungart.[‡]
- "The Critical Importance of Sustainability Risk Management," by Dan R. Anderson.[§]

So I asked Marie to order 25 copies of *Natural Capitalism* and *Cradle to Cradle*, with next day air shipment. I figured we would have fewer than 25 people in the off-site, but others might want to read them too. Any books left over I would put in the cafeteria with a sign encouraging people to read them. I also asked her to get 25 copies of each of the articles, paying royalties for the right to copy if the publisher asked.

I called a special staff meeting that afternoon to let them know of the schedule change for the next weekend and to determine who should participate in the off-site. When we were all in the room, I turned to my executive secretary, and said, "Marie, I appreciate the way you take notes at these meetings. Today I would prefer that you not take notes, and that you participate fully in our discussion. I value your years of experience and your excellent ability to see who people really are." I could see the surprise on her face; I don't think she had ever participated in a staff meeting before.

She smiled broadly, "Yes, I'd be glad to," and she put down her steno pad and picked up her coffee.

I addressed the group, "Barbara and I had a long phone call with a consultant, Dennis LeBlanc, yesterday afternoon.

[‡] McDonough, William and Michael Braungart. 2002. *Cradle to Cradle: Remaking the Way We Make Things*. New York: North Point Press.

[§] Anderson, Dan R. "The Critical Importance of Sustainability Risk Management." *Risk Management*, April, 2006. Available on-line at http://www.rmmag.com/ShowArticle.cfm?AID=3079.

He and his colleague, Karen Hoshibata, will be facilitating our off-site next weekend. Dennis pushed back when I talked about Saturday. He said that for the magnitude of change we're talking about, we would need to start Friday evening for two hours or so, like from 7:00 to 9:00, then Saturday from 9:00 to 4:00, then Sunday afternoon from 2:00 to 5:00. I was assuming that some of you would want to leave Sunday morning open for church attendance. What he said made sense—that we will need the 'soak time' to let the ideas settle in, then get back together to continue the process. Without the overnight processing time, followed by more meetings, we won't be nearly as effective. So I agreed to the entire weekend, because the fate of our company is probably riding on this meeting. I won't ask you to sacrifice your weekends for the company very often, but this time I need each of you to do that. Can you do that?" There was a little grumbling, but they all agreed.

I continued, "Dennis suggested, and Barbara recommended, that we include several key people from throughout the organization—potentially even line workers—in the planning session. The purpose of the meeting is to define our new company identity and strategy. We need to start from scratch. My dad used to remind me that the working definition of insanity is continuing to do the same things and expecting different results. Do you all concur that we will have better results, in both planning and execution, if we include people in addition to ourselves?"

After several minutes of discussion, there was a consensus to include people from outside the management staff. I asked Barbara to handle the selection process. So she took over the meeting.

"First," she said, "we'll nominate candidates, then we'll vote on them. I have given you each four slips of paper. I want each of you to nominate four people from outside this group who would be assets to an off-site. Nominate at least one person from your own department, and at least one person from another department or function; the other two can be from wherever in the company you want. When you have all filled out your slips, give them to me and I'll write the names and departments on the white board. Then we will start voting. Obviously, just because you nominate somebody does not mean they'll be participating. Let's start writing."

After collecting the slips, Barbara sorted them alphabetically, and wrote the names and departments on the white board. Sixteen people had been nominated. Two people had four nominations, three people had three, three had two nominations, and the rest had one.

She then passed out three green dots and one red dot to each person and instructed, "You each have three positive votes, and one negative vote to use if you wish. We are looking for participants who you think will do the best job in helping us create and execute our new vision and strategy. You can place as many stickers as you want on any given candidate. I also need to remind you that whatever is said and done inside this room stays here. If someone receives a red dot, all it means is that one of us would be uncomfortable with that person in this planning session. We must maintain complete confidence to protect that person's reputation. Does everyone agree?" and she waited until each head nodded in affirmation. "Then let's start placing our dots."

When all the dots had been placed, I was relieved to see there were no red ones used. Looking at the board, the top four nominees were easy to spot—each had at least three dots. They were from production (hourly), customer service, purchasing, and engineering. Barbara suggested that we also should have at least one person each from accounting, quality, and production supervision. Everyone agreed, so we picked the top-ranked persons from each of those areas. And just as we were adding them, I got the idea to add the maintenance supervisor. Somehow it just seemed right, so I suggested it. They all agreed, but the looks on their faces made it plain that they were just humoring me.

Then Tom spoke up, "What would you think if we invited our banker—Ron Meeker? He's been getting nervous about us. I think he'd be a real asset to the planning session. And that way he would understand why we'll be doing what we do in the future."

Everybody looked to me. Damn, this CEO decision-making role was still uncomfortable. Barbara spoke up in favor. "That could strengthen the outcome," she said. "It would be good to engage him and gain his commitment. And, if he participates actively in the discussion, we could all learn a lot about how the bank would react to any changes we might make."

"Anybody have any objections?" I asked. Silence. "Okay, Tom, invite him. And also give him copies of the reading materials."

I continued, "Since we're inviting Ron, we probably also should invite my mom. She's still the majority owner, and she probably knows more about the company than almost anyone sitting at this table. Are there any objections?" I didn't really expect any—how does an employee tell the owner that she is not welcome? "Okay, I'll invite her."

I closed the meeting by saying, "I'll send an e-mail to each person we nominated before I leave today. If they ask you questions about it, please tell them that their participation is very important for the company's future, and the reason they're being included is that the staff chose them. In my e-mail I'll tell them that I will be glad to talk with them myself as well. I'll also create a notice for the company bulletin board to let everyone know what's going on, naming the individuals who will take part in the off-site. Thank you for your participation today. That's it for now."

So everyone went back to work. I sent the e-mail and wrote the notice for the bulletin board.

Wednesday, I could sense some curiosity as I talked with people, but nobody would say what was on their mind. I decided just to wait until they finally started asking questions or making comments. I wanted to see who had the courage to tell the emperor he was not wearing any clothes. I called Rev. Franklin; we set up a meeting for Friday afternoon.

The books arrived from Amazon on Thursday; I was glad because I wanted people to be able to start reading the material as soon as possible. I asked Marie to e-mail people to come get them. A couple of hours later, Sam Peterson, our maintenance supervisor, asked if he could see me for a minute.

When we got into my office, he cleared his throat and said, "Mr. Brookings, I feel truly honored to be invited to this planning meeting, but I don't think I'll be able to help very much. You see, I don't feel right being there with all the rest of you."

"Sam, please call me Adam. Mr. Brookings was my dad, okay?"

"Okay, Mr. Brook . . . I mean, Adam," he said awkwardly as he looked away and then at me.

"Sam, I was the one who brought up your name in the meeting. I want you there because of all the decisions you and your staff make, day in and day out. I have a gut feeling that you are going to be one of the most important people in our new strategy. That's why I asked the staff to invite you; I think you'll have excellent ideas to contribute to the meeting."

Tom looked down at the reading materials in his hands and replied shyly, "Well, okay, if you think so. I'll start reading these tonight. Thanks." And he left, still seeming a bit puzzled.

Later in the afternoon, Barbara came in and told me she had just got off the phone with Dennis and Karen. They had put together a plan for the meeting. She was absolutely pleased to be working with them and with their expertise as organizational development professionals. (Later I would discover just how much she contributed to their understanding of who our people were and what might stimulate each one to contribute their best.) She beamed as she told me they decided to start by recreating the history of the company to set the stage the first night.

A few days earlier I had finished reading *Mid-Course Correction* and the chapter by Brown and Macy that Kelly had left me. I had given those to Mom and she had read them both.

When I came home that night, I handed Mom the reading materials for the off-site and made myself comfortable in the armchair across from her. She could tell I had something on my mind. "Mom, you know the people in the plant pretty well, right?"

"Yes, I think I do. What are you wondering about?" she asked.

"I'm trying to guess how the staff will react, person by person. Nobody has said anything to me yet, but I figure they will. The real question is, what are they thinking?"

"Adam, if you try to figure out what they're thinking, you'll drive yourself crazy. Why don't you just relax and let them tell you when they're ready."

Leaning back in the chair and stretching my arms behind my head, I responded, "Yeah, I guess there's no sense in going out looking for trouble. But the more I think about it, the more it seems that you should also participate in the off-site. You have been part of the company since it was founded. You have a lot to lose if it goes under, and a lot to gain if it succeeds. So will you join us?"

"All weekend?" she asked.

"If possible, that would be the best. But you don't have to be there the whole time if you don't want to. However, I think you should be there Friday evening and Sunday afternoon for sure. I would really appreciate it if you were there the rest of the time, too."

"Hmmm," she paused, then continued, "it makes sense for me to be there. I'll come for sure on Friday evening and Sunday afternoon. Let me decide about Saturday as we finish Friday night, okay?"

"You're the boss," I teased and smiled at her.

I was calling Kelly every night now and we talked about anything and everything for an hour or more. I missed seeing her face and holding her hands and kissing her, but even so I felt closer to her than I had ever felt to anyone before. On Tuesday night we had agreed that I would fly to Portland for a long weekend the weekend after the off-site. Tonight we decided she would come here for a long weekend a couple weeks after I visited Portland.

The questions and doubts started Friday morning. First, Tom (my CFO) closed the door as he came into my office and sat down. "Adam, I've read the chapters in those books and the articles. And I've got to tell you—as much as I *wish* that could happen here, it just can't and won't. That is just way too touchy-feely for this place. We're in the Midwest. We're solid, practical, down-to-earth people here. And I don't know how much those consultants are costing us, but we can't afford them. We barely have the cash flow to meet payroll for the next few weeks. I know you mean well. Hell, we all want to survive. But this just isn't how a real business operates—not a manufacturing business; not here. I'll be at the off-site, but I can't support this waste of time and money. Sorry."

"Tom, it takes real courage to tell the emperor that he's naked. There's probably nothing I can say right now that will change your mind, right?" He shook his head. "All I ask is that you keep an open mind until next Sunday afternoon. Then I want you to poke every hole you can into the ideas we have come up with. But until then, I need to ask you not to kill this before it has had a chance. I'll even pay for the consultants out of my own money so it won't impact the company's cash flow. I don't see many other alternatives that will keep the jobs here for the long run. Yes, I'm a little desperate. We all are. All I'm asking is that you give this hairbrained scheme a fair chance, unless you have any better ideas about how to stay competitive."

"Well, you've got me there, Adam. I don't have any better ideas, except to keep on doing what we've been doing. And you're right. The plant won't be here in three years, or maybe even one year, if we keep on doing that. I'm as frustrated as anyone else. I just don't see how this can work. The odds are so high against us! But I'll keep from saying anything bad about this to the others until next weekend."

"Thanks, Tom. I'm counting on you to show us the error of our ways next Sunday afternoon. But not a minute sooner, right?" I grinned.

He stood up, shook my hand, and said, "I watched you work here during high school and college, and thought you were a solid, hard worker. I've been watching you these last 10 weeks since Chris' death. We all have. And I've gotta tell you. You've got nerve, kid. And I, for one, admire you for it. I'll do just what you asked—I'll wait till you ask me, then I'll show you where the holes are."

"I really need you to do that. You get to be the voice of hard cash—dollars and cents—reality. That's absolutely critical, and you can do it much better than anyone else. We really need you to put on your green eyeshade at the end of that meeting. Otherwise, we're risking the whole company."

"You've got it. Keep up the good work, Adam."

"Thanks, Tom. You too."

I was refilling my coffee in the office kitchen when Wayne, the VP of operations, spotted me. "I've been reading that stuff, and I have some serious doubts. Do you have some time to talk now?"

So we headed for my office and Wayne closed the door. Compared to his usual calm disposition, the frown on his face was a little disconcerting. He also seemed nervous; he was fidgeting as he sat down and he kept looking at the desk. I just waited for him to speak. After a period of silence, he looked up at me, and said, "I don't even know how to start this conversation. So please bear with me. I want to applaud your courage for trying something to get us out of our rut. I want to support you on this. But I can't. I can't see any way that these ideas could ever apply to our industry or our company. I glanced through all of *Cradle to Cradle* to see what else it might say. One chapter talks about waste equals food. How in the world can that possibly apply here? Do you want me to buy used plastic housings and melt them down? We can't do that! You want me to buy used electronic components—a resistor here, an IC there, and reuse them? We can't do that! Your father led this company very successfully until a few months ago, and now you're coming in here with these wild, pie-in-the-sky ideas. I wish I knew where you've been getting what you've been smoking—it must be some really good stuff. I'm stuck between a rock and a hard place. I'll be honest with you. The only reason I'm not handing in my resignation right now is that I don't know where I could get another decent job without having to sell the house and move. So I'll keep doing my job as vice president of operations. But don't expect me to support this, because I can't. I think you've really gone off the deep end. I'm sorry, but that's the way I see it," he said emphatically, and then he slumped down into his chair, looking almost defeated.

Wow. What do I say after that? Dad, where are you when I need you for advice?

"Wayne, I hear you, loud and clear. And I'm glad you came in here to tell me what you're thinking. I learned from my father not to shoot the messenger. I will never criticize anyone for telling me what they think is the truth. So thank you for doing that.

"I respect your opinion that this stuff can't possibly work here. You might very well be right. When we meet next weekend, that's exactly the discussion we need to have. Because I'm as scared as I think you are. The way I see it, unless we do something *really* different, we lose the plant. First the manufacturing, and then the engineering, will go to China. That means you and all your people will lose their jobs. And I know there aren't many manufacturing jobs left around here. That's why I'm willing to try something as crazy as this." I then paused to collect my thoughts.

"Tell you what. When we discuss these ideas next weekend, we'll take it in steps. Barbara has been telling me how we'll proceed. First, we'll talk about where we came from, where we are, and where we want to be. Then we'll talk about alternatives—how to get where we want to go. Once we, as a group, have agreed on the best alternative, we'll discuss how to implement it with the lowest risk and best payback. Is there anything strange about that?" He shook his head. I continued, "Will you do that with us? I want you to bring up all your doubts and concerns, but not until the end of the meeting. Don't hold anything back, because if you're right, I don't want to go down that road either. We can't afford for anyone to be a 'yes man.' There is too much at stake. Can you do that for me?"

Looking somewhat surprised, Wayne nodded his head slowly in agreement.

"Wayne, please give these half-baked ideas a chance. Don't kill them until we have talked them out next Sunday afternoon, okay? Because we might decide sometime Saturday afternoon that these ideas won't work, but they might give us other ideas that *will* work. So we need to go through the process. And if you criticize them beforehand, we won't have anyplace to start, and the off-site will look just like our staff meetings. No hope, no future."

"Adam, I'll do that for you. I owe you, your mom, your dad, and the company at least that much courtesy, if not a lot more."

After he left, I just sat there for a few minutes, staring at my tepid coffee. Then Marie appeared in the doorway. "I'm guessing you've had an 'interesting' morning," she said, making quote signs with her fingers in the air.

"Yeah, you could say that."

"Adam, I'm impressed. Both Tom and Wayne were in much better moods when they left your office than when they arrived. I don't know what you said to them, but whatever it was, I think it worked. And as to my reaction to the reading, I don't have a clue if we can pull this off, but if we can, I think the company will win really big. I once saw a *Far Side* cartoon several years ago. Two spiders had spun a huge web at the bottom of a slide on a playground, waiting for a kid to come down. One says to the other, 'If this works, we'll eat like kings!' So keep your spirits up, okay?"

I grinned at the impossibility of it all, and said, "Thanks, Marie. I needed that."

I closed the door and called Kelly, because I needed to hear her voice. When I told her about the two conversations, she commented, "Adam, you did so well! You truly are a gifted leader. I am so proud of you."

"Really? I didn't think I did very well at all."

"Trust me, you did very, very well. So just relax for a bit, and enjoy. This is the first stage of implementing any major change—the pushback, the doubts, the fears. You remember that, don't you? You're doing fine. And remember how I told you I loved you when you were sitting in that very chair? It's still true, even more now than before."

"Thanks, Kels. I really needed to hear that." After we hung up, I just sat there in the chair remembering her being there Sunday afternoon. It seemed so long ago, but her presence was still so powerful.

At noon I headed for the cafeteria to grab some lunch. I purposely sat down with a couple of machinists that I had worked with during my third summer at the plant. "George, Henry, how's it going?" I asked.

"Hi, Adam, it's okay," Henry replied. "Wish we had more work out there—it's a little skinny in our area right now."

"Henry, you just wish you were a little skinny!" George's laugh boomed through the cafeteria. Henry was not a small man, especially around the middle; neither was George. "Yeah, all kidding aside, the volumes are off in our area. But I guess you already know that, don't you."

"Yes, I know that, all too well," I replied with a sigh.

"Hey, I hear you've got some sort of high-powered session going on next weekend, and that you're talking about stuff none of us have ever heard anything about," Henry said as he unwrapped his sandwich.

"Yeah, that's true. What are the guys in the plant saying about it?" I asked and then took a drink from my soda can.

George looked at Henry and then at me and said, "Well, most of us have only heard about it second-hand, but the buzz in the shop is that we know we hafta do *something* different, and this sure is different. They even said Annie and some other guys from the floor have been asked. Nobody here ever heard of asking us workers in the shop to tell the company what to do. That could be crazy, or it could be real productive. So we're hoping it will work, even though it sounds far-fetched."

"Thanks, guys," I said. "Tell your friends we really need their support if we start putting this stuff in. And we're hoping it will work too, although we haven't yet figured out just what 'it' is yet. That's what next weekend is all about."

I finished the last bite of my sandwich and was preparing to leave when Henry leaned across the table so only George and I could hear him. "Adam, thanks for trying. We can see the handwriting on the wall, and we were starting to get worried about our jobs. It means a lot to us that you're trying to keep the jobs here and not move them to China. I'll do anything I can to help. You just tell me what you want, and I'll do it. You hear?"

George leaned over, "Me too, Adam. All the way, me too."

"Thanks, Henry, George. I'll take you up on that," I said as I got up and left. Walking back to my office I kept thinking . . .

there were two more reasons to keep the plant open—Henry and George. I knew I could count on them.

My appointment with Reverend Franklin was at 3 p.m. On my way out the door, I told Marie that I wouldn't be back. "You've earned the rest of the day off, Adam. Go do something fun for yourself," she said cheerfully.

As I left, I realized that I didn't know what "something fun" would look like right now. Before I came back home it would have meant hanging out with my friends, maybe going to Harvard Square, or taking in a Celtics or Red Sox game. Here? Well, there weren't many friends left here from high school, and the few that I knew had families and other commitments. So I was mostly alone—alone with the pressure, the doubts, the fears. I had heard the expression "lonely at the top" while I was in college. Now I knew what it meant. I was hoping that Reverend Franklin could help with that, even if it was just a little bit.

Reverend Franklin was in his office in the church when I got there. He was seated at his desk. At about 5 ft 11 in., with light brown eyes and salt and pepper hair matching his well-trimmed beard and mustache, he looked quite physically fit.

He rose and walked toward me, smartly dressed in a blue dress shirt and tie, a dark blue v-neck sweater, grey slacks, and black penny loafers. He extended his right hand to greet me. I shook his hand warmly as he said, "Adam, I'm glad you came. I was hoping I would get a chance to get to know you better. How are things going?"

"Reverend Franklin, I guess about as well as could be expected," I said as I took a seat opposite his large wooden desk.

"Please, Adam, if you're comfortable, call me John," he said sincerely.

"I can do that. Anyhow, when Mom asked me to step in and run the company, I was intending to get it ready to sell. Then I started to realize that if we sold the company, the new owners would send all the manufacturing jobs to China. I just couldn't do that to my friends here in town. The first girl I ever loved works at the plant now; she couldn't get a job that pays that well anywhere else in the area. She's a single mom, and with her parents living here, she doesn't want to leave. My VP of operations is too old to get a job anywhere else and too young to retire. So he'd be up the creek. I just can't abandon my friends like that."

"I see, I see," he said, nodding his head. "What else?"

"I forgot to ask. Everything I tell you is confidential, isn't it?"

"Of course," John replied.

"Okay. The bad news is that unless we do something radically different, the jobs are going to China anyway. That's what our two competitors have done in the last couple of years. Their products are now 20–25% cheaper than ours, and it's hurting us badly."

"That's too bad. That's got to be causing you lots of stress," he said, looking at me with concern in his eyes.

"It sure is. But I wanted to tell you how much your sermon on Sunday meant to me. My girlfriend basically told me the same thing on Saturday, and then to hear you preach on it on Sunday, well, it must have been a sign. I never used to believe in signs, but I'm hoping that was one. Your story about the experience in Hawaii was fascinating. I just wish something like that would happen to my company."

"Did you hear what you just said? 'My' company?" John said, nodding his head.

"I did say that, didn't I? I think that's the first time I have called it that out loud. Hmmm. Anyhow, let me admit to being a little selfish. I'm finding out that the old expression about 'lonely at the top' is true. I can't share my troubles with the people at the company. I can tell Mom some things, but not all. My girlfriend is great, but she's my age. Can I talk with you from time to time just to get stuff off my chest?"

"I would be honored to listen to you, Adam, anytime. And I mean that."

"Good. Mom has been telling me lots of good things about you ever since you got here a couple of years ago. So the reason I came today was just to think out loud about what I'm hoping to do at the company. Is that okay with you?"

"Sure is," he replied.

So I told him all about last Monday's staff meeting and the upcoming off-site and Kelly's suggestion to talk with this guy she knew, my conversation with Dennis, and all the reading I had been doing on sustainability. I even showed him the article I'd brought with me.

"Hmmm, that looks really interesting. I think that might be the piece I was missing for this Sunday's sermon. Thanks," John said with a slight grin.

"So anyhow, this sustainability consulting friend of Kelly's is coming out in a week to meet people on Friday and lead the off-site. And now I actually have some hope that we can pull the company out of the fire."

Sounding a little relieved, John said, "That's really good to hear. I'm glad for you, and for the others who work there. We have at least 12 members of our congregation who work there."

"But what makes sustainability so interesting is that it no longer uses money as the only metric. It has a Triple Bottom

Line—profits, people, and planet. This might sound like a really weird question. Does the church have any dogma or teachings on the people or planet side? I assume you don't focus on profit very much."

"Good assumption on the profit angle, Adam. Yes, actually, we do have positions on both the people and planet sides, as you call them. We believe that all humans are sacred and are to be treated with respect. In fact, virtually all religions have a version of this Golden Rule. We discourage companies from exploiting or hurting workers or their communities. And we believe that we should be good stewards of the earth to honor God's creation. Virtually all religions also support that idea. So I'll be very interested in hearing how this sustainability thing works in your company. I truly hope you'll come see me again. Or I could stop by your plant sometime, if you prefer. Or, we could meet for coffee at Matilda's restaurant; they have great pies there, you know."

"Any of those sound good, especially the pie," I grinned. "If this is too pushy, let me know, but could we schedule a meeting every other Friday at 4:00 p.m.? It will give me something to look forward to."

"That sounds fine. Let's do it. I'll put those meetings in my calendar for the next three months, and then we can decide on the schedule after that." He pulled out his calendar and wrote in our appointments.

"Thanks for your time, John. And I'm looking forward to seeing you again in two weeks. Can we meet here then as well?"

"Right here will be just fine. I'm looking forward to it. See you in church on Sunday?"

"I'll be here." I stood up, we shook hands, and I headed for home.

It was almost exactly a week ago that I was driving to the airport to pick up Kelly. What a wild ride this last week had been! I could only wonder what next week would have in store, and then next weekend. That was going to be something else. Interestingly enough, given Kelly's whole-hearted endorsement of Dennis, plus my phone call with him, I wasn't at all nervous about his ability to help us. And after reading the sustainability books, plus the stuff I was getting off the net, I really thought it might work well, even in our industry, even in the Midwest.

I was expecting other people to push back on the ideas next week after they read the materials. What concerned me the most was the people who weren't reading the materials, but who were forming opinions based on what they thought other people were saying. I realized I had no real control over that, and it would probably make us or break us. Welcome to being a CEO—I was quickly learning how little direct control I had over what others do. So I planned to spend a lot of time next week practicing an old HP method—MBWA—managing by wandering around. That would be the most important thing I could do.

When I got home, I called a couple of old friends from high school and we went out for a beer. I didn't have what I would consider a great time, but it was better than sitting at home. Saturday I went down to Dad's workshop and messed around with some wood. I just needed to work with my hands and see something tangible. I wasn't really intending to make anything, but somehow I wound up with a crude knick-knack shelf.

On Sunday, Rev. Franklin's sermon was insightful and thought-provoking, again. He talked from a book by Rosamund Zander, *The Art of Possibility*.** He related the story of a college professor who inspired his students to

---

** Zander, Rosamund Stone and Benjamin Zander. 2002. *The Art of Possibility*. New York: Penguin Books, p. 27.

accomplish more than they thought possible by telling them on the first day of class, "You don't have to worry about your grade in this class. You all have an 'A' for both semesters. All you have to do is to write up a one-page description, dated next May, of what you did to earn that 'A' and give it to me within two weeks." I found myself wondering how I could use this with my staff and my people at the plant, and even customers and suppliers. And I was not at all surprised to be thinking I'd be back the next Sunday as well.

Monday at the staff meeting, I asked how many had read the off-site materials. Everybody said they had, and that the off-site participants in their departments had done so as well. I essentially repeated the points I had made with Wayne on Friday, asking each person to give the process a chance, because sustainability was just one possible way to break out of our current box. I emphasized that the group, collectively, would decide through the coming weekend how we, as a company, would proceed.

While I was in the plant Tuesday morning, Annie asked me if we could talk for five minutes. So we headed for the far corner table in the cafeteria again.

She began, "Adam, why am I in the group this weekend? Please tell me that it doesn't have anything to do with . . ." and she couldn't even say the words. All of a sudden I realized that she still had feelings for me. Simultaneously, I realized that if I weren't completely committed to Kelly, I would be tempted to develop a relationship with Annie, in spite of the fact that she worked for my company. Hey, if Bill Gates could date his employees, I could too! But I also realized that this might have tragic consequences for us all. I knew how wide the gap between us had grown since I left. Neither of us was the same; not even close.

"Annie, the reason you were asked to participate is that the staff wants you there," I said factually, ignoring her hesitation for the moment. "The staff, as a group, selected the person from each department who they thought would be the best participant. I'm personally pleased that you're part of the group, but I did not influence the selection in any way. Think of this as a huge compliment—the staff wants your ideas to help the company survive and thrive. You will be the voice of the entire shop floor as we make our decisions."

I decided to confront the relationship issue as gently as possible. "I know that we had a relationship in the past. You were my first love, and you'll always be special to me. But when Kelly was here a week ago, we finally admitted to each other that we are deeply in love, and have been for years. I suspect we'll get married some day, although we haven't discussed it yet. You and I can be friends in our own way. As your friend, I want you to have a really great life, and I'm doing the best I can to help you. Coming to this group, you will be doing the best you can to help me too, and yourself, and everyone else in this company. We need your brains in this meeting." Her eyes misted over as I said this. She nodded in agreement and went back to work.

What I was rapidly learning in the 10 weeks since Dad's death was that being a CEO was 90% about people, and 10% about technology. So maybe my psych major wasn't such a bad choice for a CEO after all. And I realized that I had quit thinking of myself as a temporary CEO, getting a company ready to be sold, or an unqualified kid who couldn't do the job. I was now feeling like what Kelly had told me was actually true—I *am* qualified. I *have* earned my "A." This is now *my* company. And we *will* make it!

CHAPTER 5
Friday Night Fights

Well, here we all were—7:00 Friday evening at our off-site strategy and planning session, at the local country club in a meeting room. The consultants had spent all day at the plant, starting with a meeting with Barbara and me, a plant tour, and then talking with participants.

The room was prepared and ready to go. Barbara had arranged for the flip charts and supplies we would need—it was like being in the third grade with magic markers and masking tape lying around. One entire wall featured a blank strip of butcher paper stretching from one end to the other. She passed out name tags, knowing that the facilitators didn't know everyone and would appreciate seeing the tags as they led. People were still dressed in what they had worn to work. We'd been business casual for a few years, especially on Fridays. I was comfortable in my jeans, loafers, and an open-collar shirt.

I kicked off the meeting at five after the hour. "Thanks for coming. I appreciate your putting the needs of the company ahead of your family and personal activities this evening and this weekend. I give you my word that we won't make a habit of weekend meetings, unless they're part of a celebration convention in the Bahamas. (There was no response to the attempted humor—either too early, too nervous, or both.)

"For those who were not at our Monday morning staff meeting almost three weeks ago, let me ask the following question again, so we can all see the result. Does anybody in this room think that we'll be in business in five years if current trends continue? Raise your hands if you think the company will still be in business." Not one hand went up. "Right—that's why we're here. My dad used to tell me that the working definition of 'insanity' is doing the same things and expecting different results. So we need to get completely creative and unconventional to figure out a way to not only survive, but thrive, long-term. And, to do that, we as a group need to trust each other and feel safe. So here are the ground rules for this weekend."

Turning the first page on the flip chart next to me, I pointed to the following rules, which were written in large black letters for all to see. I read them aloud and elaborated on each one briefly.

"1. *Each person is a unique, gifted, talented individual.* We might disagree with each other's ideas, even passionately, but we will continue to respect one another. Does everyone agree?"

All heads nodded and I proceeded to read number two out loud.

"2. *All ideas are great ideas.* Let me repeat: all ideas are great ideas. Now you say it, out loud, together. ALL IDEAS ARE GREAT IDEAS! However, only some ideas should be implemented."

I glanced across the room and thought to myself, Wayne and Tom look so uncomfortable! They had failed to repeat this along with everyone else—too nervous I supposed.

"3. *We collectively get to identify, then sacrifice, the sacred cows.* Every company has them. Each person here has them. And they're probably not what you might expect. Remember, sacred cows make the best hamburger!

"4. *Finally, and equally important, is confidentiality.* Everything said in this room stays in this room. Does each of you agree to that?"

All heads nodded in agreement.

"So, with these rules, let's start questioning everything, and changing everything, and creating something new until we can each raise our hands confidently when I ask the question, 'how many think we'll still be in business 10 years from now?'

"Before we start, I want to introduce our two facilitators, Dennis LeBlanc and Karen Hoshibata. They are seasoned business people who have skills, talents, and experience that will help us create a new strategy—one that will work. You've already done the reading on some ideas. I've learned that if I facilitate, I can't participate fully. I asked them to facilitate the weekend so I can participate.

"And since not everybody knows everybody, let's go around the room and introduce ourselves briefly. I'll start. I'm Adam Brookings, brand-new CEO." I nodded and looked at Wayne to continue the introductions.

"I'm Wayne Doernbacher—plant manager."

"Tom McCarthy—CFO."

"Cindy Haman—I work in shipping and receiving."

"I'm Jeff Holland—VP sales and marketing."

"Barbara Joiner—HR."

"Mary Pulaski—I am VP of materials and logistics."

"I'm Walter Chen—VP of engineering."

"Marie Rollins—executive secretary."

"I'm Susan Brookings—owner."

"Ron Meeker—I'm senior VP, Farmers' and Merchants' Bank—nice to meet all of you."

"Chet Schmidt—shop steward."

"Annie Zabransky—I work in the assembly area."

"I'm Heather Wilcox—quality."

"Lorraine Higginbotham—customer service supervisor."

"Carl Lewis—I'm production supervisor."

"I'm Nancy Sippinetti—purchasing manager."

"Beth Chipszak—engineer."

"Sam Peterson—I'm the maintenance manager."

Barbara then came forward on cue and led us through a five-minute icebreaker exercise called "draw a pig." It was rather hokey, but it loosened us up a little, which was the intent.

I then turned the facilitation over, saying, "Dennis and Karen will now lead us for the rest of the weekend. Dennis?"

Dennis started, "It's truly an honor for Karen and me to be here. We're here because we have led other companies, including my own, through the kind of change you are contemplating here tonight. We have achieved some remarkable results and are confident you can do the same at Brookings— nothing less than transforming your company into something beyond what you can imagine now. So we ask you to stay with us, and play along, and participate as enthusiastically as you can. We know from experience that most of you are likely to be skeptical at this point. That's good. To succeed we will base everything on one another's honest statements. Each of you will be responsible for sharing your doubts as well as your creative ideas. That's really important.

"Our role as facilitators is to make a safe place where you can be completely creative. Any questions before we start?" There were no questions, so Dennis proceeded, "Okay, let's start with a one-word check-in. Just say one word that tells how you feel right now. We won't go in any order—just speak when you want to." People said some interesting things, including nervous, excited, confused, energized, and fearful.

Dennis then said, "You've noticed that Barbara has taped butcher paper up on one entire wall. Susan, how long ago was the company started?"

"Thirty years ago," she replied.

Doing the math in his head, Dennis walked over to the left side of the paper wall and wrote the year the company started. He then walked over to the far right side and wrote the current year. Turning back to us, he said, "There are plenty of markers on the tables. Choose the ones you want, then go to the paper wall and write a major event in the life of the company at about the right place." And we did. "Okay, you can each write one more if you want to." And most of us did.

Dennis continued, "Now, moving from left to right, let me point to each one. As I point to it, the person who wrote it should read it aloud for everyone and then explain why it was important." He pointed to the first one, "patent received."

Mom said, "Chris had been working on his idea for several years. He finally got it to where he could patent it. That took more than a year and almost all our savings. But once we had the patent, we felt we could start our own company."

Dennis pointed to "company started."

Mom said, "That's when Chris and I decided to risk everything we had to start the company. Since we couldn't find a bank to loan us the money, his dad mortgaged the family farm to provide the money we needed. That farm is now in the fourth generation of Brookings' ownership. We were so moved when Dad told us he'd do that—risk the family farm for us. It was then that we realized how much he loved us and how much family meant to him. And our dream was to build a company that would operate like family—based on trust and respect."

Although Mom might have thought she was just explaining what had happened early in the company's history, her simple statement had a profound impact on the group. It was like we were suddenly all part of that family, even Ron, the banker. We were sharing Dad and Mom's dreams for their company, *our* company.

Dennis then pointed to "first order received."

Mom continued, "That was six long months after we started the company. All we had during those early days was our faith in each other and in his patent. I made the initial calls to prospects to find out who he should be talking with. Then he would call and try to talk with them. He met with several. We had to pay for all his travel expenses, of course. We were on such a tight budget that our big treat for the month was a small ice cream cone at the Dairy Queen! But finally, *finally,* we got our first real customer order. It was small, but it was a start. And they've been a customer of ours ever since. We had gotten so discouraged that we were just about to quit. That order was a godsend!"

Dennis pointed to the next event, "first hire."

Mom smiled as she looked across the room and said, "We were lucky with the people we hired. Our first hire was Wayne."

Wayne spoke, "I was fresh out of college, Michigan State, and didn't know what I wanted to do. A fraternity brother had an older brother who was friends with Chris; he told me to call Chris. So I did. I then came out here to meet with him and Susan. On the drive out, I was telling myself, 'There's no way I'm going to go to work for a startup in the middle of nowhere.' But when I met them, I caught their dream. We started talking, and the more we talked, the more I just knew that this was where I belonged. I went back to East Lansing and stayed there just long enough to pack everything I had into a trailer. I have been here ever since and never regretted it. I got to run machines, hire people, meet customers, design new plants—it's been an engineer's dream!"

And so the discussion continued, through the "next patent," "purchasing the first equipment" (used, of course), and then Dennis pointed to "first bank financing."

Ron spoke up, "I remember Susan and Chris coming to my office—a young couple, full of dreams and energy. I still had hair then, you know." We chuckled as he patted his bald head. "They didn't quite meet all the bank's criteria, but they had written a clear business plan, and my instincts said they would be a good, long-term customer. I wish more of my customers were like them. They have always been completely straight with me, telling me all the news up front, and not trying to white-wash it. Anyhow, I put my reputation on the line with my president. Brookings' performance through the years has helped me get promoted, and I am truly grateful for that."

Mom added, "That bank loan let us pay off the loan Chris' dad gave us. So the family farm was no longer at risk. We really celebrated that day."

Someone quipped, "Yeah, an ice cream sundae instead of a cone!" We all chuckled.

As the discussion continued, each person contributed.

"Air freight—now that was a day to remember," Lorraine remarked. "That was when our pick-and-place machine had broken down, and we just couldn't get it fixed right. We were getting later and later—we had missed our ship date. I was on the phone daily with our customer to keep them up to date. They kept telling me they needed the parts at their plant Thursday at 2 p.m., or their line would shut down, and it would be very difficult for them to keep using us as a supplier. Somehow, we got the machine working at the last minute, and we had to charter a private jet to get those parts to them. I think the jet cost more than the whole order. But we saved a customer, an important customer."

"Yeah," Sam said in agreement. "After that, I started focusing more on preventive maintenance. It was a real learning experience for me—let me tell you. But even when nerves were as frazzled as they could be, Chris and Wayne didn't yell at me. They kept encouraging me, telling me they knew I could do it. I wasn't sure they were right, but I sure didn't want to let them, the customer, or my company down."

"Day care," said Annie. "Yes, that's what I wrote down. It might seem like a small thing to the rest of you. But when I got divorced, I had to have affordable day care so I could work. I couldn't ask my mom to take care of Matthew every day. So I went to Barbara and asked if there was anything the company could do. Two months later, you guys opened a day care facility at the plant, just because I asked. And who am I? Just a person on the assembly line . . ." and she couldn't continue—tears were streaming down her cheeks. Barbara and Mom both went over to her. The rest of us didn't know what to do—we were uncomfortable. In a little bit, she regained control and continued, "I'm sorry, but this company, you people, you all mean so much to me. Except for my mom and Matthew, you're all I've got. You have no idea how much you mean to me. You have no idea how much it means that somebody cared enough to help me."

Carl spoke when Dennis pointed to "Lean." "Lean, now that was one scary proposition. It was actually good for the shop floor—they gained responsibility and got to learn lots of new things. But for us in management, it was scary as hell! What it meant was that we were still responsible for how things turned out, but we couldn't order people around like we had before. We needed to become coaches and advisors. I had serious doubts, huge doubts. And I walked into Chris' office and told him that, yes I did! He was like that, you know. You could tell him what you were really thinking and he wouldn't get mad at you. That day, all he did was listen to me, then he asked if I would give it a try and see what happened. He promised that if it didn't work out well, he would call a company-wide meeting and tell everyone he had blown it, big time. And that I, and several others, had told him it wouldn't work. Well, how could I say no to that? So I tried it. And funny thing, it worked, and even better than Chris had thought. I remember his speech to the entire company. He said that our pay would remain the same, but our jobs might change. As long as business held steady or improved, we would all keep our jobs. And we did."

"But only for a while," Chet butted in. "It was two years ago that you laid off the second shift—so much for keeping your promises. That's why I wrote lay-off on the time line." His tone flash-froze the feeling of camaraderie that had become palpable in the room, followed by a long, *very* uncomfortable silence.

Karen asked Chet, "So you feel like the company broke its promise?"

"Damn straight I do! And so do a lot of other people."

Karen quietly responded, "Tell me again what the promise was, Chet?"

"That the company would not lay off anyone, that's what. And they broke it!"

Karen asked, "Carl or Wayne or Tom, was that the promise?"

Wayne responded, "Not quite. It was that we wouldn't lay anybody off as long as business stayed the same or improved. Chet, do you remember how full our finished goods stockroom had gotten?"

He replied, "Yeah, it had inventory everywhere."

Wayne added, speaking to Chet, "Right. That's because customer orders had fallen off. He then turned to Jeff and asked, "What were you hearing from our customers? And I'm not blaming you or the sales force at all. What were our customers telling you?"

Jeff replied, "They were telling me that Electronic Products had lowered its prices about 20%. We figured it's because Electronic Products had shut down its plant in California and was importing the stuff from China. Some of our customers quit buying from us. Our sales fell by 30% that year, and we've never been able to get them back."

Wayne continued, "I figure if we hadn't put in Lean when we did, we would have gone out of business then. The only reason we're still here is that we got rid of all the waste that we did and were able to cut our costs."

Chet responded, "Yeah, but the owners have made a killing on the backs of my friends!"

A shocked silence settled over the room. Karen broke the silence. "I sense that we're all uncomfortable by what Chet has just said. Let's assume Chet said what he did in a spirit of openness, rather than trying to hurt anyone in this room. Let's spend two minutes in silence and just absorb it, rather than reacting quickly."

After two very long minutes, Karen resumed, "As uncomfortable as this is, I think it is actually a very good sign. Let me ask one question. Chet, were you trying to hurt anyone's feelings?"

"No, not at all," he replied. "It just came out. I didn't want to hurt anyone, especially Mrs. Brookings."

"Exactly," Karen said as she took a few steps and paused for a brief moment. She continued, "I am assuming that Chet felt comfortable enough to finally say what has been locked up inside him for a long time. And I can tell that this is very uncomfortable for the rest of you. But until these thoughts and opinions are brought to the table and dealt with openly, they will seriously impede progress. As strange as this sounds, this is actually a huge step forward for the weekend, and sooner than we expected. So let's have two more minutes of silence to allow each person to process what has just happened."

After two minutes, Karen asked, "Now, Susan, how are you feeling?"

"Shocked and hurt—but I can sort of understand why somebody might think that." She knew she needed to bring to light the reasoning behind the layoff decision.

Looking straight at Chet, she asked him, "Do you really believe that?"

"I'm sorry, but yes, I think it's true," he said.

Mom replied, "Do you think we should have kept the second shift and sent the company into bankruptcy?"

"What do you mean?" he asked.

She explained, "Well, the second shift would have still been producing products, right? And we weren't able to sell them, so we would have had to rent a warehouse to put them in. We would have continued to buy raw materials and pay the payroll and build more products that we couldn't sell, until we ran out of cash. Then we wouldn't have been able to pay the suppliers or the payroll. And we would have had to shut the company down."

"Why didn't you just cut the price to match the Chinese? You've gotta be making a killing at the prices you charge your customers."

Chet's statements were really causing an air of doubt to permeate the room. All eyes were suddenly on Mom.

After a short pause to gather her thoughts, Mom began, "I loved Chris with all my heart. But even then, sometimes we disagreed. One thing we disagreed on was how much financial information to share. He felt it was totally private, our own business, and nobody else's. I thought it would help if others knew what was going on. So I'm going to tell you some things that he didn't want to tell anyone else. And I'm counting on you, all of you, to keep this completely confidential, all right? Don't even tell your spouse. Everyone agree to that?" She looked around the room slowly; each person nodded in turn.

"Here's the deal. Our net profit right now, after all expenses, is about 2%. That's all. If we cut our prices to our customers by 20%, we would be losing 18% per year. To put that in real numbers, our company sells about $50 million per year right now. Our expenses are $49 million. If we cut our prices 20%, that means our income would be $40 million and our expenses would be $49 million. Chet, would you want to put $9 million a year into a company that couldn't pay you back?"

Looking astonished, Chet blurted out, "Hell, no!"

"Well, neither does anyone else. That's the problem. Even worse, our profit keeps falling. And it's the profit that allows us to invest in new products so we can stay competitive for the long run. That's why this meeting is happening," Susan said, addressing not only Chet, but the entire room.

Feeling like she may as well get everything out in the open, Mom continued, "The other part of that picture is this. This plant, including the equipment, is worth several million dollars. That's what Chris and I invested in. This is most of my life's savings, right here. If I could sell this plant and equipment today and put the money in a bank, I would earn more interest per year than I'm getting by keeping the company open. So tell me, Chet, why I shouldn't do that? Why should I keep this plant open?" At this, silence blanketed the room.

Chet was looking more uncomfortable as each silent second passed. He finally spoke, so quietly that I had to strain to hear him, "Mrs. Brookings, I had no idea. I really didn't know. I apologize. If you would be willing to tell the others in the plant what you just told us, it would really change some attitudes out there. I won't tell them, because I promised to not tell anyone. But it will be really, really hard to not tell them, because I don't want them to keep thinking what they've been thinking—not anymore. We were just plain wrong. I never knew."

Mom looked out at everyone as she spoke, "Chet, I accept your apology. And I'll think about your idea for a bit; I agree that people throughout the company should know more about its finances. Let's see what the rest of this weekend brings. Then I'll have a better idea what to do about that."

"Mrs. Brookings," Chet said, rising from his chair and starting to walk over to her, "I gotta tell you. You are one very classy lady. I don't know anybody else who would have reacted the way you did to what I said. Thank you." With that, he shook her hand. Then, he turned around, went back to his seat, and sat down.

Dennis suggested, "Although it was not on our original schedule, a break would probably be a good idea right now.

Let's all get up and move around some, then be back in our chairs in 10 minutes. Everyone agree?" Heads nodded. "Great—we'll see you all back here in 10 minutes."

During the break Dennis and Karen asked Mom, "How are you feeling?"

"Surprisingly good, considering," she replied.

Dennis said, "I've got to agree with Chet. You truly are one classy lady! That had to hurt, hurt a lot."

Mom remarked, "It did on the surface, but as I told the group, I could basically understand where Chet and others were coming from. If I only had the information they have, I'd probably be thinking the same things. That's why I've wanted to let everyone in the company know more about our financial situation. And I've wanted to do that for years. My experience is that if you trust people, most of them will rise to your level of trust. Those who don't, well, they eventually leave. And yes, they can do some damage, but the rewards from the people you trust are worth it."

I walked up to the group as the conversation started. "Mom, I agree with you. It's time to tell the rest of the company. I trust the people I worked with during the summers, and I've gotta believe the others are just as trustworthy, generally speaking. They all loved Dad and wouldn't do anything to hurt him. That includes you, by extension, and me, so far."

Dennis asked Mom and me, "Then by Sunday afternoon do you think you'll have some idea of what information you'd be willing to share?"

Mom and I looked at each other and I replied, "Yes. We'll talk about it tomorrow evening."

"Great! And thanks," said Dennis. Then he and Karen went to find Chet, who was outside having a smoke.

"How are you doing?" Dennis asked Chet.

"Okay," responded Chet, noncommittally.

"You know," Dennis said, looking straight at Chet, "in a month or so, people will look back on your comments today as THE turning point in the weekend. And this weekend is probably THE turning point for the company. So even if you're not sure of the effects of what you said, we think you have truly helped the company. More than you'll probably ever realize."

"Really?" Chet said, obviously having difficulty believing Dennis' statement. "Because as soon as I said it, I looked over to Mrs. Brookings and saw her face, and realized how much I had hurt her. And I *never* wanted to hurt her like that! I wanted to dig a hole, crawl in, and cover up and hide. And I still sort of want to do that. But it's too late. I don't know if I can ever face those people again. They must hate me!"

"Well," Karen said, "we were all surprised when you said that. But I don't think anybody hates you. And I think some good things will come from this, if you let them. See you in there in two minutes."

"Right," Chet replied quietly.

When the group reconvened, Karen spoke. "Dennis and I have a forecast. And you all know the accuracy of forecasts." Mild chuckles rose from the group. "Our forecast is this: a couple of months from now, you'll all realize how important Chet's comments were—how they proved to be THE pivotal point in this weekend. And that this weekend was THE pivotal point in turning the company around and getting it back to where you want it to be. So, as uncomfortable as the process was, Dennis and I want to thank Chet for breaking things open, and to thank the rest of you for responding in a positive manner. We hope that through the process you're becoming more comfortable in speaking your deepest thoughts. This kind of communication, though difficult, will make the group stronger.

"When addressing one another, keep in mind that each person here is a person of infinite worth. And respecting one another is exactly what creates great teams. You're on your way to becoming one. I'm guessing now that the sacred cow who said, 'financial information is private, and we, the owners, can't trust anybody else to have it,' is about to become hamburger. There are several others that have yet to be discovered. When they do surface, they can also become hamburger, and the team will become stronger.

"We could spend a lot more time on the timeline we've created, but to honor our commitment to take no more than two hours tonight, let's move to the final topic of the evening. You each have some sticky notes in front of you. Take a couple of minutes and write down your answers to one or more of these questions." Karen flipped to the next page and pointed to the questions:

- Why do I come to work at Brookings every day?
- What's the most wonderful thing that has happened to me at work?
- What do I value at work?

"When we're done, we'll ask each person to share one answer and put that sticky note up on the wall. You can keep the rest to yourselves if you want."

After a few minutes, people had quit writing. Then Karen began to ask each person to read one answer to the group and put it up on the wall. She started with Marie, who was sitting on her left.

"Respect—people respect me," Marie said. "Chris respected each person, which is why it's such an important part of our culture."

Cindy was next. "Compassion—when my son was in that car accident and they didn't know if he'd live, you all supported me with meals, with visits, and with thoughtful notes. I don't know what I would have done without you. You're family to me."

It was Nancy's turn. "Integrity—it is so wonderful working for a company that tells its suppliers the truth. When I hear the stories about how other purchasing people treat their suppliers, I am so glad I work here, because here, I can tell suppliers the truth."

Sam spoke next. "'Respect' here, too. Chris treated me with respect and insisted we all treat each other that way. That legacy will be part of this company forever."

It was Beth's turn. "Professional challenge—you all know I got my degree just last May. I had offers from other companies, but I came here because it looked like I would be really challenged professionally. And I have been. Thanks, Walter."

When all the sticky notes were on the wall, Karen walked over and started grouping them. "It looks like we have four general groupings: respect, integrity, compassion/family, and professional challenge. Does anyone have a sticky note they would like to add that would be in a different grouping? If you do, please say it out loud to the group and add it to the wall." We looked at one other, but there was no other response.

Karen concluded, "Thanks for coming tonight, everyone. It's been intense, more so than we anticipated. But you are doing very, very well. We're proud of you, and what you've been able to accomplish so far. So go home and get a good night's sleep. We'll see you all at 9:00 a.m. sharp tomorrow. We'll have fruit, muffins, and yogurt here tomorrow, so you don't have to worry about getting breakfast. Adam, do you have any final comments?"

I stood up and looked out at everyone. "Thank you all for being here and participating tonight. I think we've made a major breakthrough. I'm truly proud to be part of this company. And I'm really interested to find out what we'll learn about ourselves tomorrow." I then turned to Dennis, Karen, and Barbara. "Thank you, Dennis and Karen and Barbara, for creating this safe space for us. We couldn't have done this without you. I'll see you all tomorrow morning at 9:00. Have a good night."

And with that, everybody got up and left, walking out in twos and threes, talking with each other. Mom, Dennis, Karen, Barbara, and I were left in the room.

"Wow," I said. "That was intense!"

"Sure was," replied Karen and Dennis in unison. They looked at each other and started grinning, then laughing. Karen continued, "We have been around each other so much we have started talking like each other."

"Now that the rest are gone, I can admit I was not sure what was going to happen when Chet blurted out his surprise," added Dennis. "The mood was so mellow and comfortable and, well, intimate, just before then. It was sort of like a skunk suddenly appearing at a wedding reception and spraying the bride, the groom, *and* the cake just as it is being cut." We all started snickering at that image, then laughing. I guess we needed to relieve our tension as well.

"Is there anything you need from us?" I asked.

"Just be here at 9:00," replied Karen.

"You've got it," I replied.

"I wouldn't miss this for anything," added Mom. I turned to look at her; she was smiling, a smile I hadn't seen since Dad died. Amazing! I never would have figured that.

Then Mom said to me, "We need to talk about how much information we're willing to share with the rest of the company. But let's wait until tomorrow night. Tonight was intense enough. I need to process it some more."

"Sounds good," I replied.

As we were leaving, we noticed Dennis, Karen, and Barbara removing the sticky notes from the walls. I suddenly remembered that we were in a public space, and that the cleaning crew, setup crew, and catering people would be in that space before we returned. Once again, I appreciated Dennis and Karen's thoroughness and professional competence, and the support Barbara was giving them.

Mom and I drove home in a companionable silence. As soon as we got home, I called Kelly to fill her in on everything that had happened. Although I knew this weekend was critical to the company's survival, I was starting to wish it was next Friday, when I would be with her again. I had lived without her for five years, and had been okay. But now I had come to miss her so much—next Friday seemed so long from now!

CHAPTER 6
Weeding the Garden

The entire group was actually gathered and in place at 9:00 Saturday morning, which was highly unusual. Several of the participants were habitually late for meetings; their punctuality this morning spoke highly of their regard for the process. And I noticed that everything in the room was back in place. Dennis and Karen must have been there before 8:15 to accomplish that.

I again opened with a brief statement. "Thank you all for being here and being so prompt. We'll quit no later than 4:00 this afternoon or earlier if we've done what we need to do. I hope that we'll keep making excellent progress like we did yesterday. I'm really heartened by what I have seen happening so far." I glanced at Mom, who nodded slightly back to me, and then I turned to Chet.

"Chet, I just want to say thank you for speaking what you thought was true yesterday. Although it hurt at the time, you have really helped us move forward."

I nodded to Dennis and Karen. Dennis stood up and gazed around the room, holding each person's eyes for a couple of seconds. Then he began, "We all checked in yesterday when we began the meeting to help us come together. Let's do that again today. The check-in question this morning is, 'how are you feeling now?' Let's go around the room, starting with whoever speaks first. Then we'll proceed with the person to his or her right."

Chet started, "I'm nervous and hopeful."

And the group continued, one at a time. I was surprised at the variety of responses.

Next, Karen asked, "Does anyone want to make any additions or changes to the timeline? If so, grab a marker and write it there. And if there is something left over from yesterday that you think the group needs to hear, please bring it up now."

Several people added items—highlighting events they felt were an integral part of our history and culture. I learned a lot about our company, as did many of the people there, including some of the old-timers.

Then Dennis and Karen started with the first new topic of the day. Dennis said, "Now we'll start to record the company's current strategic position. First, what are the company's strengths?" He picked up the marker and wrote the word "Strengths" across the top of a new flip chart page. The answers came in spurts and he wrote each one down.

- Family owned.
- Nimble.
- Close to our customers.
- Known for quality.
- Loyal employees.
- Community support.
- Known for integrity.
- We go the extra mile.

"Next," Karen said, "let's record the company's weaknesses." Dennis wrote the word "Weaknesses" across the top of the next flip chart page. But this time the response was like popcorn popping—Dennis could hardly keep up with the answers at the start.

- Costs too high.
- Lack of capital.
- Aging product line.
- Not big enough to fight the big guys.
- Not part of a large corporation, which could make volume discount arrangements across a wide offering of products.
- Sagging morale.
- Fear of layoffs.

Karen then asked, "Could you have talked openly about these weaknesses before this weekend?"

Various people answered, "No," "Not really," "Not comfortably," "Only in private."

"How does it feel to be able to tell the truth, the whole truth, as you see it, openly in a group like this?" Karen added, looking at the facial expressions of everyone.

There was silence for a while. Then someone said, "Free." Others said, "Amazing," "Real," "Different," "Big relief!" and "Uncomfortable."

I suddenly realized the importance of the open interaction and response Karen had just invoked. So I stood up and commented, "I want this to be how we work together from now on. We have to tell each other the truth, period. Because if we don't, I don't know how we can survive. And if we do, we'll be a company I want to work for."

"Time for the third chart," said Dennis. "Let's look at opportunities." He said, pointing to the word written across the top of a clean flip chart page. There was silence for a while. The answers, when they came, were spaced out quite a bit. He wrote them down one by one.

- Bring out a new product line.

To this somebody asked, "How are we gonna do that?" Dennis reminded him, "Let's just get the ideas down now; we can figure out the 'how' later," and he continued to write.

- Merge with another company in the same industry.
- Merge with another company in another industry that has a compatible/synergistic product line.
- Sustainability, I guess (now that was a resounding vote of confidence!).
- Move production to China.
- Form a co-op of companies such as ours to jointly market products and purchase materials and services.
- Implement a new ERP package.
- Implement a six sigma program.
- Hire more salespeople on straight commission.

There was a long silence. Dennis asked the group, "Anyone have anything else to add?" There were heads shaking "no."

"Finally," Karen said, "let's look at threats." The same process was used to capture all the ideas coming from the group. When she finished writing, the list was composed of the following.

- We're going out of business slowly.
- Our competitors have 25% lower prices, and probably even lower costs than that.

- Our major customers sound like they're getting ready to drop us, as are some of the medium and small customers.
- If our profitability drops much lower, we'll start to violate our loan covenants.
- Morale is dropping.

Dennis finished the exercise, explaining, "What we've just done is called 'SWOT' analysis—Strengths, Weaknesses, Opportunities, Threats. The technique has been around for a while, but it still works really well. Now I think it's time for a coffee break."

We did need a break right then. The mood was not as euphoric as during the early part of the previous evening, but I figured Dennis and Karen knew what they were doing.

After the coffee break, Dennis asked the group, "Are there any items that were missed on any of the four SWOT charts we just did?" A couple of people added some ideas, but otherwise the lists looked relatively complete—and relatively grim, as a whole. I didn't have much confidence that we could pull our company, *my* company, out of its tailspin. It seemed as if others felt the same way—the mood was serious, even somber.

Dennis sensed the mood in the room and asked, "Let's try the question one more time. How many here think the company will be here in its present form in 10 years?" No hands went up. "Five years from now?" Again, no hands were raised. "Good," he said. "We're all still on the same page."

I thought to myself, "Good? He said *good*? I'd like to know where he's getting that!" I looked around; from the looks on other people's faces, they were thinking the same thing. As hard as it was to stay silent, I decided to bite my tongue and trust Dennis.

"So since you all think the company is going down the tubes, you'll be willing to humor me for a bit, right?" Dennis continued. We murmured assent. "Okay, let's do something completely different. I want you to use the sticky note pads and write down at least two of your deepest values, the things most important to you. When we're done writing, I'll ask each person to share one. You can keep the others to yourself, or you can share them if you want. Are there any questions?" There was silence. "Okay, then please start writing."

People, including me, seemed a bit uncomfortable. It was hard for me to sit still; I squirmed, and others were doing the same. I finally decided to write the one I was going to keep to myself: Kelly. Then I realized that I could generalize that—love. I could also write another one, family. And a third, children—I really wanted to have some with Kelly—and this was the first time I ever had that thought. It felt so right, I couldn't imagine why I hadn't realized it before. I wasn't going to share *that* one with the group! So I surreptitiously put it in my pocket. I'd tell Kelly when I saw her next weekend. I added a fourth, health, and a fifth, freedom of choice. Hey, this was not as hard as I thought! I could share those last two really easily.

Finally, Dennis looked at me and asked, "Adam, would you mind sharing one of yours first?" I felt all eyes turn toward me. Should I take the safe route and say "health" or "freedom of choice," or should I expose my soft side, and become vulnerable? Dad had always told me that leading by example was the only kind of leadership that mattered. The only way we could survive is if we took risks, big risks, so I decided to put it out on the table. I paused, looked around, and swallowed hard.

"Love," I said sheepishly. I guess I was halfway expecting derision from the group for being "soft" or, at the least, general discomfort. But none of that happened. Instead, there was a palpable feeling of relief. I suddenly realized that more than half the people in the room had probably written "love" as well but were probably too embarrassed to say it, and they were so relieved to have someone else say it first. (It turned out that it was actually over 75%.)

So Dennis went around the room, asking each person, while Karen recorded the answers. "Love" got more votes than anything else on the first round. After that, we all started just saying the rest of the ones we wanted to share. We wound up with many different values, some of which overlapped. The other heavy hitters were family, creativity, joy, health, making a difference, and learning. The exercise was a very interesting detour off the main reason why we were here.

Then Karen seriously stretched our comfort zones. She said, "I would like each of you to come up to this flip chart, write the values that are most important to you, and sign it. Will you do that?" Again, I decided that leading by example was important, so I walked up, took the deep green marker (green is my favorite color), and wrote "Love, Family, Joy, Making a Difference, Health," each on its own line, drew a red box around them, then signed my name inside the box. As I went back to my seat, others started forming a line to do the same. Watching that flip chart come to life with our deepest values was moving, much more so than I ever expected.

As we were getting used to what we had just revealed publicly, Dennis went back to the earlier flip chart, which had the values as we had spoken them, and asked, "How many of these values are directly expressed in the work you do at Brookings? How many are in the Brookings vision and mission statements? How many do you actively consider when you make decisions inside the company?"

There was dead silence.

Then Karen blew our minds completely, taking us by surprise when she said, "What would the company be like if you could bring those values to work with you every day and use them in your decisions? Would that make a difference to the company . . . to your city . . . to your customers and suppliers? I want you to be completely silent for two minutes, a mere two minutes, while you think that over." And she sat down.

We were silent all right. We were more than just silent; we were totally shell-shocked. It was not possible. It was *not* possible! *It couldn't be possible*, could it? But what if it were? Some of the readings started seeping back into my mind. Maybe it was possible!

After two very long minutes, Dennis stood up. "Let me try to help you. We had you read a couple of articles on sustainability before this workshop to provide just enough background so that you could at least entertain a possibility. Most of you would have dismissed that possibility out of hand if you hadn't read the articles beforehand. I can see most of you are still highly skeptical, if I'm reading your body language right." There were several vigorous nods.

Dennis continued, "So here it is. I've been in lots of companies in my career, and so has Karen. What we've noticed is one common theme. It doesn't matter where we are, anywhere in the world. It doesn't matter what industry. It doesn't matter whether it's the lowest-paid or highest-paid person. The one common theme among humans is—that's right—their families. If they're older, they have pictures of their grandchildren. If they're middle-aged, they have pictures of their children. If they're younger, they have pictures of their spouses or closest friends. Barring that, they'll have pictures of their parents. Are you with me so far? This is *important*." We all nodded.

"So the most powerful, motivating force on earth is love for family. That shouldn't be a surprise—your own flip chart shows that in spades. But this is not how businesses are organized. They are organized to measure widgets and dollars, not love and family. So each day, each of us has to put aside our deepest values and come to work in a place that values things, not people. Each of us has to sacrifice what we truly value, for that which the company values. Susan, Adam, please understand that I'm not criticizing your company; virtually *all* companies operate under these same principles. Am I right, Tom?" Dennis said as he looked at him for affirmation.

"Yes, the purpose of any company is to make money for its owners," Tom said heartily as he looked around the room.

"Right," agreed Dennis. "But there have been a few pioneering companies who have chosen to operate differently. They have based their decisions on the Triple Bottom Line—putting people and the environment on an equal level with profitability when making decisions. And they are winning against normal companies most of the time." He nodded to Karen and sat down.

Karen stood up and continued, "From what Dennis and I have seen and heard, you have those values strongly built into your culture already. It wouldn't be that difficult to use them to make decisions. You already care deeply about each other; we heard that loud and clear last night. All you'd have to do is to change your decision-making processes to include your real values. This is not easy, as you remember from your transformation to Lean, but it's doable, especially here at Brookings."

Karen walked over to the "Opportunities" chart that was taped to the wall, and said, "Tell me, except for sustainability, do any of these opportunities sound like something you really want? Do you want to move production to China? Do you want to sell to or merge with another company? Do you think that just creating a marketing co-op is going to keep you healthy, long term? I think that's why the mood was so somber after we completed this exercise, right? Sort of like a cancer patient that has six months to live, except there is this one experimental drug?" We all nodded, although we weren't sure we wanted to go where she was taking us.

"So before lunch we'd like to show you a little more about what sustainability is, and how it operates in some very real companies, in various industries. After lunch, we'll start the discussion about how that might fit here at Brookings. At the end of that discussion, we'll ask if you want to continue exploring sustainability, or if we should look at other alternatives instead or just go home and roast marshmallows in the fireplace. We've gotta warn you, though, the first part of this presentation can be pretty uncomfortable. But our commitment to you is to tell the truth, the whole truth. Are you ready?" While she was talking, Dennis had turned on his laptop and the LCD projector.

We all nodded with puzzled looks on our faces, wondering what she meant by "pretty uncomfortable."

"Where's the popcorn?" I quipped; a few people chuckled nervously.

"Here's the United Nations' definition of sustainability," said Karen, as she read the first slide (see Figure 6-1): "'Meeting the needs of the current generation without compromising the ability of future generations to meet their needs.' And here's a good working definition—'The Golden Rule, applied across generations.' Our definition, which you just encountered, is 'Making decisions based on our deepest values, which honor people and our planet as well as profitability.' This works with most companies, because most people's values do indeed promote long-term sustainability. Look at all the sacrifices that parents make for their children—they work long hours and save so their children can have college educations. They will willingly risk their lives for their children. They will not knowingly poison or hurt their children. So all we're suggesting is that you bring those same values here and use them openly, collectively, rather than trying to live them when the decision-making system does not honor them. More than once while I was working in a large company I found myself making decisions that violated my deepest values, but they were required because they looked like they would improve profits. Those decisions turned out to be mistakes, but I couldn't justify doing what I knew was right while I was making them. Has anyone here had a similar experience?"

"Yeah," spoke up Annie, which surprised us a bit; she hadn't participated very much so far. "A while back our Lean team determined that switching from an aqueous cleaner to a dangerous chemical cleaner would reduce cycle time. So we switched. We were all uncomfortable doing that, because

---

Sustainability

- Meeting the needs of the present without compromising the ability of future generations to meet their needs*

- The Golden Rule, applied across generations

* "Brundtland Commission Report." United Nations, 1987.

Figure 6-1.

we didn't want to be around that new chemical. But we felt we had no choice, because we needed to cut cycle time to help our company stay in business. Is that what you're talking about?"

"Exactly," replied Karen. "Thank you for sharing that. And what is the true cost of the new cleaner?"

"Well, we have to put on special protective clothing, and be very careful. We're not supposed to breathe it. What are our choices—quit breathing? So of course we breathe it. And the warning label says it could interfere with human reproduction. If we ever spill that stuff, we'll have a real mess. But all we were looking at was cycle time when the decision was made." Annie sighed heavily.

"Bingo. If you had been looking at the people side, and the environmental side, would you have made the same decision?" Karen asked, looking at Annie and then around the room.

"NO WAY!" Annie shouted, surprising us with the force of her answer. "We would have kept the old cleaner." She turned to Wayne who looked a little uneasy, "May I tell the team on Monday that I want to get the chemical out of our plant, and never, ever, see it again?"

"Absolutely," Wayne replied. "I was never that comfortable with it either, but I didn't want to second-guess the team's decision."

"The prosecution rests its case, ladies and gentlemen," quipped Karen. "Do you see what I mean? It's called listening to the wisdom that you've acquired through years and years of learning. And that wisdom has come at quite a price.

"The next slide shows the Triple Bottom Line—profits, people, and planet (see Figure 6-2). Companies have been refining the profit side of decision-making for years. Tom,

```
┌─────────────────────────────────────────────────────────┐
│                                                           │
│                   Triple Bottom Line                      │
│                                                           │
│      • Profit                                             │
│                                                           │
│      • People                                             │
│                                                           │
│      • Planet                                             │
│                                                           │
│      (Companies that embrace the Triple Bottom Line usually │
│      outperform those that do not.)                       │
│                                                           │
└─────────────────────────────────────────────────────────┘
```

Figure 6-2.

you're computing monthly P&L using standard costing based on FASB and GAAP, right?" Karen rattled off quickly.

"Right," said Tom. But many of the others in the room had really puzzled looks on their faces, myself included.

"Sorry for the acronyms," Karen said as she looked around the room. "FASB is the Financial Accounting Standards Board; GAAP is generally accepted accounting principles; and P&L is profit and loss, which tells whether the company is making money. Tom, you do that monthly, right?"

"Right again," he said.

"So is there anything in those standards that prevents management from making decisions based on factors other than financial profitability?" Karen asked, and then took a drink from her bottle of water.

"I guess not . . ." Tom replied hesitantly. He thought for a moment, and then said confidently, "No, there is not."

"So the accounting profession doesn't care how a company makes its decisions. It only cares whether the company is reporting its financial status according to the accepted standards, right?" Karen prodded.

"Right," Tom agreed, but he looked quite uncomfortable at this point.

"Tom, were you here when the company put in Lean?" she asked.

"Yes," Tom said as he shifted in his seat.

"Were you uncomfortable when you first heard that decisions would be made in a different manner as you started the Lean journey?" Karen said, realizing she was really putting him on the spot.

"Absolutely!" he said loudly. Karen smiled.

"And what have been the results of that Lean journey?" she asked.

Tom paused a moment and said, "We improved profits and our competitive edge, until the other two big players moved production to China."

"So would you be willing to try still another decision-making approach if it would help the company?" Karen asked and then looked around the quiet room. Everyone was listening closely, waiting for Tom's answer.

After a slight hesitation, he replied, "Yes, I would be willing to try one."

"Thanks—that takes a lot of courage. We really appreciate it," she replied graciously.

Karen turned to the rest of us again, "When companies implement sustainability, one of the major stumbling blocks is accounting, because they tend to keep using traditional metrics. And those metrics cause decisions like the one Annie was telling us about earlier. So when we help a client implement sustainability, one of the most important aspects is to define the new metrics. And to do it in such a way that we don't give the CFO ulcers, because we want to sustain Tom's health too, right?" and she grinned at Tom.

"Damn straight!" exclaimed Tom, smiling.

"Tom, this was one of the most important topics to be covered this weekend. It just showed up here before I had a chance to talk with you off-line. I apologize for surprising you like that, especially in public," Karen said sincerely.

"No major harm done, Karen. I understand. But please don't do that to me very often," Tom said, patting his heart to chuckles in the room.

"We'll do our best. And the rest of you, please notice what happened. I surprised Tom by questioning the fundamental basis of his profession, and therefore his worth to the company. He stayed in the discussion, which took real strength—somebody else might have gone silent, or gotten mad, or whatever else. I was lucky. You're lucky to have Tom," Karen explained.

I couldn't help myself. "Thanks, Tom," I said, and I started clapping; several others joined me.

Dennis elaborated on what had just happened. "You clapped for Tom—good job. I think we just made another sacred cow into hamburger—the sacred cow of predictability and non-emotionalism. It's okay to show enthusiasm. Actually, not just okay, but absolutely necessary if a company wants to be truly healthy and sustainable."

He thought for a bit more and then said, "Let's list the sacred cows we have sacrificed so far. What are they?"

And Dennis wrote our answers on the flip chart.

- Financial information must be kept private.
- The only purpose of a company is to make money; we have to check our real values at the door.

- Positive emotions like laughter and applause don't belong in a company.
- We can't speak what we really believe; we can't tell the whole truth.

Dennis ripped the page off the pad, taped it to the wall, and said, "Any time we find another sacred cow, make sure we write it down, okay?" We all nodded. Then he signaled to Karen that she could continue. She clicked to the next slide (see Figure 6-3).

She began, "Let's talk about the planet, or environmental, side of sustainability next. Before we leave tomorrow, you'll need to create strategies, tactics, and metrics for this. Let's review the *Cradle-to-Cradle* material just a bit. Most businesses, actually most Western societies, operate on a model that says we take stuff from the ground, we process it, transport it many times across thousands of miles, then use it up, and throw away what's left into a landfill. Does that sound basically correct?" Everyone nodded. "That's called the Take-Make-Waste model, and it assumes two things we might want to question:

- Raw materials will remain abundant and cheap for a long time to come.

Take-Make-Waste Model

Assumptions:
- Natural resources will remain cheap
- There is an "away"

Figure 6-3.

- There is an "away" where we can throw things and not have to worry about them.

"Let's take the first assumption. Do you really think that raw materials will remain abundant and cheap forever?"

"No," responded Mary. "The prices of many of our raw materials have increased. And I don't see why it would stop."

"You're completely correct, Mary," Karen said earnestly. "Most people don't talk about it much, but raw materials are finite, and the supplies are slowly decreasing. And, as population and affluence increase, the demand increases. Therefore, prices must rise over time. The most obvious poster child is crude oil, which doubled in price from $30/barrel to $60/barrel in two years from January 2003 to January 2005. Natural gas rose almost as fast. And that put pressure on coal. One critical part of becoming more sustainable is to deliberately design your business to use less of these fossil fuels and materials." She clicked to the next slide (see Figure 6-4).

"However, there's something else happening here, more insidious and far more serious than future oil shortages. Humans can survive without oil; we did it for millennia. What's far more important than oil is the earth's basic ability to support life for humans and other species. This basic ability is being seriously degraded. There are three very disturbing long-term trends:

1. The *population* of the world has grown dramatically, and continues to increase. The earth's population was 2.3 billion people in 1945. It is over 6.5 billion now, and projected to hit 9 billion around 2050.

2. *Water*, clean and fit for drinking, is becoming scarce in many parts of the globe. The World Bank says 80 countries now have water shortages that threaten health

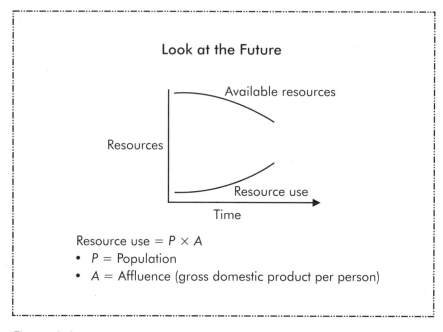

Look at the Future

Available resources

Resources

Resource use

Time

Resource use = $P \times A$
- P = Population
- A = Affluence (gross domestic product per person)

Figure 6-4.

and economies.* By 2025, half the world's population could have trouble finding enough fresh water for drinking and irrigation.† In China, serious water shortages are constraining economic growth. Here in the U.S., the mighty Colorado River doesn't even reach the Pacific Ocean much of the time. The Oglala aquifer provides water for thousands of square miles of the high plains and the Southwestern U.S., including several cities. We're mining that water at a rate of 10 feet per year, and nature is replenishing it at 1/4 inch per year. When it runs out, life will become very diffi-

---

* *Arizona Water Resource*, November-December 1999, http://ag.arizona.edu/AZWATER/awr/dec99/Feature2.htm.

† BBC News, December 15, 1999, http://news.bbc.co.uk/1/hi/world/americas/566809.stm.

cult in that area. The Aral Sea in the former Soviet Union was once the fourth largest inland sea in the world. It is now less than 25% of its former size.

3. The amount of *arable land* in the world is shrinking, as is the total production of grain. Deserts are taking over areas that used to be grassland. Harvests of the world's five major grains have shrunk 15% since 1985. And we keep putting houses and shopping centers on land that used to grow crops.

"Any one of these trends alone would make life difficult for our children and their children. The combination is almost overwhelming. I think there is a cultural reason for this. If you look at Europe or China, you'll find cultures based on the assumptions that people are born, live their lives, and finally die in the same town. That was the way life was for thousands of years. So they have made decisions based on the underlying assumption that their children would live with the consequences of those decisions.

"Now let's look at America. For the first 250 years of our history, we were blessed with an unprecedented, and unrepeatable, gift: the ability to move west, to go to a place that was not yet spoiled. So our culture developed the understanding that there was always a fresh start in the next valley over. If we cut down this forest, there is another one. If we ruin this farm, we can find another one. That's not true anymore, but we keep making decisions as if it were. And our decisions are irrevocably shaping the lives our grandchildren will live. We are ruining the lives of future generations."

Karen clicked and the next slide came on the screen (see Figure 6-5). She began, "One example of hurting future generations is the use of toxic chemicals. We humans keep creating and using toxic substances and then disposing of them. We pretend that once they're out of sight, they're gone. But

Toxic Chemical Pollution in the USA*

Year	Billion lbs
1999	7.3
2000	6.6
2001	5.6
2002	4.7
2003	4.4
2004	4.2
Total	32.8

* www.epa.gov/triexplorer/

Figure 6-5.

they're not really gone; they're just out of sight, mixing with whatever else they contact, and slowly poisoning our planet. Between 1999 and 2004, companies in the U.S. released 32.8 *billion* pounds of toxic chemicals into the environment. And many of these are highly persistent; they don't just go away. This chart covers *only* the U.S., and for *only* six years. You can try to extrapolate these figures for the rest of the world if you want."

Then the next slide came on the screen (see Figure 6-6). Karen's voice became soft, so soft we could barely hear her. She was obviously having difficulty keeping her emotions in check. She cleared her throat and said, "This is where we get personal. Each one of us has toxins in our body. We all will continue to accumulate them until we die. Recent studies have found carcinogens, hormone disrupters, and neurotoxins in every child that has been examined. *Every child!* What

Poisoning Our Children

- A child carries an average of 23 carcinogens, hormone disrupters, and neurotoxins, including PCBs and DDT.*

- Breast milk has been found to contain flame retardants (U.S. mothers have rates 10 to 100 times higher than mothers in Europe or Japan), DDT, PCBs (both banned for more than 30 years!), dioxin, lead, arsenic, and mercury.†

* Mittelstoedt, Martin. "Toxic Cocktail Found in Children." *Toronto Globe and Mail,* June 2, 2006.
† Williams, Florence. "Toxic Breast Milk?" *New York Times,* January 9, 2005.

Figure 6-6.

is most alarming is that DDT and PCBs have been banned from use for about 30 years, and they *still* are showing up in children. These chemicals just won't go away! In another study, *each person* tested in the state of Washington had between five and seven classes of chemicals in their bodies, including flame retardants, mercury, pesticides, lead, and phthalates. One surgeon, a woman, had a PBDE (polybrominated diphenyl ether, a flame retardant) level almost high enough to cause reproductive problems.‡

"Men carry their chemical burden with them forever. Unfortunately, women pass some of their chemical burden on to their babies in their breast milk. This slide also shows some of the compounds that have been found in women's

‡ Phinney, Susan. *Seattle Post-Intelligencer,* May 24, 2006.

breast milk. My daughter just had her first child six months ago, and she is breast-feeding, because we think it's still better than formula. And she can't help that she's feeding chemicals like this to my granddaughter. We are poisoning our babies." Karen paused for a moment, blinked to clear the moisture from her eyes, then continued, "I presented this slide at a Starbucks meeting in Seattle a couple of months ago. Somehow, I had ignored the fact that most of the people in the room would be young women, many of whom had very young children or who were about to start their families. They just broke down; they couldn't help themselves. How in the world could we do this to our babies?" Her voice became an anguished whisper, "How could we?" and then she sat down.

We all just sat there silently. Karen was right—how could we do this? I thought of Kelly, and the children I hoped we would have together, and I had real difficulty keeping control of my emotions. Then I remembered my earlier quip about "where's the popcorn?" I fervently wished there was a way to retract those words.

After allowing us some quiet time to absorb the full significance of THAT slide, Karen continued with the next one (see Figure 6-7). "Global warming is real. Scientists have been sounding the alarm for a while. In a review of 928 papers on climate change in peer-reviewed scientific journals, three quarters of them concluded that global warming is real and that it is primarily caused by human activity; the other quarter of the papers were focused on past events. *None* of them disputed that global warming is happening or that humans are causing most of it. The author of that study concluded, 'The scientific consensus might, of course, be wrong. If the history of science teaches anything, it is humility, and no one can be faulted for failing to act on what is not known. But our grandchildren will surely blame us if they find that we

---

Global Warming is Real

• Happening much faster than anyone predicted
  - Glaciers and ice caps melting faster than ever
  - More land devastated by drought
  - Rising waters drowning low-lying areas
  - Responsible for >150,000 deaths/year (will be >300,000 deaths/year by 2030*)

• Weather more violent in the past 35 years
  - Occurrence of category 4 and 5 hurricanes has doubled
  - Average hurricane wind speed is up 50%[†]

* According to the World Health Organization.
† *Time*, April 3, 2006.

Figure 6-7.

understood the reality of anthropogenic climate change and failed to do anything about it . . . There is a scientific consensus on the reality of anthropogenic climate change. Climate scientists have repeatedly tried to make this clear. It is time for the rest of us to listen.'[§] Unfortunately, more than half the articles in the popular press have discounted it. But now, even most of the skeptics are convinced. The bad news is that it seems to be happening faster, and more pervasively, than was forecasted just a few years ago. That is one more reason to reduce the use of fossil fuels as quickly as possible.

---

§ Oreskes, Naomi. "Beyond the Ivory Tower: The Scientific Consensus on Climate Change." *Science,* December 3, 2004.

We have no idea what the real impact will be on our lives or on our companies."

Karen continued, "Thanks for reading the material that we requested. You may recall from the materials that natural savings is the natural resources component of natural capitalism (see Figure 6-8). One of the most important ways to become more sustainable as a company, and as a society, is to understand the difference between natural savings and natural income. Any time we use natural savings, we are creating two problems:

1. We're depleting the resources available for future generations *unless* we ensure that the materials remain in use indefinitely. This means we have to design products so they don't wind up in a landfill.

2. We're making ourselves vulnerable to potential materials shortages and price fluctuations. To the ex-

---

Natural Savings vs. Income

- Natural savings: anything not replenished (quickly) by nature
  - Iron
  - Oil
  - Topsoil

- Natural income: anything that naturally arrives daily
  - Sunshine/solar energy
  - Wind
  - Water power
  - Geothermal energy

Figure 6-8.

The Squeeze

tent we can depend less on natural savings than our competitors, we will have a long-term competitive advantage.

"This is just an overview of the situation in our country and the world. But Dennis and I truly hope that as you create your new vision, you base that vision on what we have just told you. We'll be glad to go into more details on any of this if you want. Trust me; we have just scratched the surface of the data available from reputable sources."

I had to speak. "We need to add some more sacred cows to the list. Who has one?"

One by one, we added the following:

- Raw materials will remain abundant and cheap.
- There is an "away" where we can throw things.
- Chemicals are safe unless proven otherwise.
- Our actions and decisions in our company and our personal lives don't matter to future generations.
- What we don't know can't hurt us.
- Everything is just fine.
- Our government will protect us from the consequences of our decisions; its rules will keep us from hurting ourselves.

Dennis stood up, picked up the remote clicker and the next slide appeared on the screen (see Figure 6-9). He said, "You're doing well. The good news is that the heavy part of the slide show is over. We've thrown a lot of bad news at you that might not look like it applies to business. So let's look at sustainability again. The United Nations' definition is fine, but it doesn't help companies make day-to-day decisions. For that, we prefer the Triple Bottom Line— profit, people, and planet. The good news is that companies

---

The Timberland Company

- Combat social ills; improve conditions for workers around the globe.

- Help the environment.

- For the last five years, increases in:
  - Profits: 9.7%/year*
  - Return on investment: 20%/year*
  - Stock: 64%[†]

* Reingold, Jennifer. "Walking the Walk." *Fast Company*, November, 2005.
† Timberland web site, www.timberland.com, March, 2006.

Figure 6-9.

that embrace the Triple Bottom Line usually outperform those that don't. For example, Timberland is a for-profit company, as you well know. But its mission is to 'save the world.' It has two goals: 1) to combat social ills, improving conditions for workers around the world; and 2) to help the environment. Jeff Schwartz, the CEO, maintains that this mission helps him attract and retain the best work force, and energizes them for their jobs. The financial results seem to support this. Over the last five years, the company's profits increased 9.7% per year, ROI increased 20% per year, and its stock increased in value by 64%.

"I'll relate two more stories about large, well-known companies. Jeff Immelt, the CEO of GE, unveiled his Ecomagination campaign in 2005, not to be trendy or moral, but to accelerate GE's economic growth. He intends to develop solutions for a world whose oil supplies are increasingly limited and whose constraints on greenhouse gas emissions are increasingly stringent.

"In November 2005, Lee Scott, CEO of Wal-Mart, committed his company to increase efficiency of its vehicle fleet by 25% in three years and double it in 10 years, reduce energy consumption in the stores by 30%, and reduce the solid waste from U.S. stores by 25% in three years. The cover of *Fortune* magazine quotes Scott as saying, 'What I thought was going to be a defensive strategy is turning out to be precisely the opposite.' He goes on to say, 'There can't be anything good about putting chemicals in the air. There can't be anything good about the smog you see in cities. There can't be anything good about putting chemicals in the rivers in Third-World countries so somebody can buy an item for less money in a developed country. Those things are just inherently wrong, whether you are an environmentalist or not.**'

"One more piece of data about the social side: Companies that were on the *Fortune* '100 Best Companies to Work For' list outperformed the S&P 500 in return on investment to shareholders by more than 50% (see Figure 6-10). To be more precise, the difference between the S&P 500 and the *Fortune* '100 Best Companies to Work For' was 65% for one year, 79% for three years, 80% for five years, and 54% for 10 years.

"Leading investors, such as Goldman Sachs[††], now view sustainable companies as safer investments. Such companies

---

** Gunther, Marc. "The Green Machine." *Fortune*, July 2006. Also available online at http://money.cnn.com/magazines/fortune/fortune_archive/2006/08/07/8382593/index.htm.

†† Dahle, Cheryl. "The Greening of Goldman." *Fast Company,* June, 2006, p. 40.

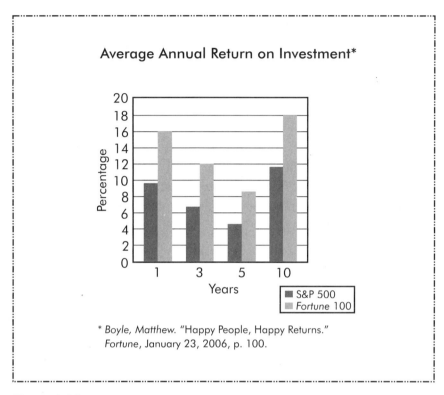

Average Annual Return on Investment*

* Boyle, Matthew. "Happy People, Happy Returns."
Fortune, January 23, 2006, p. 100.

Figure 6-10.

are less likely to have executives bleed the company dry, or be subject to lawsuits with respect to environmental degradation. Reinsurance companies are looking at the carbon footprint of companies, because those with a higher carbon footprint are a higher risk.

"So how can sustainability help a company? The answer is in both strategy and tactics. If you decide to use sustainability as a value, an identity, you will be a more attractive supplier to customers who have the same values. Those customers will probably thrive for the long term, and do better than the 'we're in it for the money' customer." Dennis looked around the room and said, "You seem skeptical. I was too, until I read *Built to Last*. The authors researched 18 pairs of competitors. In each pair, one had the single goal of making money, while the other had the goals of making money *and* something else, such as improving health in the world. Out of the 18 pairs, 17 that outperformed their counterparts were in business to do something more than just make money.[‡‡] Your best customers will value your sustainable initiatives because they are no longer shopping for just the lowest price. Likewise, you could choose a strategy of being way ahead of the EPA, so you don't have to worry about EPA audits any more. One term for that is, 'beyond compliance.' And just as you would be attractive to the best customers, you would be an even more attractive customer to the best suppliers—those who are also interested in sustainability. Just like the sustainability-oriented customers, they will probably out-survive their conventional competitors and will help you on your journey.

"From a tactical standpoint, sustainability helps prioritize a company's many alternative projects, investments, and opportunities. It also creates a whole host of possible projects to work on that probably would not have been otherwise considered. It provides the basis for getting the Lean teams excited again. It allows you to start including the community as you make your decisions."

Dennis paused briefly, and then said, "If you start embracing sustainability, you'll want to rethink your metrics. As you well know, the old metrics in most companies were all created to focus on the financial bottom line, and only the financial bottom line. So you'll need to create some metrics for the people side and the planet side. You'll notice that I said 'most.' The concept of the Balanced Scorecard has been

---

[‡‡] Collins, James C., and Jerry L. Porras. *Built to Last: Successful Habits of Visionary Companies*. New York: Harper Business, 1994, p. 55.

around since the early 1990s. Many of the larger, well-managed companies have implemented it. It measures businesses on four perspectives:

- Financial—traditional profit calculations and market value are used.
- Customers—are they happy?
- Business processes—are they effective and efficient?
- Learning and growth—are employees learning and growing?

"The Balanced Scorecard values customers and employees, but not the environment or the community that surrounds the company. It also understands, and rightly so, that financial results do not occur in a vacuum. If processes are ineffective or inefficient, customers are unhappy, or employees are not learning and growing, the future financial outlook is not good. So we can use some of these concepts as we create metrics for sustainability.

"Any questions so far?" Dennis asked. We were all silent, just thinking about all that had been presented since the coffee break. I felt like I had lived through a lifetime or two since then, and it had been less than two hours!

I spoke up. "Dennis and Karen, you've given us so much to think about. I think it's time for lunch. And actually, since we're 15 minutes early for lunch, why don't we just get up and walk around for a bit, then meet back here at noon for our food? It's a buffet today, so if you want to take an extra five or ten minutes to clear your head, that will be fine."

Dennis replied, "Sounds good. We have plenty left to discuss this afternoon."

As I got up and stretched, I felt really tired, but also sensed that something important had just taken place. I needed to get outside to stretch my legs and get some fresh air. So I did. While I was outside, I called Kelly and told her what we'd experienced during the morning session. She was excited for us, and for me. As we talked, I began to get a better sense of the real power and possibility of sustainability. I now knew that I was going to propose to her when I saw her again next weekend. It was like she fit perfectly with me; she perfectly filled the piece of me that had been missing for so long. I was complete with her, and incomplete without her. But I was also nervous about whether she would be willing to move back to the Midwest from Portland. And I couldn't even contemplate leaving the company at this point—it needed me too much, and I needed it, too. Clearly, I was meant to be here, in "my" company, at this time and place.

I led off the afternoon. "It's time for a reality check. Should we continue to spend time on sustainability, or do you want to look at one of the other alternatives, or do you want to try to find new alternatives that we haven't listed yet? Or do we want to just fold up shop and go home, and be back in the same old, same old, on Monday morning?"

"No way I want to go back to the same old, same old!" Annie blurted out.

"Me neither," added Wayne.

"Let's try some other alternatives," said Tom. So we created a couple more possibilities—voice of the customer and improved supply chain. But they didn't cause any excitement in the group. The obvious consensus was sustain-ability. None of the other alternatives addressed the heart of the matter— telling the truth, tapping the passion and creativity of each person, respecting the next generation, and valuing human relationships.

Then Dennis stood up. "Adam is right. It is time for a reality check. If sustainability is so wonderful, why aren't more companies doing it? Let's count off in threes to form groups. Each group will take 15 minutes to talk about the barriers and problems that you might encounter as you implement sustainability. After 15 minutes, we'll all get together again, and a spokesperson from each group will report the group's ideas back to the large group. This is the time to bring up all your doubts, your fears, and the things you're not sure about."

Soon, each group was actively discussing all the problems Brookings Manufacturing might have if it started trying to implement sustainability. The discussions were so vigorous that Karen announced, "Let's take an additional 10 minutes." Finally, we got up and stretched; some grabbed a cold can of soda or water and then we regrouped.

Marie reported back for the first group. "We brainstormed for a while, and then we organized the issues. So here's our list," she said, pointing to a colorful flip chart page.

"Internal:

- How do we implement it? It's so new; there is no clear path yet.
- Fear of change—how will this affect my job? Will I have to do new things, learn new things?
- Fear of failure—what if I fail when I try to do the sustainability stuff?
- No metrics—how do we measure the non-financial stuff—people and planet?
- We still think this will cost too much money, no matter what Dennis and Karen say. (Sorry, Dennis and Karen.)"

Marie flipped the chart to the next page and began with an audible sigh.

"*External*:

- Will our customers be interested? Will they think this is important? Or will they think we're being non-business-like, and take their business to the competition?
- Will our suppliers be interested? Will they think this is important?
- We can't imagine being an EPA poster child!" Marie concluded loudly, and then took her seat.

The second group, led by Chet, had many of the same items, adding the following:

Internal:

- If there are three bottom lines, how do we decide when they're in conflict? For example, if something will help the environment and the people, but costs a lot of money, do we do it?
- Education and training—what education and training do we need? Who is going to do it? When?

External:

- Will this help or hurt our relationship with the bank? Will this make them more willing or less willing to lend us money?

The third group, led by Annie, said the first two groups had documented virtually all of their questions. They only added two:

- How much will this cost? Where will the money to pay for it come from?
- If we start putting this in, will it be enough to turn the company around and sustain it?

Karen addressed the group with a smile, "I know it's nowhere close to 4 o'clock, but we've covered everything we had hoped to cover today. So with your permission," and she smiled, "let's call it a day, and be here tomorrow at 2:00 in the afternoon. We'll be through by 5:00 p.m. Let me answer one question that I suspect some of you are thinking about, but you're too polite to ask out loud. The reason we're coming back tomorrow, and not finishing this afternoon, is that you have had a lot of information presented to you today, and you've looked hard at a new way of possibly doing business. We need for you to have some time to just let it soak in, and let the insights and questions arise. Sort of like letting spices marry in your favorite recipe. Thank you all for your participation. It has really been an honor to be with you today."

I stood and said, "See you tomorrow. Have a great night." And they all left, except for Mom and me. As Karen, Dennis, and Barbara were rolling up all the flip charts from the walls and the easels, I asked Karen and Dennis, "Could we take you out to dinner tonight to help us understand the process better and get prepared for tomorrow?"

"Sure," Dennis said.

"Great," I said enthusiastically. "We'll pick you up at 7:00 and head for Charley's. It has excellent food and overlooks the lake—nice and peaceful."

"Sounds good," replied Karen. "We'll be ready—business casual okay?"

"Sure," I said with a smile.

On the way home, I felt like I couldn't put off any longer something that had been gnawing on me for a while. "Mom, what would you say to letting the employees own part of the company? And increasing that percentage through the years?"

After thinking a moment she replied, "That might be a really good idea; I've thought about it through the years, as did your dad. We obviously never did anything about it, but I have the suspicion that if the employees owned a piece of the company, they would start to think more like owners and less like employees."

"That's why I suggested it. I really appreciate the way you were able to transfer 49% of the stock to me. I was thinking of putting 10% of my shares into a bank, awarding half of it to the employees right now based on years of service, and keeping the other half for use as bonuses for exceptional performance and the like. That would leave you safely in control, because you'd still own 51%."

"Sounds like something we could talk over with Dennis and Karen tonight," Mom said as she turned to look at me.

"And Mom, you know that when I first came back here, I was intending to help get the company ready to sell? I'm not thinking that way now. I've learned more, and grown more in the last 11 weeks than any other time in my life. And I'm actually enjoying the process. So I'd like to stay for the foreseeable future, anyhow."

"Thanks. I was hoping you'd start feeling that way. We need you—the company AND me. Without you, I don't see how the company can survive." Wow. That felt really good, like a huge vote of confidence, and really scary at the same time. The future of the company was indeed resting on my shoulders!

I then decided to initiate the conversation we had put off from the previous day. "So how much financial information are we willing to share with the employees, with all of them?"

"I guess the basics—profit and loss, balance sheet, cash flow, and then eventually the budget. But we'd have to educate them first," she replied.

"I agree. And the profit and loss should be high level, especially at first. I think I remember hearing about a company that introduced its employees to financial statements, providing a little more detail each month. Maybe we could do that here."

"Sounds good—you could call an all-employee meeting each month; one of the topics would be the financial statements, plus education on the new sections," Mom said.

"The other thing I want to do is to tell the employees important news, both good and bad, like when we get a new contract, or lose a customer. They'll find out anyhow, and I'd rather have them hear it as soon as we do."

"I agree," Mom said softly. "I think they'll appreciate that."

"Yeah, I know some companies only tell the good news. But that's not being honest, not telling the *whole* truth. Employees learn to discount what the company says, because they know they're only getting half the truth."

The rest of the ride home was quiet—we were both deep in thought. After we got home I puttered around the house for a bit, working on the odds and ends that occupy a homeowner's time. I cleared sticks and winter debris from the lawn, which was almost snow-free at this point. But while I was doing that, my mind was completely focused on the company and, more specifically, the people who were at the off-site this weekend. I found myself wondering what they would be thinking about tonight and how they would react tomorrow after they'd slept on it. Tom had taken a hard hit to his profession this morning. I really hoped he would be okay tomorrow, because he was a good accountant and a good business executive. I was pleased that Marie, Chet, and Annie were the people to report out from their respective groups. It would have been so easy for the group just to let a VP do that, because of their stature in the company. I might have been underestimating Chet, and I might have been too careful to avoid any appearance of favoritism toward Annie.

Then it was time to clean up and take Dennis and Karen to dinner.

Although it was dark outside when we reached the restaurant, floodlights were illuminating the dock and a bit of the lake, and we could hear the waves lapping gently onto the shore. Barbara was already there waiting when we pulled up with our guests in tow. Once we were seated and the waiter had taken our drink order, I asked Dennis and Karen, "How do you think we're doing?"

"Very well, actually," replied Dennis.

Karen added, "I agree; your team handled a lot of difficult stuff today. I was watching their moods and body language carefully; they seemed to be doing well. Of course, we'll know more tomorrow afternoon."

"What do you think of the idea of giving some stock in the company to employees?" I asked.

"I'm glad you're asking the easy questions *before* dinner!" laughed Dennis. "The short answer is, I think it is usually an excellent idea. What it requires, however, is that management be willing to share financial information with all the owners. Are you really willing to do that?"

Mom answered, "Yes, so that we don't have the type of misunderstanding we had with Chet last night."

"My experience," added Karen, "is that employees who are owners, even of just a few shares, think much more like owners than employees. They watch the financials closely and are much more careful with company money and resources, even office supplies! Tec Labs is a privately held company in Albany, Oregon. It was voted the #1 small company to work for worldwide, by *Scientist* magazine[§§]. Small companies in this survey have fewer than 5,000 employees— Tec Labs has fewer than 50. Anyhow, each employee there is responsible for a line item in the budget. For example, the person at the front desk might be responsible for the office supplies budget. Because of its culture, Tec Labs can attract and retain the best and brightest people."

"Sounds like it could help the company survive and thrive," mused Mom out loud.

After a comfortable silence, Mom asked, "Dennis and Karen, why do you consult?" She immediately added, "You're required to travel a lot, your clients probably don't implement your ideas very well, your income is uncertain, and your profession is the butt of lots of jokes. So why do you do it?"

Dennis thought for a minute. "Because I have to," he replied softly. "Now that I know what I know about how our way of life, especially here in the U.S., is irrevocably damaging the ability of future generations to be healthy and have enough to live on comfortably, I have to. If I didn't, I couldn't look my grandkids in the eye. I don't have any yet, but when I do, I want to be able to say that I did everything I possibly could for them."

"That's it for me, too," Karen concurred. "Except I now have a granddaughter, and I'd do anything to help her have a full, rich life."

"And because this way I get to hear lots more consultant jokes," quipped Dennis, and we all chuckled.

"So what's the most frustrating part of consulting . . . the travel, the clients who don't implement your ideas, the lack of respect?" I asked.

---

§§ Survey results. *Scientist*, June 6, 2005. http://www.licefreee.com/press_scientistMag.htm.

"None of those, although they are all real," replied Karen. "The most frustrating part of consulting is not being able to influence the majority of companies that are doing okay or reasonably well, and who won't even talk to us!" She paused, and then continued pensively, "We provide business advice. Companies that use consultants like us fall into two basic camps. The first, which is pretty small, is companies that are doing well and want to do even better. The second is companies in trouble who are finally willing to admit they don't have all the answers."

"And we fall in the second camp," I stated.

"Yes. Although from talking with you and watching you around your people, I believe you'll be in the first camp in a couple years," replied Karen. "But to answer your question, Adam, the most frustrating thing about consulting is that we *know* so many companies who could benefit from implementing sustainability, but they won't even consider it. They're doing okay right now. They can't see the opportunities; and they can't see the damage they're causing. I guess you could say that doing okay is the enemy of doing great."

Then the food arrived. My stuffed flounder was superb. Dennis kept complimenting the prime rib, and Karen enjoyed her lobster, which she had seen in the tank when we walked in. Mom had the lake trout almondine, her favorite.

After we had enjoyed our dinner and were waiting for the dessert and coffee to arrive, I asked, "So what happens tomorrow? What do I need to know and to do?"

Karen responded, "Tomorrow, we'll have people create, or design, a company that reflects their deepest personal values. Then we will help the group translate that into why customers, suppliers, and employees will do business with this new company instead of the competition. One of the most fun parts of that process is describing a customer from hell—

that normally really gets the juices flowing. And that's often the easiest way to define the perfect customer, because the perfect customer is just the opposite of the customer from hell. People realize rather quickly that when we talk about a perfect customer for us, we're describing the way suppliers would like us to be, and ditto for employees wanting us to be like that too. Then we'll ask the group to get practical and start defining how this perfect company will actually operate in the people and environmental dimensions on a daily basis. What will be different from how you operate today?"

"Sounds like a really productive meeting!" I said enthusiastically.

"Yes, the one tomorrow will be a lot more fun than the one today," said Dennis.

I added, "One more thing—I promised to give Wayne and Tom a chance to poke holes in the ideas at the end of tomorrow's meeting. So I need to honor that promise."

"No problem," replied Karen.

After we dropped off Dennis and Karen, I finally got the courage to bring up the one topic that I needed to talk to Mom about, the one that had been in my heart for a while. "There's one other thing I want to talk with you about, Mom."

"Is it about Kelly, by any chance?" she said with a smile.

"Yeah, and you probably know the next statement too," I said, grinning.

"Well, I might be able to guess, but I'd rather hear you tell me in your own words," she replied.

"I want to have her near me for the rest of my life. I realized that last weekend, and it became painfully obvious when I missed her so much this week. We belong together, for the rest of our lives. When I go there next weekend, I'm going to ask her to marry me."

"That's wonderful, Adam, I think you two are perfect for each other!" she exclaimed.

When I got home, I called Kelly, of course, and talked with her some more. I felt a little guilty not telling her about my intention to propose.

Then I slept well, surprisingly well. Maybe this sustainability stuff was a good idea after all . . .

CHAPTER 7
Creating the Vision

Sunday morning's sermon was provocative—it caused me to think, and to put things in a different perspective, again. The theme was that a friend is one who remembers your song and who will sing it to you when you forget the words. I couldn't help but think of Kelly. She and I had been doing that for each other for years now. And Mom and Dad—they did that for each other too. How could this translate to work? Could team-mates do that? Could we do that as part of our culture? I had lots to think about. And in that vein, I was glad we scheduled the meeting to start at 2:00 to allow for families to have dinner together.

As I arrived at the country club, I noticed that Karen and Dennis had once again recreated the space we had left the night before. I knew they had removed everything on Saturday afternoon, because I had watched them start to do it as I left.

When it was time to start, Dennis and Karen got up and went to the front of the room; Karen picked up a marker. Dennis asked, "We have started each meeting with a check-in. Because the group has established a level of trust, we can now ask a more important question. What is your deepest hope for today? Whoever wishes to speak can speak, in any order."

"Figuring out how to move forward," came the first response.

"Clarity and strategy," came the second.

And so on, until Lorraine, who had been relatively quiet throughout the weekend, said, "I hope Susan and Adam will commit to keeping the company going. I'm afraid Adam will leave and they'll sell the company."

"Lorraine! You can't ask that in front of everyone!" was Wayne's shocked reply.

Mom and I looked at each other quickly. I was really glad we had the conversation last night; she now knew I was committed to stay and help the company thrive. So she nodded for me to answer. "Oh, that's okay," I said as I looked at Lorraine, only a little taken aback by her forwardness. "You probably need to know that, don't you, along with everyone else here. If we're going to do this, we're all going to have to be committed to making it work.

"Now, to address your concern, Mom and I had a long talk last night about that, and we agreed. I am completely committed to staying here for the next few years, and to doing whatever it takes to build Brookings Manufacturing to be the biggest, best, most profitable, and most fun company in the industry. I haven't had time to move my stuff here from Boston yet, but that will happen soon. Right now, the company is more important than my move."

Mom told me later that she felt something shift in the room—the group seemed more relaxed, more confident, and ready to move forward boldly.

After the check-in was completed, and with that one important detour, Dennis said, "Now, let's design a company where your decisions are made based on your deepest values. Describe in detail how the company will operate five years from now based on those values. Why do customers, employees, and suppliers choose you instead of the competition? Talk about how you make decisions in your own job, and how others around you make their decisions. The rules are very simple: all ideas are great ideas. *Some* should be implemented; some should not. But this is *not* the time to decide which ones will be implemented. This is the time to bring *all* ideas forward, and let those great ideas cause other great ideas. Remember, this is just talk. At the end of the day you can throw all this away and go back to the company just the way it currently operates, or to any other design you choose. Let's allow for 45 minutes to talk about it and see how that works."

Lorraine jumped in and began talking animatedly, "It is wonderful to work in a company where people truly care about each other. We already do that. But in the future, it would be so wonderful to be able to think of people, including my children, when I'm making decisions at work. Of course, I don't make that many decisions that would directly affect them. But Sam, you make decisions about the chemicals you use for maintaining the plant and office. When you make them, please think of the health of our workers, our families, and our community."

Sam responded, "Lorraine, I feel the same way. If I can make decisions based on people and the environment, as well as money, I can replace some of those really dangerous chemicals with others, which may cost just a bit more or may be a little less efficient, but a lot less damaging. And I can look for others that are even more benign; I now have a reason to spend time doing that."

Barbara contributed, "I've been thinking about the Triple Bottom Line. I think it could help us keep the people we've got and, when we start to grow, to attract and retain some really good people. It's not easy to get the cream of the crop to move here to a small city in the Midwest—we don't have the draw of New York or Boston or Chicago or Denver or Silicon Valley. I've lost too many really good candidates in the past when they realized where we're located. And," she enthused, "I really like the idea of 'people' being included as a primary criterion for decision-making. My deepest desire is to be in the top 10 in *Fortune* magazine's '100 Best Companies to Work For' list."

Walter added, "I suspect this Triple Bottom Line stuff will affect engineering in ways we don't yet anticipate. I do know that the European Union requires manufacturers of most major consumer electronics, cars, and other consumer goods to actually take back their products at the end of their useful life. So BMW has drastically reduced the types of plastic in its cars to make them easier to recycle. I'm wondering about the possibility of bringing back our older units, rebuilding them, then reselling them or sending them back to the original customer. We'd have to change some designs, but I think we could do that. I think it would save money, allowing us to reduce our prices to meet customer pricing requirements. And it would reduce the amount of stuff going into landfills."

After a short pause, he continued, "And as for my deepest desires, I want to change our design criteria so we eliminate as many toxic substances as possible. I've gotta tell you that slide of the chemicals in breast milk really got to me. Heather is still nursing our second child, and we'd like to have one more. And I now know that the decisions I make at work do make a difference in my babies' world."

Ron said, "I've been feeling like an outsider during these last few discussions, because I *am* one. But I want to tell you that I really envy you the chance to redesign your company this way. I have been so inspired by what you've done this weekend that I want to have my bank do the same. And, to answer one of the questions raised yesterday afternoon, I will be more inclined to review loan applications favorably now that I understand why you'll be doing what you'll be doing. I might be a banker, but I'm also a father, and my son and daughter-in-law just had their first child. So I want to help you, and every other company in town, eliminate the use of toxic chemicals. And I'm really interested to find out how this 'people' dimension will play out. I am glad Adam invited me to participate this weekend."

Marie spoke from her heart. "I've worked here for 20 years now. I think Chris was a wonderful man and a great boss. But this idea of having each of us bring our deepest values to work and make decisions based on them, and not just profitability, excites me more than anything else since I joined the company. I know Chris sometimes agonized over decisions, weighing what the financial picture told him he had to do against what his heart was telling him he *should* do. If we had started this process a couple of years ago, he might still be with us. I am convinced it was stress from trying to keep the company running that killed him. I'm all for this, even though I won't be able to make that big of a difference in my job."

I said, "You might not know this, but I'm as scared as anyone else about the way we're changing the company. I've worked for an industrial products distribution company in Boston for the last five years. They're good people, with an owner who is the same kind of person as my dad was—honest, hard-working, caring. But they're still focused on money. So, all decisions are made based on money—that's the only criterion. I really want to work in a company that honors people and the environment. My gut tells me it's the right thing to do. But I don't know how to do that any more than anyone else here, except Dennis and Karen. So I can't lead you all there, because leading implies I know where we're going and how we're going to get there. All I can do is help design it and trust each person to help create it with me. I have promised you I will tell the truth, the whole truth, and I will keep my commitments.

"I do have one more idea though, from Ray Anderson's book," I added, and then looked at Walter. "Maybe we don't have to worry about selling the refurbished units. Maybe all we have to do is lease the units for an annual fee, and we would be responsible for upgrading the units in our customers' equipment. They wouldn't know or even care if the unit we put in is new or used; we would stand by our craftsmanship and they would get the performance they're paying for."

Walter responded, "Sounds interesting. That would drastically change our sales model, wouldn't it?"

Jeff retorted, "It sure would, and I don't think our customers will like it one bit!"

I said, "Well, it's an idea, and all ideas are good ideas, to quote Dennis. We'll let it germinate for a while to see if it is something we want to think about implementing." Jeff glowered at me.

Dennis took the lead. "So let's design the new Brookings. Let's start with our customers—who are they and why are they buying from us instead of our competitors?"

And the answers started coming, like popcorn popping once again. Karen walked to the flip chart and started writing down the key points.

Why Customers Buy from Us:

- They want a reliable, long-term supplier they can trust.
- They're looking for integrity.
- They want to keep jobs in the U.S.

- They want to be able to talk face to face with our staff—engineers, assembly people, and quality people.
- They want quick response.
- They want a company that reflects their values—one that values people and the planet as well as profits.
- They recognize that the price they pay is not the same as the total cost; it is only one part of that total cost.
- It's all about relationships.
- It's because all of our products are purple.

This last addition was followed by incredulous stares, then general laughter from the group.

I reminded everyone, "Remember, *all* ideas are great ideas." Then somebody asked, "Why not all purple?"—and we all started thinking about that for a bit—what could we do to be distinctive? Like the orange semi-trailers on the road—you know they're Schneider. And the green tractors out in the farmers' fields—you know they're John Deere. We continued until we were out of ideas.

Then Dennis asked, "Which customers do we choose *not* to sell to?" A couple of people looked like they'd been slapped. They couldn't imagine ever intentionally turning a customer away. I could understand why; business had been slowly sliding south for several years. If a customer could pay, we would take their business, and gladly. "Let's define the customer from hell," he said.

It was like a cloudburst. Dennis began writing frantically on the flip chart.

Customer from Hell:

- One that beats us up on price—price, price, price.
- Pays our invoice late, and only after several phone calls and claiming they lost it.

- Constantly threatens to take their business else-where.
- Treats us like dog doo-doo (general laughter).
- Takes the discount for prompt payment when they finally pay in 100 days!
- Constantly changes their minds, even after the product has been shipped.
- No way to please them.
- Insists on ridiculous specifications.
- Arrogant.
- Rude.
- Condescending—"Oh, you're so *lucky* that you're selling to *us*!"
- Gives away our ideas to competitors.
- Does not listen when we have ideas that could help them.
- Takes three months to finally sign the contract, then wants delivery on a custom-designed part in three weeks.
- Blames us for their screw-ups.

Dennis continued, "Let's assume you're so successful that you can choose which customers you want to sell to. Let's assume you don't want to grow as fast as potential customers want you to. So how do you choose? What does a perfect customer look like?"

Wow. It was Carl, of all people, who started grinning first—I had never seen him grin like that! Then Lorraine and the others caught on. You'd think they had just won the Powerball for $200 million.

Finally, people started speaking. Dennis picked up the marker again and began to write on a clean flip chart page.

Perfect Customer:

- They value people and the environment as well. That means they're going to value a long-term relationship with a supplier who has the same values—and they won't drop us for the first hot-shot who underbids us by a nickel on a $100,000 contract.
- They treat us with respect, and they earn our respect.
- When something goes wrong, it is viewed as an opportunity to improve; and they work with us to correct the problem.
- They are willing to help us improve.
- They take the time to learn who we are.
- They invite us to work with them on their new products. They might even invite us to visit their customers with them!
- Integrity—they honor their word.
- They pay on time and in full—no games and no holdbacks!
- They honor confidentiality.
- They admit when they've made a mistake.
- Help us meet our objectives.
- Invite us to develop new products for them.
- They tell us the truth, and the whole truth!

I don't know where the idea I was about to divulge came from. I was either crazy or on a workshop high. And I've been known to blurt things out before I think them through. So maybe that's what happened. But I was amazed as I heard my mouth say, "I'll tell you what. Before this meeting closes, let's identify one customer who we want to quit doing business with. After we identify that customer, we'll figure out later how to quit selling to them without leaving them in the lurch." There was dead silence in the room. I mean, DEAD SILENCE. I guess my remark really surprised everyone.

Then, like a slow sunrise, Wayne said, "Yeah, I could do that." And he started laughing, not just chuckling, laughing!

Then Lorraine did too. "I wish I could see their faces when somebody tells them we won't sell to them anymore. I would give anything to be there!"

I asked, "Are you both thinking of the same customer?"

"Oh, yeah!" they replied in unison. Somehow, I think the decision as to which customer it was had already been made.

When the laughter subsided, I asked the final question, "So who do we have to be in order for this perfect customer to buy from us?"

Dennis flipped to a new page and began to write quickly.

Perfect Supplier to Perfect Customer:
- Treat our customers with respect.
- Help them improve—delight their customers, fulfill their long-term vision.
- Learn who they are.
- See the world through their eyes—help them achieve their goals.
- Invite them to help us create new products.
- Provide products that help them excel in the market-place.
- Honor our word.
- Admit when we've made a mistake.
- Show them that we value people and the environment.
- Respect them—earn their respect.
- Invite them to visit our suppliers.

- Honor their confidentiality.
- Tell the truth, the whole truth.

The group very quickly realized that this list was basically just the obverse of the Perfect Customer list—it had the same characteristics, only from the customer's viewpoint. And most of it repeated what we had put on the first flip chart page. Such is the way of brainstorming and creativity—it is not necessarily very efficient. But that's okay; it's not supposed to be.

Then Walter said, "I once heard that you can't buy coffee—you can only rent it. I agree with that thought; I need a five-minute break." It's fun to watch a group move in unison without any external coordination. Everybody got up at the same time. Of course, the five minutes was closer to 10 when we finally all got back.

When we returned, Dennis said, "Now let's define our suppliers the same way."

Marie interjected, "Why don't we just use our customer lists, and put a green checkmark by all the lines that apply to supplier relationships?" So we did. Nobody was really surprised when every line had a green check mark next to it.

Then there was a long, uncomfortable pause, and I was wondering who would finally ask the question. It was Wayne who finally said, "Well, if we're going to identify a customer that we want to drop, will we do the same with a supplier?"

"What does the group want to do?" I asked.

"Yes," "Um hum," "Absolutely!" resounded, along with a few nodding heads.

"And do you have one in mind?" I asked.

Wayne replied, "Actually, several."

Sam piped up, "I've got a couple, too."

Walter added, "Me, too."

Amazing—totally amazing—we had been buying from suppliers that we didn't want to do business with. Why? I was sure I'd find out soon enough. They were probably good reasons, unless you looked at things from a longer perspective.

It was Marie who asked, "And how about employees?"

"Good question," I responded. "So let's define the perfect employer, as seen from the employee's viewpoint."

Again, Dennis picked up a marker and began writing on a clean page.

Perfect Employer:

- Honest—tells the whole truth and does not manipulate.
- Employer's products and services "make a difference"—help the world be a better place.
- Invests in workers—helps them gain new skills and knowledge on the job and off-site (for example, offering reimbursement for community college classes).
- Respects workers as people of equal worth.
- Invites and challenges the workers to grow and advance.
- Recognizes and praises a person's contributions.
- Pays fair wages; the minimum pay is a living wage.
- Encourages teamwork.
- Provides day care on site or nearby.
- Offers flex and sick time/personal time.
- Trusts workers—does not watch over them like a hawk—believes them and believes *in* them.
- Supports the local community—for example, United Way, and provides scholarships for college-bound youth.
- Works with local high schools and colleges to employ students part time, and to help classes be more relevant.

- Provides a safe work environment, physically (no toxics, dangerous machines, etc.).
- Provides a safe work environment, psychologically (no threats, no rule by fear, no bigotry/slurs/gender issues).
- Provides a light, airy workplace, preferably with natural light.
- Work is fun—people are laughing and smiling a lot.
- Its products help companies and people become more sustainable—for example, making wind turbines, growing Fair Trade coffee, making clothes from organic cotton, etc.
- Participates in outreach programs for the community.
- Provides assistance to help customers and suppliers become more sustainable.

As we completed the list, Dennis reminded us we had not done what he had asked. We had defined the "perfect" customer, supplier, and employer, but had not talked about how the company would be operating and how people would be making decisions. The group greeted the news with good-natured groans. He added, "To help our creative process, consider Toyota's four True North metrics and their hierarchy*," and he pointed to the flip chart next to him. "The metrics are:

1. Human development.
2. Quality.
3. Delivery/cycle time.
4. Cost/productivity.

---

* Koenigsaecker, George. "Strategy Deployment: Linking Lean to Business Strategy." *Manufacturing Engineering,* March, 2006.

"Inside Toyota, managers who have to choose between these metrics will sacrifice the last one (cost/productivity) first. They will never sacrifice human development. Their motto is, 'We build people before we build cars.'"

I asked, somewhat rhetorically, "I wonder where GM and Ford and Chrysler would be today if they had adopted Toyota's metrics and motto 30 years ago?"

The ideas started to flow and get vocalized. Dennis again took a marker in hand and wrote them down one by one.

Perfect Company Operations/Decision-making:

- Full communications—people at all levels know what's going on.
- Sufficient financial disclosure is made so people can make intelligent decisions in the trenches.
- Decision-making is pushed to the point of greatest knowledge and impact.
- Old-style hierarchy is replaced by overlapping teams.
- Decisions are made based on the Triple Bottom Line, not just profitability. They are based on the greatest total good—profits can be lower if the gain in the other two is greater.

Dennis flipped to a new page and continued writing.

Regarding the environment:

- We will cause no harm with any of our processes, products, or services.
- Our ultimate goal is to cap all emissions sources so that we emit no liquids or gases into the environment.
- Our ultimate goal is for all liquids inside the company to be safe enough for a person to drink.

Again, Dennis flipped the chart, writing furiously to keep up with the flow of ideas.

Regarding social aspects/people:

- Like Toyota, we're in the human development business first, because people are the foundation of our company. With motivated people, we will treat our customers and suppliers well, develop new products, and thrive.

- Community and society at large are included, not just the workforce. We will offer education and training to the community on subjects such as English as a second language, basic financial skills (investments and managing a checking account), parenting, etc. Each employee will be encouraged to give 40 hours of paid time to community causes.

- The highest paid persons at Brookings will have a cap on earnings of 14 times the average salary.[†]

- Ownership of the company will devolve to the employees.

"Well, that's a good start," said Wayne, "but let's talk about how we'll interact with customers—making quotations, taking orders, answering questions. What will be different?" We talked for a while, and couldn't discern any major outwardly visible differences a customer would notice on the phone, or when requesting or receiving a quotation. Those processes would remain pretty much the same.

"So what difference *does* sustainability make for our customers?" asked Wayne. When Chet glowered at him,

---

[†] Quinn, Steve. "Whole Foods Expands by Selling Not Just Good Eats, But also Ideals." *The Oregonian,* April 17, 2006, p. E2.

Wayne got a bit defensive. "Hey," he said, "I'm not trying to kill the idea; I'm just trying to understand how it would work day-to-day."

Lorraine replied, "Let me think out loud for a bit." (Guess who is an extrovert?) "On a given quote, the customer might not see much of a difference. However, we will be giving each of our top- and middle-tier customers a tour of our plant or we will be visiting them at their facilities to tell them about sustainability, and how it will help them gain a competitive advantage. As we implement sustainability, I hope we'll be reducing our cost, which will show up in our pricing, although it might not totally match the lower China prices. And we'll be asking our customers to partner with us to reduce toxic chemicals, reduce packaging, and reduce transportation, which they will notice. It just won't be for specific quotations; it will be how we work with them routinely. We'll probably win more 'supplier of the year' awards, too."

"How about the manufacturing floor itself?" Wayne asked. "What differences will we see there?"

Carl responded, "Let me try this one, and you can tell me where I'm wrong or missing stuff. The floor will be cleaner and even better organized. People will be happier, and that will show. There will be less waste of materials and energy. People will have more ideas. We've done pretty well with Lean, but this will take us to the next level. There should be virtually no toxic chemicals in use, so the hazmat book should be a thing of the past. We will have at least one area dedicated to refurbishing our products. We also might be receiving competitors' products and upgrading them."

Wayne said, "Sounds good so far. You're sure you're talking about our company?"

I smiled, then picked up the thread, "We'll have at least one, probably two or three classrooms that we'll use for employees during the day, and make available to the community during the evening. We'll offer classes on topics that will help our employees and the community's citizens improve their skills or live life better. For example, we'll be offering classes on English as a second language, and we can also offer classes on financial planning, how to buy a house for first-time home buyers, how to read blueprints, and even on how to run some of our machines. I'm guessing there are some potential machinists outside this company who didn't take high school very seriously. They may be very interested in learning a trade to earn more money, and will certainly have a lot more fun doing it than slinging fries at a fast food restaurant or restocking a retailer's shelves."

Barbara interjected, "Adam, I've wanted to do this for years. Our employees will love this!"

I continued excitedly, "Mom and I have decided that we want our employees to own part of the company."

Barbara interrupted exuberantly, "That's just amazing. That could change everything. So we'll want to teach them about how to understand company financials."

Dennis said, "I visited American Cast Iron Pipe Company in Birmingham, Alabama, several years ago. It was very different from other companies because the employees thought and acted like owners and entrepreneurs. That's because they were—it was employee-owned. I was amazed at their attitude. It was on *Fortune* magazine's '100 Best Companies to Work For' list recently as well."

I continued, "Exactly. And we'll have people from our shop floor visit customers from time to time, and suppliers as well. We might even have them help us present our plans to the bank!"

Ron looked a little taken aback at this, then started smiling.

Chet looked pensive and then asked, "Do you really mean that, Adam? I don't mean to doubt you, but I've never heard of anything like that before. That would really change things."

I concluded, "We'll do everything we can to ensure that our employees have full, rich, productive lives. If we do this, will our employees give us their loyalty and energy, and productivity like we've never seen before? What am I missing here?"

Wayne replied, "I think you're right. As strange as this idea sounds, I think I like it. And you've probably missed several things, but I'm not sure they matter right now. This is a good enough picture for me."

"Oh, I forgot," I said, tapping my chin. "We'll be an EPA poster child. They'll use us as their demo lab to show other companies that it can be done—a company can respect the environment and improve profits. So instead of fearing those unannounced audits, we'll be getting phone calls from them asking if they can schedule another plant tour. And other companies, not just those invited by the EPA, will want tours, too. We'll probably give three tours a week, and turn down as many requests as we say 'yes' to."

"One other thing," I was really on a roll now, "once our prices are close to the China prices, we should gain market share because of the additional value provided by sustainability, as well as our ability to respond quickly to market changes. So we might have to add a second shift. I would be delighted if this happened—that layoff still hurts."

I just couldn't stop! "And people on the floor will be even more involved in the design process. We want their expertise included as we design. That's one of the reasons they'll go on customer visits—to learn how customers really use our products, and to watch what happens on the customer's floor and out in the field. In other words, we'll expand the boundaries of their jobs and let people grow into them. I know that not all people are interested in growing that much, but some probably want to. And that's the biggest waste there is—the waste of unused human potential. To me that's much more expensive than any of Lean's seven wastes."

I thought to myself how I really must sound like a psych major. All these new insights about the potential impact of sustainability surprised me. I thought I had been committed to sustainability before, but now that commitment was deepened, touching the bedrock of my psyche.

"I really like what you said," Wayne remarked.

Chet chimed in, "Me, too!"

"Let me try the engineering piece," volunteered Walter. "We'll be designing products to be rebuilt and reused for several life cycles. And we'll be eliminating toxics from our products and our processes as quickly as we can. Now, keep in mind that we're dealing with electronics manufacturing, which historically has used some really ugly chemicals. But we'll keep working on it, and working with others. I still have some contacts back at MIT—I'll bet one of my professors would be willing to create a class project to reduce the use of toxic chemicals in electronics manufacturing. I'm not sure how much of that you will see when you walk the floor, but it will be there."

Sam really surprised us when he said, "I've got so much stuff to do it isn't even funny! I'm going to start researching alternatives to the chemicals I've been using in maintenance. That's obvious. What's more interesting is how I'm starting to think about cutting our fuel costs. I know how much we spend to heat our plant in the winter and how much we spend on our electrical bill monthly. I'm going to try to cut those numbers in half, or even more. That might require some capital investment, but I'm going to look at getting natural light into the plant and the offices. I'll look into windows that open, and see what I can do to have natural ventilation. And I'll start looking at solar panels so we can generate some of our own electricity. I'll check into how we power our machines up every morning—I think we're probably paying a demand charge right now due to all the machines being started at the same time. I'd like to see if we can avoid that. That's just for starters. I'll need help on some of these things. Even if I work 24 hours a day, there's just too much for me to do alone."

I replied, "Sam, I am really impressed with your ideas! I'll be glad to get you some help."

Tom interjected, "Hey, how much are you planning on spending here? You're talking like we have lots of money sitting around just waiting for a place to spend it."

I responded, "Tom, you're right. We'll need to look at the cost of each project before we start it. We want to keep the brainstorming going now though."

Dennis said, "You know, there are federal and state programs to help companies become more energy efficient. Let me put you in touch with some people who can help you make the right connections."

"Thanks," replied Sam.

"Sounds great!" said Tom. "Any time somebody else is willing to pay the bill, I'm all for that!" and we all laughed.

Glancing at my watch, I said, "We've all been at this for more than an hour, and we really need a break. It's amazing how time flies when you're having fun!"

After the break, Nancy, from purchasing, declared, "I'm going to start including sustainability as an important decision criterion when awarding contracts, especially long-term contracts. If a supplier is not practicing sustainability now, that would not stop us from using them as long as they are willing to start down the path. We might offer them some assistance—and maybe even get paid for it! Just think—the Brookings Manufacturing and Consulting Company!" Everyone laughed at that. But still, it was an interesting idea. She continued, "Given the rise in fuel prices and the probability that they will continue to rise over the long term, I'm going to start sourcing as close to our plant as possible."

Mary, her boss, was nodding, saying, "Keep going, Nancy . . . that's great."

Chet commented, "I really had my doubts about this, but I can see how it will really help my fellow workers out in the plant. I like the improvements to safety by eliminating the toxic chemicals, the idea of natural light and natural ventilation, and the idea of classes to help our people and community learn more skills and have better lives. I'll tell the people in the plant that this will be good for them, for their families, and their jobs. And when they start learning what this is and how it works, I can guarantee that you'll be getting some really innovative ideas from them."

Jeff was silent as we talked; he was crossing his arms, leaning back and frowning. He basically came across as "Just show me how I can increase my commissions." It was like he was digging in, getting more rigid and more strident. Unless something changed, I suspected he would be gone from the company within six months.

Karen noticed that Tom was looking concerned so she asked him, "What are you thinking?"

After a short pause, Tom replied, "All this actually sounds good. I'm a little surprised because I didn't think when I came here Friday night that I would find any of it believable, and now I am beginning to believe. But the bottom line is that somebody has to measure how we're doing. That's accounting's job. And I don't know how to measure any of this yet." I glanced around the room and could tell people were taking Tom's remarks as being constructive rather than critical. That was good.

Dennis responded, "Tom, that's a great observation. Please keep asking that question. Our experience with companies is that they actually define the metrics when they start approving specific projects and programs. It's too early to define specific metrics yet."

Karen then got up and taped a couple of flip charts up on the wall. "Okay folks. Now let's look at the barriers to implementation that you came up with yesterday afternoon. And let's see what we can do about each of them." She proceeded to lead the discussion, talking about each barrier, and writing the plan for resolution after each one. She found herself taping up additional pages to accommodate the ideas.

- *Barrier*. How do we implement sustainability? It's so new there is no clear path yet.

  Resolution. Use the same approach we used for Lean. We know up front that we'll make mistakes, but that's okay. It's part of the learning process. Institute a 'most creative mistake of the month' award.

- *Barrier*. How do we address the fear of change?

  Resolution. Use the same approach as for Lean implementation. We will support people and let them know that honest mistakes are expected—it just means they are learning.

- *Barrier*. How do we address the fear of failure?

  Resolution. Same—their paycheck is safe. If they aren't capable of doing the new aspects of their job, we'll help them transfer inside the company. If they want to leave the company, we'll help them find a good job that fits them. There should not be as much culture shock as when we put in Lean.

- *Barrier*. No metrics—how do we measure non-financial stuff (people and planet)?

  Resolution. We'll have to invent this as we go. We'll also be reading a lot and asking Dennis about who else is doing this stuff so we can call them.

- *Barrier*. It will still cost too much money.

  Resolution. This is no longer an issue. It might cost money, but we'll get it back and then some. It's the best choice we have. Each project will be cost-justified before we start it.

- *Barrier*. Will our customers be interested?

  Resolution. We hope so. At least, the customers we want to sell to will be—it is up to us to educate them. When we do, we'll form tighter relationships.

- *Barrier*. Will our suppliers be interested?

  Resolution. Same as customers, see above.

- *Barrier*. We can't imagine being an EPA poster child!

  Resolution. We can now imagine that (with difficulty).

- *Barrier*. How do we decide when the bottom lines are in conflict?

  Resolution. Create a formula as a guide and listen to our gut as a reality check.

- *Barrier*. Education and training—what do we need, who will provide it, and when?

  Resolution. We'll create a schedule and modify it as we go along. We'll need a lot of education and training, just like with Lean. The companies that have been most successful have invested heavily in education, double and triple that of the typical company.

- *Barrier.* Will this help or hurt our relationship with the bank?

  Resolution. Help—we'll be a better long-term risk for them. And they can use us as a model to help other customers implement sustainability.

- *Barrier.* How much will this cost? Where will the money for it come from?

  Resolution. We don't know yet. But major expenditures will have to be approved based on their merits.

- *Barrier.* Will this be enough to turn the company around?

  Resolution. We hope so—it's the best alternative we've got!

Dennis nodded to me, and I got up and said, "About a week ago, Tom and Wayne came into my office, at different times, to tell me they had some serious concerns about this sustainability stuff. I promised them that if they'd participate fully this weekend, I would give them a chance to share their reservations with the group. I wanted them to be our acid test—to spot any weaknesses in strategy or tactics. So Tom, Wayne, here's your chance. Where are the weaknesses? What won't work?"

Tom stood up. He slowly looked around to each person then said, "Adam is right. I walked into his office a week ago Friday and told him point blank that I didn't see how this sustainability stuff could help the company survive. It seemed too soft, too 'new age.' And I know the comments I just made might have sounded critical, but I was only trying to understand how to measure results. I've been watching what's been happening this weekend. I'm an accountant, and not an HR pro, but from everything I've seen, we should move forward with this as fast as we can. I don't see that any other alternatives give us any real hope at all. Sustainability does. I don't yet know if we'll succeed; we have a long way to go. We'll probably encounter lots of surprises. But I can't see any glaring weaknesses. This is our best chance of succeeding, and it looks like we'll have fun trying. I say we go for it."

Wayne stood up and said, "I agree with Tom. This should reduce costs and improve our relationships with customers. I don't see any glaring weaknesses either. Adam, if you'll help me find the crow, I'll eat it, with or without ketchup and mustard. I'm behind this 100%."

I turned to the group, "Well, now that you've had a chance to create a company strategy and a few tactics based on sustainability, what do you think? Do you want to try this or one of our other options? Or, do you want to brainstorm something new that we haven't discussed yet?"

From the murmurs, there seemed to be unanimous consent. Karen said, "Since there seems to be a lot of support for the idea, someone who doesn't support it might not feel comfortable speaking out right now. Why don't we have each person write their answer on a sticky note—that way, everyone will feel safe." So we did. Karen read the results to the group. We had 15 in favor of sustainability, three who were okay with moving forward but who still wanted more information, and one who didn't like sustainability. I figured I could easily guess the identity of that one person.

"I will personally support this initiative with everything I've got," I told the group. "But I shouldn't be the sustainability leader. We should choose a person who has been in this group this weekend, who has the respect of people throughout the organization, and who can make this work on a day-to-day basis. Are there any volunteers—any nominations?"

After some discussion, we selected Carl; he'd been with the company for 20 years, starting as an apprentice machinist. He had gone to night school at the local community college to get his associate's degree and continued to take courses when he could. He was respected and well-liked by virtually everyone, and was instrumental in our Lean transformation. He was even-handed, even-tempered, and an excellent leader.

I stood up and addressed the group, "The steering committee will be the executive staff; we meet every Monday morning. Carl will come to our meetings to report progress and ask for resources. One of your first tasks, Carl, will be to create a project team of people from across the company who will be the sustainability coordinators in their departments. Can you have that committee defined by a week from tomorrow?"

"Yes," Carl replied.

"Good," I said, nodding. "Now let's each write down three to five things we could do in our departments as possible first projects. When you get back to the plant tomorrow, I want each of you to pick the top two and perform a rough cost-benefits analysis. It should include estimates of time and resources required. You'll need to get this information to Carl by Friday morning. Also give Carl the ideas for the other projects—we don't want to lose track of them.

"Carl, meet with me tomorrow morning at 10 and we'll start defining the education and training needs for our people.

"I will be calling an all-employee meeting tomorrow afternoon to let everyone know what we've talked about and where we're going. I'll explain that this is still very new, so we don't have all the answers yet. Each person who was here this weekend will be asked to stand so employees will know who they can talk to."

"Now, I think we've done what we came to do. I, for one, am proud of you for your hard work and your commitment. We've made huge progress. I know we have a long, long way to go, but I am delighted and amazed with what we've done this weekend. Thank you all. Does anyone else have any final comments?" No one responded, so I nodded to Dennis and Karen and sat down.

Dennis and Karen both stood. Karen started, "It has truly been an honor and a privilege to be here this weekend. Lots of things can happen in the next few years, but I have a really good feeling about how things will work out for you. You have so much going for you!"

Dennis continued, "I also want to thank you for inviting us to lead this workshop. I've led lots of them, and you are truly special. I'm with Karen; I think you'll make it."

I stood back up. "Karen and Dennis, we couldn't have done this without you. Thanks so much for being the catalyst we needed, and for giving up a weekend with your families." At that I started clapping and everyone else stood up, clapping loudly.

As the clapping was dying down, Tom held up his hands to get everybody's attention. "Adam, please order a second serving of crow. I'll be joining Wayne in eating it." He turned to the group, "A week ago I told Adam I thought the money he was spending on this weekend was a complete waste of our precious resources. He replied that he'd take it out of his own pocket so the company would not have to spend anything. Adam, this was the best use possible of our company's funds. It will be a privilege for me, as CFO, to write the check to cover the weekend."

"Thanks, Tom," I replied. "Okay, everyone, let's go home!" And with that, the group dispersed in pairs and trios, everyone talking as they gathered up their things and headed for their cars.

Wayne, Tom, Mom, Barbara, and I stayed behind for a bit to have a little time with Karen and Dennis.

"So what do you think?" I asked them.

Karen answered, "I meant what I said at the end. I think you guys will make it. And I'm glad, because you have a lot of good people here. They really care. If Chet and Annie represent the people in your plant, you're very lucky."

"I'd like you to continue to guide us on our journey. Would you be willing to do that?" I asked.

"Absolutely! We really enjoy working with you," Karen said as she put her handbag on her shoulder.

"When can you come back?" I asked.

"Let's plan on a month from now, and make it during the week this time," Dennis grinned. "If you'll be a little flexible, we might be able to stop here while we're working with other clients in the general area. It will save us a lot of wear and tear on our bottoms in airplane seats, and save you some travel expenses."

"We can easily do that. Let's talk in a week or two and set a date," I said.

"Sounds good," Dennis said as he picked up his brief-case. "We've got to get moving to make our flight. Thanks again for the opportunity to help. You've got our numbers and e-mail addresses—feel free to contact either of us if you have any questions."

"You know I will!" I chuckled.

After handshakes, Dennis and Karen headed quickly for their car.

On the drive home, I turned to Mom and said, "Wow. What an intense weekend. I hope this week cuts us a little slack." Unfortunately, Murphy (as in "Murphy's Law") had other ideas.

CHAPTER 8
Monday, Monday.
Can't Trust That Day . . .*

For a Monday, it started out pretty well. The weekend had tired us out, but we were still pretty high from what we accomplished, and we had hope for the future. The staff meeting was short. I told everyone that Dennis and Karen would be back in about a month. I asked Tom to prepare a couple of overheads showing our financial situation for my use at the all-company meeting at 3:00 that afternoon. Then I spent some time with Carl on the education and training plan for our people. We agreed to educate everyone on the basics of sustainability, starting with the meeting that afternoon.

Just before lunch Jeff came into my office and closed the door. He didn't even ask if I had time, he just walked in. "Here's my resignation and my two weeks' notice. I'm taking a position with Electronic Products" (our largest competitor), he announced.

"Why?" I asked.

---

* Mamas and the Papas. April, 1966. Song, "Monday, Monday."

Jeff curtly replied, "Four reasons." He held up his hand showing all four fingers. Then he ticked off one finger at a time as he continued, "1) They've got a major cost advantage by sending their manufacturing to China and they'll be outsourcing their engineering to India this year to further cut costs. 2) They have the capital backing of a Fortune 100 company. 3) They're offering me a substantial increase, so I'll finally get paid what I'm worth. 4) No offense, but I don't think Brookings is going to survive, and I'd rather go with a winner." After a short pause, he leaned forward, almost into my face, and said, "And I don't think you've got what it takes to be the CEO of a successful company. You're too young, too soft. That off-site was pure touchy-feely crap. The only thing that counts in business is money . . . profit . . . bottom line . . . and nothing else. So I'm out of here. I've joined the winner. Thanks for the training and the contacts in the industry." This last statement was delivered with a malevolent grin.

"Are you staying in town?" I asked as I stood up from my chair.

"No, I'll be in their executive offices in California," Jeff said coolly. I wondered briefly if his wife would be moving to California with him, since her parents still lived here.

I thought for a minute. I'd never had an employee go to a competitor before. Controlling my growing anger, I said, "Since you're going to the competition, you can't stay here any longer. I'll call security. They'll escort you to your office. Pack your personal things and give me your key and your laptop when you leave." I was trying to stay outwardly calm, but my insides were churning. I was facing a traitor, somebody who knew all our weak spots and would exploit them to the best of his ability in his new position at our competitor. I also realized that anything he wanted (such as customer contact information) he would have already taken.

As soon as he left my office with the security guard, I called Tom, Wayne, and Barbara into my office, and announced, "Jeff just quit; he's going to Electronic Products." I waited for them to absorb the news. Then I said, "We have three issues to deal with: 1) Who will take over his accounts? Who will become VP of sales and marketing? 2) He told me, 'Thanks for the training and the contacts.' That doesn't sound good. How do we keep him from taking our major customers? If we lose one major or even two medium customers, we're in serious trouble. 3) He knows about our plans to move toward sustainability. Even though he doesn't believe it will work, he will probably still tell Electronic Products what we're going to be doing. So we just lost the element of surprise."

Barbara broke the silence. "We don't have to answer any of those questions right now, do we? Let's think about it for a couple of days. You can be acting VP of sales and marketing until we find the right person. The question we *do* have to answer now is, do we tell everyone at the 3 p.m. meeting?"

I looked around and saw three heads nodding. I was surprised when I realized mine was nodding too. "Yes, I guess I will tell everyone at 3:00. This means I'll also brief them on our SWOT analysis, just so they know what's really going on. I'll tell the rest of the executive staff about Jeff beforehand; I don't want them to learn about it at that meeting. And I'll call a special staff meeting Wednesday morning to discuss the three issues."

Just then Jeff came into my office, gave me his key and his laptop, then left, without saying a word to any of us. We all looked at each other, shaking our heads.

I walked down the hall to the sales and marketing department and called an impromptu meeting. "You are probably all aware that Jeff resigned today. He will be working for Electronic Products. Since he is going to a direct competitor, I had him pack up his personal items and leave the premises immediately. I've just met with my staff to discuss how we'll handle this. We're meeting again Wednesday morning to make some decisions. So for the time being, if someone asks for Jeff, you can tell them he is no longer with our company and find the appropriate person to handle the situation. Until we find a replacement, I'll be acting VP of sales and marketing. We don't yet know what we'll do about filling his position. I'll tell the entire company at our 3 o'clock meeting. I'd rather you didn't discuss this with anyone else for now—just focus on keeping our customers as happy as possible."

At 3 p.m. I addressed the entire company at the staging area of our shipping dock. It was the only place large enough to hold all of our employees at one time. Lucky for me, our shipping foreman's office was on the second floor, which had an outside stairway that faced the staging area where everyone was standing. So I stood at the top of the stairs, facing the crowd, using a portable microphone Barbara found somewhere. "I've been here 11 weeks now, and it's time I told you what is going on. This is your company as much as it is Mom's and mine, and you deserve to know. But before we get into the details, I need to ask you to not tell this to outsiders. You can tell your spouse, but only if they promise to keep it confidential. We're going to treat you like adults, like partners in the business, and we need to know that you'll treat us the same way. Are you ready to hear what's really going on?" Lots of people were saying yes and nodding their heads. "And will you keep this information confidential?" There was the same response.

I told them about our off-site, and briefed them on sustainability and the Triple Bottom Line. I asked each person who had been at the off-site to raise their hand as I called their name. I told them that Carl was the day-to-day sustainability leader, and that I backed him 100%. I had Carl come up beside me and present the first draft of the education and training plan; we would be presenting a one-hour overview of sustainability to all employees, with sessions starting next week. I told them a few of our ideas about places to look for improvements, and that we hoped to cut our costs 25% or more within two years, while keeping all our people. I finished that part of the presentation by saying, "Think of Toyota, then think of GM. Toyota has no debt, $30 billion in cash, and makes money on each car it sells. Toyota has four measurements: 1) human development, 2) quality, 3) on-time delivery and short cycle times, and 4) low cost and high productivity. Toyota's fundamental operating principle is human development. Their motto is, 'We build people before we build cars.' I want us to follow their example. From this day forward, Brookings Manufacturing is in the human development business. You'll find out more during your sustainability overview next week."

I asked Chet to come up beside me, then I said, "We all owe Chet our thanks. He had the courage to say what he thought was the truth during the off-site. He didn't have any idea how the company was doing financially. And it wasn't his fault; we have intentionally kept that information private for years. We now realize that keeping information about the company's performance private basically sent the message that you weren't important and we couldn't trust you. So Mom and I decided to change that, starting right now. Thanks, Chet." I started clapping and others did too.

"Mom, please come and stand beside me while I tell people where we are financially." She joined me and I began in a serious tone, "The situation is not good. Sales have been dropping, slowly, yes, but they are still dropping. And you probably know the basic reason: our two major competitors have outsourced their production to China. Mom and I are committed to keeping production here—we can't even conceive laying off our friends and neighbors who work in our plant. Unfortunately, profits have been dropping even faster than sales." I continued with the grim financial news, concluding, "A fundamental part of sustainability is trust. We will trust you by telling you the truth, the whole truth, and trust that you will use the information wisely. This picture is not pleasant. But it's the truth. We'll give you updates on the 10th of each month, just so you'll know, and so you can make intelligent decisions." Everyone looked somewhat stunned.

"I have two more topics to discuss so that you will have a complete picture." I gave them the SWOT overview. They gasped when I said we decided to stop selling to one customer, effective almost immediately, even though they understood why. Here we were, desperate for sales, and we were firing a customer?! Then I said, "Jeff Holland was our VP of sales and marketing. He quit this morning and is going to work for Electronic Products. He said he wanted to be with a winner, and that wasn't us. So we're going to discuss how to make sure we keep all the customers we want to keep. Right now, we're very vulnerable, even more so because of Jeff. But in spite of his resignation, I think we can make it, and even take over the number one position in our industry again. With your help and ingenuity, we can make it. Will you help us keep the jobs here?"

First one person, then a couple of others, and then finally everyone started applauding.

"The door to my office is open to anyone, at any time. Now let's get back to work, so we can turn our company around."

Tuesday morning I was walking the floor just to see how things were running when Annie motioned me over. "Looking for another cup of coffee?" I asked.

"Yeah," she grinned. "How did you guess?"

When we were sitting at what was by now our table, she said, "You did a really good thing yesterday, trusting us enough to tell us what was really going on with the company. That's all I've been hearing about ever since the meeting—how the company is really doing. You'd be amazed at some of the things people thought were true! Like the company making $10 million in profits each year, and stuff like that. And we're also a little scared. That was a huge load to dump on us all at once. What can we do? Most of us are just hourly employees with high school degrees."

"Would it help if I came to a team meeting or two?" I said, and then took a drink from my cup.

"Would you really? That would be great!" she said with excitement.

"But you have to invite me, remember?" I said as I looked at her. "I can't just show up without being invited. And I want to bring Carl with me, because he's the sustainability leader."

Annie raised her coffee cup and was about to take a sip, but paused and said, "Oh, yeah. I forgot. I'll make sure you're invited to our meeting tomorrow afternoon. And it's cool to bring Carl too."

"What time?" I asked.

"Let's make it 2:00 in the meeting room. I'll check with the others and call you," Annie replied, rising up from her chair.

"Good. I'm looking forward to it," I said and we both returned to work.

When I got back to my office, I called Barbara and the two of us went by Carl's office to talk about what we could do and say in the team meeting tomorrow.

"Why don't we use them as guinea pigs for our sustainability education? With their permission, of course," Carl suggested.

"Could we have it ready in time?" I asked, knowing it would take a little time to put together the curricula and presentation.

"I think so," said Carl. "Barbara, could you get those slides from Dennis and Karen? If we had those, we'd have an excellent start."

I jumped in before Barbara could answer, "I already have them. I asked Dennis and Karen for a copy Saturday evening, and they gave me one. It's on my hard drive now; I'll send it to you as soon as I get back to my office."

"Great," Carl said. "I'll start working on it right away."

So I e-mailed Carl the slide file. I stopped by his office that afternoon and we decided who would present each topic. I wanted him to be the main "go-to" person on sustainability, but I also needed to make sure people knew I was truly behind this new way of conducting business. And I needed to get comfortable with the details myself, because I sensed I would soon be tested. I hate it when I'm right like that . . .

Wednesday morning I called another staff meeting to discuss the answers to the questions caused by Jeff's departure. We were still struggling until Barbara gave us the proper perspective. She said, "Let's pretend like we're five years into the future, looking back on this moment, and saying that Jeff's departure was one of the best things that could have happened. Why would that be true?"

"Because he was basically selfish, loud, and arrogant," said Wayne.

"Because he only focused on money and himself, and he wouldn't fit with our new values," added Marie.

Walter said, "Because his attitude would actually alienate the customers and employees we want the most." Bingo! That was it.

I commented, "I just had another insight—we used to refrain from talking like this because it didn't seem professional or nice or something. But now we can speak the truth as we see it, when we're in a safe place. It doesn't seem wrong when it helps us move our company forward.

"We need to have the right people on our bus. And Jeff wasn't one of them. He actually did us a favor by leaving when he did. If he had stayed longer, he would have slowed down, or even damaged, our sustainability initiative. So, who do we replace Jeff with?"

They all started looking at me. That was not a good sign! Wayne said, "I think it would be a good idea for you to take our three largest customers for the time being. They're nervous as it is because of Chris' death. They've never had a chance to meet you face to face, and Jeff will probably tell them you're a naïve, incompetent kid who is not fit to be the CEO."

"And that description is wrong where?" I quipped.

"Adam, trust me on this," Wayne responded. "When you meet those customers face to face, they'll start respecting you. You have enough charisma to do this. Look how you have been leading us—first the off-site, and then the employee meeting Monday. You're the only one who can show them that Jeff is lying, because it's you he's lying about. If anybody else met with them, they'd still have doubts about the long-term prospects of Brookings just because they wouldn't have met you.

And you're the best person to start talking with them about sustainability and our strategic direction. In fact, you should be making plans to meet with the big three right now. And as soon as you're done with the big guys, you get to meet the five medium customers. We can't afford to lose any of them either."

Barbara picked up that train of thought. "Wayne's right. As for the day-to-day stuff, Lorraine and her crew can pick up the slack. From what I've heard from her, Jeff wasn't that great on the details anyhow—he was more of a glad-handing, 'take them for a round of golf' type. So we didn't lose much as far as the actual quotation and order functions."

I looked at Walter, and said, "I'll need you, Walter, and your team to back me up on this. I don't want to promise something we can't deliver."

"No problem, Adam," he said. "Honestly, I feel better having you attend to our customers instead of Jeff. He figured that if he could sell it, we could build it. A couple of times he sold stuff that didn't exist, and we made him go back to the customer and tell them we couldn't do it, which didn't sit very well with him, or with them either. And he blamed us for that. We can only push the state of the art so far; we're not magicians, in spite of our reputation. So we're behind you all the way."

"Thanks. I'll talk with Lorraine to make appointments to meet with our large and medium customers," I said, wondering how I would ever accomplish all that lay ahead of me.

Lorraine was able to get me appointments with two of our largest customers and two of our medium customers, all in California, the following Monday and Tuesday. This meant I could spend all day Sunday with Kelly! I sure was looking forward to seeing her again. And my appointment with BayTech, our other large customer, in Boston, was arranged for a couple of weeks later. Lorraine said not to worry about BayTech because they were completely loyal to us. She also made appointments with the other medium customers. As she made the appointments, she deftly failed to mention Jeff's change of loyalties; instead, she merely said that the new CEO wanted to meet our customers face to face. They seemed pleased to oblige.

That afternoon at 2:00, Carl, Barbara, and I were in the meeting with the assembly team, which included Annie. They seemed excited to be the guinea pigs for the one-hour sustainability overview. We spent about 20 minutes on the why of sustainability, and what was happening in the world. Another 20 was spent on the Triple Bottom Line, especially the environmental and social aspects of it. The final 20 minutes was all questions from the team. Carl was writing down questions during the whole hour, so he would be better prepared for them in the future. He was proving to be an excellent choice for sustainability leader. The most important questions were, "Will this work? Will it save our jobs?" and "Tell me again how this actually saves money?" These were interspersed with "Finally, decisions will be made for the right reasons," and "Is this really true? This concept (Triple Bottom Line) sounds too good to be true." We left that meeting with some excellent feedback for the sustainability overview for our company.

Wednesday night Mom and I talked about the staff's idea over dinner. "I like it, Adam," she said. "Wayne was completely right. You need to do this; nobody else can. And Walter was right, too, about having the right people on the bus, and about Jeff's style. Jeff schmoozed your dad with the promise that he could increase sales. When things kept getting worse instead of better, Jeff found other people to blame. And your dad got so wrapped up in trying to turn things around he couldn't see that Jeff was a major part of the problem. I'm glad he's gone. And I'm glad he went to Electronic Products—he'll reinforce their image of MCP salesmen."

"MCP?" I asked, puzzled.

"Male chauvinist pig—a popular expression back in the 1970s," she said with a grin as she poured us each a glass of iced tea.

"It's almost funny, us sitting here basically thinking that Jeff will do more good for us working for the competition. I really like that! Here's to Jeff! May he increase our business!" I smiled, raising my glass in salute.

We were silent for a while as we both began to eat. Then I brought up the topic that had been in the back of my mind most of the week. "Mom, I don't know what to do about Kelly. Do I buy a ring here and take it with me, or do I propose and then we pick out her ring together?"

"Well, I think having the ring with you is more romantic. And you can always get it sized there, after she says 'yes.'"

"I know she will say 'yes.' I mean, I hope she will. I think she will . . . I'm so scared that she might not! I wouldn't blame her for wanting to stay in Portland. I mean, it's so beautiful out there."

"Trust me, Adam; she loves you as much as you love her," Mom said as she placed her hand over mine. "You are much more important to her than Portland. She will say 'yes.' Everything else is details, which you two can work out together."

"I hope you're right. Do I *ever* hope you're right," I said. Mom squeezed my hand reassuringly.

"Adam, did you remember to call Rev. Franklin to reschedule your meeting for this Friday?"

My face turned red. "Oops!"

"That's okay, just call him tonight and leave him a message. He'll understand."

"Okay, Mom."

When I called Kelly that night, she squealed with delight when she heard I would need to be in California Monday morning to meet with our customers. "That means we can spend all day Sunday together here!" We talked about how we could spend the day. And I told her about the task ahead of me on Monday. She agreed with the staff, that I needed to meet the customers myself, face to face.

Friday morning, all of the off-site participants met to discuss what they'd gotten accomplished so far. Carl went through the one-hour sustainability overview quickly (the team had already seen the slides the previous weekend and just needed to know which ones were included and what the main focus would be for the training). Nancy had started calling suppliers to ask if they were doing anything with the environment, sustainability, or social responsibility. Most of them were not, yet. She also scheduled meetings with them to ask how they could reduce their costs to us so we could keep our plant open here. The alternative, of course, was sending production overseas to China, at which point they would lose the volume permanently. As we hoped, they were eager to do everything they could. Chet had asked people on the floor to identify all the toxic materials, and Sam had started doing the same thing in maintenance. Walter asked his engineers to start researching the utilization of used or recycled materials in our products in place of virgin materials. Barbara had done some research on classes we could offer our employees. The one that seemed most popular was a two-hour introduction to personal financial management. Interestingly enough, Ron was willing to teach it! I was very pleased when I heard that. We would follow it up with an introduction to company financial statements, led by Tom and his people. Barbara had also contacted the English as a second language people downtown to see about setting up classes in our building.

Finally it was Friday afternoon, and I was driving to the airport to fly to my soon-to-be fiancée. Nervous? Absolutely. And it had very little to do with the sales calls on Monday or Tuesday. They were merely about the business; the weekend was about my life. Hmmm . . . was there a Triple Bottom Line message in there somewhere?

CHAPTER 9
The Shortest Weekend Ever

My flight reached the gate at 6:42 p.m. Portland time. I was out of the plane five minutes later (finally!). And there she was—I couldn't believe how beautiful she looked! We kissed. I mean, we *kissed!* One of those traffic-stopping, I want to wrap myself all around you, movie kisses. I just couldn't get enough of being near her, and it had only been two weeks. We walked to the luggage claim with our arms around each other's waist. I could hardly wait to ask her to marry me, but I didn't want to do it at the airport.

Her condo was a converted loft in the Pearl District, a recently renewed part of Portland adjacent to the downtown area. It had high ceilings, lots of windows, wood floors—really, really nice—a place that I would enjoy living in. But such was not to be the case, not for a while anyway.

We talked throughout dinner, about big things, little things, everything, and nothing. The dinner itself was quite a treat—she prepared small filet mignons with a special sauce, baked red potatoes brushed with garlic butter, asparagus with Hollandaise sauce, and a delightful chocolate mousse. The meal was accompanied by an excellent red wine from Oregon, and illuminated by two candles on the small table. She noticed my jitters. "Adam, you look nervous. Is it about meeting those customers on Monday?"

"That's a lot of it," I said, glad I could find a way to answer truthfully without giving anything away. She didn't push the question further, for which I was grateful.

Finally, the perfect moment arrived. When dinner was finished, I reached in my pocket for the ring, which I had removed from the box a few minutes earlier. I walked over to where Kelly was seated, knelt, took her hand, and looked into her eyes lovingly. I began, "You are my light and my life. You are my soul mate. When I see you the world lights up. When I'm away from you, I'm only half alive. I want to spend the rest of my life with you by my side. I love you. I promise to cherish you and honor you till death finally parts us. Will you marry me?" Trembling while I awaited her answer, I lifted up her left hand to put the ring on her finger.

Her eyes widened and began misting over, and she started beaming joyously. "Yes, Adam, YES!" and she sprang from her chair, lifting me up, and kissing me all over my face. I almost dropped the ring, but managed to keep it in my right hand. After a bit, she gasped, "My ring! Where is my ring?" She called it *"MY"* ring. That sounded so good!

"Right here—let's see if it will fit your finger. If not, we'll get it sized tomorrow," I said as I awkwardly put it on her finger. It was a bit loose, so our first stop tomorrow would be a jewelry store.

Leaving the dishes on the table, we managed to stumble into her living room and finally sat down. Actually, I sat on the couch, and she sat on my lap, reminding me of that time in my office two weeks earlier.

"Kelly, I need to ask you to move back to be with me. I can't abandon the company at this point. If I did, it would probably go under, and too many of my friends would have trouble finding new jobs. I'm really sorry; I wish I could move out here instead."

"Adam, I understand. I was hoping you'd ask me to marry you, and was expecting that you wouldn't be able to leave the company right now. So I've already thought that through. And yes, I'll move back to be with you. But someday I'd like to move back to Portland to live. I love it here—the mountains, the uncrowded beaches, the mild winters, the long gentle spring, the friendly people. It's where I want to live, and I think you'll love it here too. I understand why you need to be the CEO of Brookings for a while, and I'll be by your side while you return the company to prosperity. Adam, I want to be with you. You are much more important to me than where we live."

Our love-making that night completely surpassed any experience I ever had—making love with one's soul mate is a spiritual union, in addition to the physical bonding. If I had died that night, I would have felt my life was complete.

I wasn't used to sleeping with another person in my bed; she wasn't either. So we wound up waking each other up a few times during the night. Sometimes we just snuggled and went back to sleep. Then there were the other times . . .

As I woke up the next morning, I first realized that I was in a strange bed. Then I became conscious there was someone in bed with me, comforted in the realization it was my Kelly snuggled against me. "My Kelly," I thought to myself. That sounded so right. She was still sleeping, her head on my shoulder. I didn't want to get up; I just wanted to hold her forever. When she started to waken, I just watched her eyes. First they opened a bit, then she looked at me, and our souls seemed to merge one more time. I was complete . . . finally complete. And she was, too.

"Kelly," I whispered.

"Hmm?" she said groggily.

"When did you first realize you were in love with me?"

"Remember that night during our junior year at Clark when I almost got raped by that Neanderthal at that dance?"

"Yeah, I'll never forget that! You were so scared, so vulnerable, so hurt," I said, looking into her deep-brown eyes.

"You were in our living room when I got back to the dorm. You knew immediately there was something wrong, that something bad happened. You sat down on the couch, opened up your arms, and I crawled inside. I felt safe. I felt warm. I felt loved by you, unconditionally. Right then I knew, way down deep inside, I wanted to spend the rest of my life with you. But I was afraid to let you know; I didn't know if you felt the same way. And if you didn't it would have ruined our friendship, which was the best thing I had at Clark. So I didn't risk it."

I just held her for a while, stroking her hair and face.

"Adam?"

"Yes, my beautiful wife-to-be?"

"When did you first realize you were in love with me?" she asked, looking into my eyes.

"At the end of our sophomore year," I replied. "Remember the water balloon fight on the quad, our dorm against the other one? You were soaked. And you were beautiful— my Amazon warrior princess. I fell for the fire in your eyes, your laughter, your grace as you dodged the water balloons. I was completely hooked. You were the only woman I wanted to spend the rest of my life with. There has never been anyone else. But I was afraid to tell you . . ."

"It was because you didn't want to ruin our friendship, right?" Kelly asked.

"Got it in one, beautiful," I replied.

"So why did it take us so long?" she said, stroking my forearm.

"I don't know, Kelly. I kept believing you wanted to be in Portland, and that I wanted to be in Boston. Our separate lives seemed more important than us being together. I guess I was basically afraid of the depth of my feelings for you. I was afraid of . . . I don't know what. But after you came out to see me two weeks ago, I knew that I never wanted to let you out of my sight again."

"Same here—I kept trying to tell myself that you were my college boyfriend, a youthful flame, and that now that I'm an important professional woman I would find an important, professional man to love. I was fooling myself. As soon as I saw you when I got off the plane two weeks ago, I knew you were my man, for the rest of our lives."

When we finally left her condo late in the morning, we took her ring to get resized so it would not fall off her finger. Then we went to the Saturday Market, a myriad booths of various artisans and craftspeople, mingled with merchants and food vendors. We lunched there. Kelly was just beaming; her smile outshone the one-carat, solitaire diamond in her engagement ring. We went to Powell's Books, another Portland landmark, a whole city block of nothing but books. What a neat store! New and used books interspersed, and more books than I had ever seen in one store in my life—larger than many public libraries! I bought several more books on sustainability. Then we hopped the trolley to the EcoTrust building.

"This is a prime example of sustainable architecture," Kelly said. "This building was recycled; it was originally a transfer and storage building. They kept the original floors, sanding and resealing them. They added an earthquake-proof steel structure externally. And the walls were painted with recycled paint, which is higher quality than new paint, at 20% of the price. Come on, let me show you an eco-roof." So I followed her up the outside stairway until we got to the roof. It didn't look like any roof I'd ever seen—it was grass and some wildflowers!

"So what is this?" I asked. "Do they have to mow it?"

"It's an eco-roof. It's designed to keep most of the rain from running off the building. And the rain that does run off goes into the bioswale below where it is purified. This way, the load on the storm sewer is reduced. Places that have used an eco-roof, like Ford Motor Company on its River Rouge plant, have saved money over conventional roofs. And no, they don't have to mow it; the whole idea is for it to be natural."

We then went back to her condo for dinner, and...

On Sunday she wanted me to see Multnomah Falls. They were 620 feet tall, she said, and the second-highest, year-round waterfall in the nation. That was okay with me; anything she wanted to do was okay with me. I was just happy to be with Kelly. So we drove her Miata® east into the Columbia Gorge. We chose the older scenic highway rather than the interstate so we could see other falls as well. I was surprised when the mountains began to pile up on both sides of the river until they were rising 2,000 feet up from the highway. Huge basalt cliffs piled one on another up into the forests. We passed lots of waterfalls as we drove east until we reached the one you see on the postcards, a high, narrow ribbon falling hundreds of feet into a pool that then tumbles down the lower falls almost to the road and lodge. Parking in the lot, we hiked to the top of the cliff along with a bunch of other tourists, and I didn't care if we were in a crowd, as long as I was with Kelly. I floated up the trail and back down feeling like my life had just started. We returned in time to have an excellent dinner at McCormick and Schmicks, and to catch a glimpse of the sunset turning Mt. Hood a light salmon hue.

Our last night together was again wonderful. I just couldn't get enough of her—her presence, her touch, her smell, her smile, her eyes, the way her hair swished when she walked, and the way she expressed herself with her hands as well as words . . . I wanted to spend every possible minute with my fiancée. She apparently felt likewise. Whenever we were awake, we were constantly touching each other. And even when we were sleeping, we were snuggled together. I now understood why my parents' marriage was so strong, and so able to withstand the pressures of business problems, child raising, money problems, etc. They were soul mates too; I knew that even when I was much younger. And now I finally recognized mine. My only regret was that it had taken me eight years to realize it, and five irrecoverable years had passed without our being together . . . but no longer.

CHAPTER 10

Monday, Monday, Redux

I hate Mondays! This was the third one out of four that damn near killed me. Hey, it's not what you think. The flights were on time. I even arrived at SVE (Silicon Valley Electronics) early, and was greeted warmly by the receptionist. And Jessica Gomez, their purchasing professional, was cordial, even sympathetic. But her message was not at all what I wanted to hear. After getting me a cup of coffee—Starbucks, no less!—she started our conversation very directly.

"Adam, thanks for coming to see us. I'm glad you're here in person. I'd much rather have this conversation face-to-face instead of over the phone or by e-mail."

Those words didn't sound very comforting, but I decided to ignore what they might mean. "You're entirely welcome. As you know, my father died suddenly a few weeks ago, and I've taken over as CEO. I wanted to meet our most important customers face to face, and you're the most important customer we've got, so I'm meeting you first."

"Unfortunately, that makes this an even more difficult conversation," Jessica said.

"Oh?" I was trying to remain calm, cool, and relaxed.

She began, "Yes, our corporate parent has instructed us to cut costs by 10% across the board or they'll shut us down and send the manufacturing overseas. We have 90 days to make it happen. We can't cut wages, plant expenses, etc., by 10% that fast, so purchasing has to achieve 20% reductions on all contracts. Electronic Products gave us a quote last week that is 25% lower than your price. I am going to have to take it. I hope you understand. And it's clearly no reflection on your quality, delivery, or customer service. They have been superb. That's why I was able to keep buying from you for the last few years. But at this point I have no choice. I'm so sorry. I wish there was something I could do."

"Me, too," I said, trying desperately to keep my disappointment from showing. Grasping at straws, I asked, "Is there any way you could let me think out loud for a moment to see if we could create some way that it could possibly work?"

Jessica replied, "I'll give you the 25 minutes until my next appointment, but I don't know what you can do unless you can meet their price."

I realized I had nothing left to lose, so I let my thoughts flow. "I've only been a CEO for 11 weeks now. But let me tell you a little about our company so you can understand why this is so important to me. Until 11 weeks ago, I was working for an industrial products distribution company in Boston. I had encouraged, even urged, my dad to sell the company and retire. But he wouldn't do it, and I couldn't understand why.

"When I first took over as CEO, my original intention was to pretty the company up and sell it so Mom could retire. But after I'd been there a few weeks, I realized I couldn't do that. If we sold the company, the corporate buyer would in all probability send the manufacturing overseas, followed by the engineering. And we're the last manufacturer of any size left in town; the others are all shut down except for sales and finished goods distribution. It's my high-school classmates, and their parents, who are working in my company. If we shut down, about 200 of them will lose their jobs and have no possibility of finding employment at decent wages without moving. If they move, they leave their parents and siblings behind, so their children won't have grandparents, aunts, uncles, or cousins nearby anymore. Even worse, manufacturing keeps going overseas, so it is very difficult even for excellent people to find any manufacturing work at all. So I'm basically fighting for the life of my home town. And I'll do anything I can to keep the plant open.

"Unfortunately, we can't match Electronic Products' prices today. Our financials are not public information, so I'll ask you to keep what I am about to tell you confidential. Our net profit is only 2%, so if we give up more than that in our price, we will go out of business.

"However, we are starting to implement sustainability; we had our initial vision-setting workshop the weekend before last. It has the promise of reducing our costs, and therefore our prices, the same way that Lean has done over the last five years. The benefits are not as straightforward as Lean. With Lean, we could expect to cut inventories by 75% or more. We could expect to reduce the total cost of quality by 80% or 90%. Sustainability is softer, if you will. But all the research I've done on it so far has convinced me that it will have the same financial effect. And we're betting our survival on it, because if it doesn't work, our company will have to ship the manufacturing and then the engineering overseas, just like our competitors.

"Jessica, may I ask you a question?" I said looking at some photos on a nearby desk.

"Sure," she replied, following my gaze.

"Are those pictures of your children?" I asked, nodding to the photos.

"Yes," she replied. I was sure she was wondering where this was all going.

"How old are they now?" I felt her growing impatient with my questioning.

She answered curtly, "Matthew is 18; he'll graduate from high school this year. He's gotten early admission into Stanford. Jenny is 15, and Eric is 13."

I continued, "What can we do, you and I, so that Matthew, Jenny, and Eric have jobs that will sustain them and an earth that will support them and their children?

"What do you mean?" she asked with a puzzled look.

"Well, that's what sustainability is all about," I said confidently. "It's about meeting the needs of the current generation without compromising the ability of future generations to meet their needs. It's about keeping corporations fiscally sound while honoring people and preserving the environment. That's what we're just starting to do inside Brookings. And it's exciting."

Jessica responded, "That sounds interesting, but we only have five minutes left. And as much as I would like to keep the contract with Brookings, I have to show savings or I'll lose my job. Or worse, this division gets closed down. Is there any way you can give me some savings right now?"

"How about a plan for phased-in savings . . . say 10% right now and 10% more in a year? My company will lose money at the beginning, but I'm confident our sustainability program will provide those savings. Actually, I'm betting my company on this."

"Adam, I wish I could, but I don't have the authority to do that. Let me talk with the VP of materials and logistics. I'll need you to put your offer in writing or an e-mail. But I'm also curious about sustainability. How can I find out more about it?"

"I'll e-mail you a couple of articles from my hotel tonight, if you'd like, along with my offer," I replied.

"I'd like that," she said, rising up from her chair. "We have to stop now; I have another appointment in a couple of minutes."

"Thank you so much for trying, Jessica. That means a lot to me."

"You're welcome, Adam. It sounds like our companies are basically in the same boat." She escorted me to the lobby. We shook hands and I left, saying goodbye to the receptionist as I exited.

I was totally drained when I arrived in the parking lot of Quark, Inc., a medium-sized customer. Kent Case, the company's purchasing agent, was very cordial and seemed happy to meet me in person. After the initial pleasantries and his condolences about the loss of my father, he said, "I don't know if you're aware, but Jeff called me last week and asked to meet with us. Now that I've met you in person, I'll tell you what I never would have said over the phone. I didn't really like Jeff. We have been doing business with Brookings for years and were always treated well. But when Jeff took over our account, I got the feeling I couldn't trust him as much as your dad or the other salespeople we had through the years. I know he has left your company. If he had stayed with you, we probably would have changed to Electronic Products. But now that he's there, we're very happy to stay with you."

I thanked Kent for the information and for his trust. And then I told him about our commitment to sustainability. He listened intently, asking several questions. When I finished, he was smiling.

"Adam, I'm glad you came out here. It's nice to see a person face to face. I have an off-the-wall question if you don't mind."

"Yes?" I said, wondering what was to come.

"This sustainability stuff sounds interesting enough that I think I'd like my president and executives to hear about it. The next time you're in the area, do you think you could tell them what you just told me and answer their questions? We're being squeezed just like Brookings. And, if this is half as good as you hope, I'd like us to find out more about it."

"Kent, I'd be delighted to do that. I'm not yet sure when I'll be back—it might be a month, or two or three months."

"Not a problem," he said. "Anyhow, I'm glad I had the chance to meet you, and I wish you and Brookings Manufacturing the best. I wish more of our suppliers were like you guys."

I got to the airport for my flight to Los Angeles in spite of the legendary Bay Area traffic. While I was waiting for my flight, I called Mom. She was much more pleased with my report on my day's activities than I was as I was telling her. So at the end I asked, "I don't get it, Mom. I thought today went okay at best, but you seem extremely happy. We could lose our biggest customer. What am I missing?"

"Adam, SVE likes us enough that they're willing to negotiate. And if we have to, we can actually cut our price to them as much as they demand. They're happy with us except for the price. And based on what Quark told you, Jeff's switching confirms our suspicions—that when he switched to Electronic Products he helped our business. Step back for a moment and think about it: they like what you're telling them about sustainability. They're two important customers, out of two, who think we're doing the right thing. And at least one of them was honest enough to tell you Jeff was the wrong person to have in our company. So we're in much better shape with both of them than we were two weeks ago."

I sighed, "Hmm . . . I hadn't looked at it that way. That really helped. I love you, Mom."

"I love you too, Son. You can tell Kelly 'hello' from me and that I am ecstatic about the engagement. I've wanted to call her 'daughter' for years."

"I will, Mom," I assured her.

After I got to my hotel in LA, I spent more than an hour on the phone with Kelly. We were planning for her to fly out to be with me a week from Friday. I could hardly wait . . . 11 days, that's 264 hours . . . It just seemed like forever. After being together last weekend, I didn't ever want to be alone again. I wanted us to be together every day. I was amazed at how much one weekend, one glorious, phenomenal, loving, joyful, playful weekend with the person I love changed my whole life so profoundly. I had teased my friends when this happened to them. And now I didn't even care if they teased me back; it wouldn't even bother me! That was saying a lot. Suddenly, all those time-worn clichés resonated; I finally understood what the poets and writers and lyricists were saying, after all these years. Now I knew.

Maybe Mondays weren't always bad after all. They sure were full of surprises though. What was that ancient Chinese curse? "May you live in interesting times?" Well, I was, and it was anything but dull and boring. I couldn't even imagine going back to my job in Boston. This was so much more fulfilling, so much more challenging, so much more important, worth so much more. I was hooked. And I still had more sales calls Tuesday, including one more major customer. Who knew what surprises I would get?

So, after talking with Kelly, and saying "good-bye" and "I love you" for at least 15 minutes, I started reading one of the books I had bought at Powell's. It was *Plan B,* by Lester Brown*—not an easy read, but it removed the insulation from my eyes. Deep awareness might be painful at times, but it's worth it in the long run.

Tuesday started as a repeat of Monday, but at least I had a little better idea of what to expect. My morning call was to California Machines and Electronics, or CME, our second largest customer, in City of Industry. Bob Moorehead greeted me warmly, "Adam, it's nice of you to come see us. I'm so sorry to hear about your father. We started working with him 20 years ago when he was not only CEO, but VP of sales and marketing too. We developed a deep respect for his values and commitment to total customer satisfaction. Did he ever tell you about the time he saved my career?"

I shook my head.

"No?" he said with a slight smile. "Well, that sounds just like him—among his many strengths was his modesty. Anyhow, I had ordered the wrong item and didn't realize it until the materials planner called me in a panic. He said we were out of that special AC/DC device you build for us, and that we were intending to start production in two days. I quickly checked my records. It was my fault all the way; I had just ordered the wrong part. So I called your dad and he made a special order just for us. Didn't even charge us extra, although I know it must have cost him a bundle to rush it through your plant. Luckily, he had the components. He knew I was a rela-

---

* Brown, Lester. 2003. *Plan B: Rescuing a Planet Under Stress and a Civilization in Trouble.* New York: Norton.

tively new purchasing agent; he told me later that he was expecting an order for what we really needed, so he was already prepared to produce it. I insisted on paying the air freight charges, and we got it here just in time. I made sure our system didn't 'ding' him for bringing stuff in by air freight like we usually do, because air freight normally means the supplier is out of control and could miss a due date. And he never mentioned it again, even during contract negotiations.

"What he didn't know, and I never told him, was that I had screwed up on delivery of another component the prior month and shut the plant down for two days while they were waiting for the part. During that shutdown, the president called me into his office and told me that he could forgive me once, but only once, and that if I did that again, my career would be toast. So your dad pulled my career out of the dumpster without even knowing it. I personally owe him, and your company, a huge debt that I'll never be able to repay.

"I assume you know your competitors are now pricing close to 25% below you?"

I nodded.

Bob continued, "I need to work with you to help you reduce prices, but this is *not*, repeat, *not* a threat to take our business elsewhere. We really believe in partnerships; your component is a small enough portion of our total material cost that I can defend the difference. But having said that, I would like to work with you, so you can reduce the price you charge us, while you still make a fair profit. Yes, I want you to make a profit, because I want you to stay in business. And if you can reduce the price you charge us, you will have reduced your costs, and have the ability to keep your other customers happy too."

"Bob, I never heard that story. All I know is sometimes at dinner Dad would talk about a rush shipment, and I saw several of them leave the plant when I worked there during the summers. I never really thought about what might have caused them. I feel even more proud of Dad than I did before. And yes, we want very much to work with you so we can reduce our costs and still make a fair profit. Can you spare 10 minutes so I can fill you in on what has happened in the last 11 weeks at Brookings?"

"Sure," he replied with a smile.

So I told him about my initial intention to just sell the company and how instead we planned to keep it open, and then about our off-site and our expectations that we could reduce cost and prices.

"Adam, I have two thoughts," he continued, "First, I'm glad you're here, not Jeff. I don't know what it was about him, but he didn't seem to have the same values as your dad, or as you have based on what I've heard so far this morning. Second, we've been on our Lean journey for a while, and it's lost some of its juice. We'll be very interested to watch what happens with your sustainability effort. If it's half as good as you hope, we'll probably want to start using that here, too."

That was three out of three . . . nice! I was feeling pretty good as I headed for my afternoon appointment with another medium-sized customer. I was beginning to think this sustainability stuff really was attractive to our customers and would give us a competitive edge.

The grounds and facilities at E-Tech-Tronix looked like they were straight out of an architectural magazine. Not one blade of grass was out of place; the flowers were blooming in beautifully landscaped beds. Natural light from floor-to-ceiling windows suffused the entry lobby, and the receptionist could have been on the cover of any women's magazine.

Then Heather Gillespie, the purchasing agent, shook my confidence with her first sentence. "Mr. Brookings, I assume you're here to try to save our account. I don't know why you didn't respond to our earlier communications, but we were not impressed. We have quotes from Electronic Products for an identical product at a much lower price than you're offering. I was about to accept their quotation when your *secretary* (and the way she made the word sound was not at all pleasant) asked for this meeting. Well, you have five minutes, and only five minutes, to meet their price."

I just sat there, too stunned to even say anything.

After a few long moments, she continued, "I'm sorry you wasted your trip. I'll escort you to the door now."

"Excuse me, Ms. Gillespie," I said brazenly. (After all, at this point what did I have to lose?) "Can you give me the rest of my five minutes?"

"You only have 3-1/2 left," she said, tapping her fingernails against the desktop.

I continued, "The reason we did not respond is that this is the first time I have heard about your earlier communications."

"And you expect me to believe that?" she said in a voice that was dangerously icy.

"All I can do is tell you I've been with the company for 11 weeks and have not heard a word about this."

"Sounds like you've got a serious problem with communication," she replied.

"I think we used to; but we don't anymore."

"Oh?" she said.

"Jeff has left our company to accept a position with Electronic Products," I replied.

"Interesting . . . but as interesting as that is, their price is substantially lower than yours. You have to meet it or we go with them."

"Ms. Gillespie, how long have you had us as one of your suppliers?"

She actually bristled a bit. Damn, she was touchy! "For more than 20 years. But I took this area over as purchasing professional six months ago, and I've been reviewing all relationships." Suddenly her voice had become lower and softer, and more intense. I knew I was in deep trouble.

"So are the 20-plus years of history we have as an excellent supplier to your company worth anything?" I asked in a desperate bid to stay alive.

"The other two vendors also have an excellent track record in the industry. For the last time, are you going to meet their price?" she asked firmly.

"May I have 24 hours to see if we can meet it?"

"I'm sorry," she snapped. "You've taken much more than the five minutes I allowed. It's time for you to leave. We're going with Electronic Products. I'll show you out."

And it was over, just like that. I wanted to scream that she was being completely unfair. But I didn't. I wanted to impugn her professionalism. But I didn't. I wanted to curse a blue streak. But I didn't. I just got up and followed her out. When my dad taught me to play poker, he told me the age-old adage, "You gotta know when to hold 'em and know when to fold 'em." There was no way I was going to change her mind; that much was *perfectly* clear. So why expend any more effort into a completely lost cause—the only thing it would do is irritate her further, and she was already highly irritated.

I could actually understand what she was doing and why. She was new to the company and wanted to impress somebody by saving money. That's how purchasing agents get measured—the single bottom line, the financial one. So I left.

And I called on every reserve of grace within me to turn, smile, shake her hand, and say, "Thanks for seeing me." And I meant it (well, at least part of me did). I learned why she was doing what she was doing, and I probably wouldn't have learned that by phone or fax or e-mail. I also learned Jeff had sabotaged our relationship with E-Tech-Tronix. And I could only assume Electronic Products would be rewarding him in some way for bringing in the account.

It was just late enough that there were no more flights out to get me home that night. I didn't feel like catching the red-eye—I needed some sleep to recover from that last meeting. So I was going to spend the night in California—unless, of course, a certain fiancée wouldn't mind putting me up for the night. I could get home from Portland just as easily as from LA. And I could sure use some comforting right now.

So I called Kelly to ask if I could fly up and spend the night with her. Go figure—we just lost one of our medium customers, which meant cash flow would be even worse, and there I was spending extra money for another flight. But there are some things more important than money.

Before I got on the plane, I called Mom. She wasn't as upset as I figured she might be; she had been through things like this with Dad before. This was going to require some more belt-tightening back at the plant, effective immediately. I could feel the squeeze tightening one more notch and we didn't have many notches left. We discussed the possibility of legal action. If Jeff couldn't prove he responded in a timely manner to E-Tech-Tronix, we might be able to get some sort of compensation from Electronic Products. The problem was it would distract us from what we really needed to focus on—keeping our customers, getting new customers, and getting our costs and prices in line with China. This was just one more thing to talk about at the staff meeting next Monday—as if we needed more topics right now.

I caught the 4:22 p.m. United flight at LAX, and 2 hours and 30 minutes later I was walking into the welcoming arms of my soul mate.

That night as I was trying to get to sleep, the word "relationship" kept echoing through my brain. It didn't make a lot of sense until I told Kelly about it as we were driving to the airport the next morning so I could fly home. Change that—so I could fly back to the plant. "Home" for me, right now, was with Kelly, no matter where we happened to be.

Kelly started thinking aloud. "Adam, maybe relationship is more important in business than financial profit, the financial bottom line. Let's look at your two customers from yesterday. The one would walk through hell for you, because of what your dad did for him when he needed a friend. The other was looking purely at money, and nothing else much mattered. Which one do you want for a customer? When you get right down to it, business is not about profits, it's about relationships. And relationships are built on trust. Healthy relationships result in profits for both parties. In unhealthy relationships, one party is taking advantage of the other. Unfortunately, companies, per se, don't remember anything. Only people do. So when people change, like that new purchasing agent at the second company, the relationship-building has to start basically from ground zero."

I continued the thought, "I guess the same would be true for the relationship between a company and its employees too. It has to be based on trust. The difference is employees are around each other, so if the company has a good relationship with its existing employees, a new employee will soon pick up on the culture. Customers don't congregate together, so good relationships with some customers don't form a culture that a new customer quickly adapts to."

"Or even new employees at an old customer, as so skillfully demonstrated by Exhibit B, your afternoon sales call," added Kelly.

"Yeah, you're right. I'm thinking that we need to have at least one backup salesperson in contact with each of our major and medium customers to create deeper relationships. We also want to have relationships with more than just the purchasing agents. Like we want to talk with the engineers . . . damn! Why didn't I think of that sooner? I might have been able to save the . . ."

"Adam," Kelly interrupted sharply. "*Don't go there!* Don't even *think* about going there! You didn't stand a chance. The umpire had called three strikes before you walked up to the plate. There is nothing you could have done, and the more you tried, the more you would have irritated the new purchasing agent. Better to just walk away from that one for a while. If all she's interested in is money, then they're not a good prospect for you anyhow. You're looking for customers who want a relationship, creativity, and the lowest total cost of ownership, not just the lowest purchase price."

"I know, I know, but that doesn't make this any easier," I said gloomily. "They were a $2 million account, and our net profits last year were only $1 million. So we're $1 million in the hole, starting right now."

"You're too stressed to think clearly right now," Kelly observed. "You won't be buying the raw materials to make those products. So best guess is you'll be breaking even, not going in the red. And that's before your employees start getting creative."

"Thanks. That helped. But I still feel like shit. I've let the company down. I don't want anybody to lose their job over this." I was beginning to wonder if we could still pull this off with everything we had going against us now.

The problem with flying east from the West Coast is you lose a whole business day due to the flying time and the time change. I had chosen to get a decent night's sleep, knowing I wouldn't get into my office until Thursday. During the flight, I was feeling somewhat guilty for not having caught the red-eye out of LA and proceeded to the office Wednesday. But I also knew that I don't sleep worth anything on planes. So yes, I would have been in the office physically on Wednesday, but I wouldn't have been worth anything. And I would have been beating myself up pretty badly for passing up a chance to see Kelly again. I finally put that out of my mind and started working on my laptop, trying to see if I could figure out how much the loss of E-Tech-Tronix would really cost us. But I didn't have enough data to form any conclusions.

So I tried to work some more on our sustainability program. But there wasn't a whole lot I could do on that either, except to remember that we should probably be using value stream mapping to map the processes so we would be able to easily identify the high-priority opportunities. How could we have missed that? We used it so much during our Lean journey. (Value stream mapping is a visual tool that uses flow charts to show the total value-added time at each step, the changeover time for each step, the total time between steps, and the scrap rates or quality problems at each step. It enables a team to quickly spot the areas that are the best candidates for improvement efforts.[†] This tool can be equally

---

† Rother, Mike, and John Shook. 1999. *Learning to See*. Brookline, MA: Lean Enterprise Institute.

effectively for use in office and other non-manufacturing set-tings.) And I was wondering if we could incorporate any theory of constraint ideas into this sustainability stuff too. Flying is such a supreme waste of time. I wanted to be back in my office!

I held a quick staff meeting Thursday morning. The staff knew, of course, what had happened with E-Tech-Tronix, because I had sent an e-mail Tuesday night. So Tom had worked up the financial impact. Kelly had been pretty close; we would be barely profitable if everything else lined up just right. Unfortunately, I knew Murphy visited our company on a regular basis, so we would probably end a couple of hundred thousand in the red, on an annual basis. We could handle that for the short term until the expected savings from sustainability started kicking in.

After we had discussed the impact of E-Tech-Tronix, I said, "I want to tell all our staff exactly what's going on, and I want to do it this afternoon."

"But we've never done that before," responded Tom.

I retorted, "Yeah, and look at what Chet was thinking as we started our off-site. The foundation for a relationship is trust. If we don't tell them what's going on, what does that say about our level of trust? What are we afraid of? They'll already know something is going on, and when they don't see any orders, they'll figure it out. We might as well tell them up front. I don't see that we have anything to lose, and we sure as hell have something to gain."

So I called a general meeting and gave the troops the story. I told them that we were basically at break-even right now, so they needed to watch every expense, even the little ones. I told them about how Jeff had not responded to E-Tech-Tronix's request for a lower quote. They were furious.

"Traitor" was one of the nicer terms muttered from the group.

Friday morning as I walked the floor, Annie motioned me over. "Adam, we're glad you told us. That's what was missing all these years; your dad was honest and he cared about us, but we never knew what was going on. This is the incentive we needed to really get moving. We can do this; I know we can."

Later, I reviewed the plans to visit our other large customer and the three remaining medium-sized customers next week. It looked like I was going to be a road warrior again. I would be arriving back home about the same time as Kelly. I had once heard a comedian joke, "There are only two kinds of people who say they enjoy living on the road: those who've never done it, and liars." I wondered why the older guys in the audience cracked up at that; I hadn't thought it was that funny. Now I was beginning to understand. I also set up meetings with the sales support person and the engineer who dealt with each of these accounts to learn as much as possible before my trip. I didn't want to get blindsided again!

I called our weekly sustainability team meeting for early Friday afternoon. It was headed by Carl, with his choice of a key person from each major area. They reported on their progress. I asked about value stream mapping; they were embarrassed that it had slipped their minds. They promised to start using it to highlight and help prioritize the opportunities. I told Carl to make them copies of the article from *Target* magazine, which showed how Baxter used value stream mapping to map water usage. Tom promised to give them the detailed cost estimates (material, labor, and factory overhead) of the major products that ran through their areas before the next meeting. The plant-floor teams would then use fishbone diagrams and their experience to choose which costs and processes to map first. So the paint booth might start mapping the cost of a changeover (the time, plus the paint lost in bleeding the lines, plus the cost of disposing of the flushed-out paint, plus . . .). The injection molding area could ask about the cost of virgin pellets compared to recycled, plus the maximum percentage of regrind allowed by engineering into a batch, plus the cost of the energy to melt the plastic. Sam suspected his first priority would be to check our compressed air system, which was about 20 years old. He had read an article about a company that cut its electric bill by 10% by finding and plugging all the leaks in its compressed air pipes throughout the plant. The company was able to take its oldest and biggest electric motor completely off-line because it was no longer required. He also wanted to look at adding insulation in areas not currently insulated, but needed to determine how much area there was and how much the insulation would cost.

When the meeting was over, I was completely whipped. If I hadn't been looking forward to seeing Kelly in only seven more days, I don't know how I would have kept my sanity. We were right on the edge, and I had a gut instinct we would wind up losing at least one more customer. If that happened, it would really hurt. I was both glad and irritated that I had scheduled a meeting with Rev. Franklin for 4:00 that afternoon. Part of me just wanted to go home and collapse, but I also knew he might help with some insight and wisdom.

After greeting him and sitting down, I figured I might just as well start the conversation by being totally honest. "John, it's been such a tough week that I'm not even sure I want to be here."

"If you'd rather leave, that's okay. It won't hurt my feelings at all; I understand what pressure is like," he said gently.

"No, it's probably a good idea for me to stay," I sighed.

"I'm glad you chose that. So why don't you tell me what's happening?" he said as he sat down at his desk. So I told him. He listened, asking for clarification from time to time. I could feel my tension dissipating as I talked; somehow he created a space that was peaceful and calm.

"Interesting . . ." he replied after I finished talking. "So, let me ask you a question. Let's pretend it's five years from now. You're looking back at the experiences from these last few weeks. What did you learn about yourself?"

"Well . . ." and I paused while I thought for a bit, "I learned I can be flexible and go with the flow . . . I learned I shouldn't trust all people. I learned I could treat people with respect and civility even when they were hurting me, and that honesty was even more important than I used to think . . . And I learned that I can't imagine going through life without Kelly. I never knew I could miss someone so much that I physically ache."

"Good," he said, nodding. "And what did you learn about others?"

"That some people, and some companies, treat people well. They follow the Golden Rule. And when we're open and honest with each other, even in a sales call, wonderful things can happen. That some customers are worth their weight in gold, while others aren't people we want to do business with. That my company is more creative and more committed than I ever had any right to expect. The people there are truly amazing! And that Kelly is the most wonderful woman I have ever known (except for my Mom, of course). I am amazed that she loves me and wants to be my wife. I still don't understand why. And she says the same things about me. She helped me see that, in the long run, it's about relationship, even when we're in business.

Relationships are more important than profits, because they're what cause the profits."

"Good. Anything else?" he said as he leaned forward in his chair.

"Yes. This sustainability movement is about relationships. That's why it will succeed and eventually be the predominant model for businesses. Sustainability is not optional—every action we take today will directly affect our children and grandchildren. So I want to help each person, and each company, understand how important they are, and how their decisions affect future generations. Visiting with you is really helpful because you help me take a longer view and keep my priorities focused."

"Now," he said, "the big question: Who are you?"

"What do you mean?" I asked, a little perplexed.

"Just what I said, Adam—who are you?"

"Well, I'm the CEO of Brookings, I'm engaged to Kelly, and I'm Mom's son."

"Those are all roles, Adam."

I thought a moment and added, "I need to become a truly effective leader to help Brookings survive."

"That's still a role, Adam. Let me ask it differently. What are your core values? What matters the most?"

I paused for a while. "People matter, especially my family and friends. My children, which I hope Kelly and I will have someday. My relationships with others and theirs with me are important. Health, joy—I want to have joy in my life and see it in the lives of those around me."

"Good, Adam. Those are your core values—they were just as true when you were in college and working at the plant as a summer job as they are now, right?"

"Yes," I replied, wondering where he was going with this discussion.

"Let me tell you a little more about leadership from my own personal experience. Every truly effective leader that I know has had to go through tremendous personal growth. A shallow person, a selfish person cannot be a truly effective leader. People see through it and won't willingly follow. Only those who have done the difficult work of discovering who they are can be effective leaders. You're well along on your journey, Adam, especially for your age."

"Thank you, John."

"See you Sunday?"

"Yes, I'll be here Sunday. See you then."

So I went home to have dinner with Mom and catch her up on everything. Then I called Kelly and talked with her for another hour. I was really glad we had one of those cell phone plans that considered all in-network calls free; otherwise, our cell bills would have been astronomical!

CHAPTER 11
Where's the Value?

On Sunday, Rev. Franklin preached on "inner fire, public voice," saying that people frequently ignore or hide their inner fire and don't give it voice, making them not feel as good as they could about themselves. But when they actually give voice to their inner fire, they grow and serve the world. That was so true—we had seen it at our off-site, and now it was starting to permeate the entire company. It meshed rather nicely with Toyota's top priority—human development.

The Monday staff meeting was relatively short; since we had discussed my trip to the coast late last week, there wasn't much more to be said on that. We needed to start educating the teams on sustainability. We could build on the one-hour overview that Carl created. So after the meeting, Carl and I reviewed the overview and decided on the various topics that needed more depth.

Monday the teams started examining their processes and the costs of their products. They did fishbone diagrams to record all the possible causes. Then they created Pareto diagrams to find the most important causes and kept repeating the process until they found a root cause. (Pareto diagrams show which sub-items are the most important causes of the result you're looking at. For example, if a particular model of toaster keeps having warranty issues, the team would fishbone the possible causes, such as burnt-out element, broken slide knob, disconnected power cord, etc. Then the team would look at the percentage of each cause. In this example, burnt-out element is the cause 55% of the time, broken slide knob is 20%, and disconnected power cord is 12%. So they would start looking at the heating element to find out why it burns out so quickly, and then create a fishbone for that. That fishbone also would have several causes, including vibration, inferior materials, poor design, etc. The team would Pareto those causes, then start discussing those that are most important.)

The teams used value stream mapping to figure out where the largest uses of energy, water, and other non-conventional materials were consumed, as well as the conventional ones (e.g. circuit boards, plastic cases, etc.). They also started using value stream mapping on hazardous chemicals, starting with the worst first.

The Lean teams were familiar with these activities—they were the same ones they used for five years as they implemented Lean throughout the company. And yes, they used these same approaches in the office areas as well—especially in customer service and accounting. So why was sustainability any different from Lean? Because it embraces the Triple Bottom Line, and it promotes making decisions from a non-financial as well as financial perspective.

The first education sessions for the teams focused on the overall "what" and "why" of sustainability and the non-financial components of the Triple Bottom Line. Each team got a copy of the potential metrics Dennis sent me so they could start exploring non-financial opportunities.

So I asked Carl to coach the teams on not only the traditional Lean approaches to identifying and reducing waste (and therefore reducing cost, which we desperately needed!), but also on the Triple Bottom Line. I asked him to have each team identify and implement one improvement effort for each of the three bottom lines—profits, planet, and people. When I got back from my road trip, I was amazed and delighted at the creativity, wisdom, and entrepreneurial spirit the teams had unleashed. They had come up with the following ideas.

Profits:

- Reduce packaging on inbound materials and on finished goods.
- Buy recycled plastic to use in our injection-molded cases.
- Drop the lights from the ceiling in the shop to just above the work areas. Leave enough in the ceiling so people can move around, find materials, etc. This will reduce the number of light bulbs by about 30%.
- Visit customers to find out how they actually use our products so we can understand what adds value to them and what doesn't, and quit doing the things that don't add value.
- Invite engineers and shop-floor people from key suppliers to visit us and work with us to reduce costs.

Planet (notice some of these were also in the "profit" category!):

- Buy recycled plastic to use in our injection-molded cases.
- Drop the lights from the ceiling in the shop to just above the work areas. Leave enough in the ceiling so

people can move around, find materials, etc. This will reduce the number of light bulbs by about 30%.

- Replace chemical cleaners with earth-friendly cleaners throughout the company.

- Encourage car-pooling among employees. (We were too far out in the country for the city bus line to come nearby.)

- Hire a van to carry people to and from the city bus stop closest to our plant at the start and end of the shifts.

- Put recycling containers for plastics and glass throughout the company (we were already recycling our paper).

- Switch to permanent plates, tableware, cups, and glasses in the cafeteria for eat-in meals. This could potentially increase labor cost (for washing and putting away dishes).

- Replace foam cups with paper cups for take-out coffee.

- Reduce the coffee price 10 cents/cup if people use a permanent cup (ours or theirs).

- Replace foam filler with recycled paper filler for our shipments.

- Plant trees in our parking lot and around our grounds—the trees will absorb CO_2 and shade our cars in the summer. We might be able to get the trees free from a local arbor foundation.

People:

- Reward learning—create a pay-for-knowledge matrix for shop employees (this would need to be approved by the union as well as management).

- Teach employees how to read the financial statements of our company.

- Hold classes before or after work on various topics, such as personal finance, parenting, how to buy a house, and English as a second language.
- Open those classes up to the public, but give first priority to our employees and their immediate families.
- Host community college classes on site.
- Host professional organization classes on site (such as American Production and Inventory Control Society [APICS] certification review courses).
- Pay the tuition and book fees for each person in an employee's immediate family so they can attend the local community college or pay an equivalent amount if they go elsewhere.
- Change the company benefits plan to a cafeteria plan— let employees opt in or out of individual benefits as they choose.
- Work with the high school and community college to start an internship program for students interested in becoming machinists, etc.

Because of the urgency to reduce costs as quickly as possible, this was not a well-organized, top-down implementation. It was more like a stampede to escape a forest fire, with everybody trying to go in somewhat the same direction as rapidly as possible. Some of the projects interfered with others, some failed publicly and miserably, and the confusion level was high. Whether it was in spite of this atmosphere or because of it, morale had never been higher. A sense of excitement permeated the entire facility, from the front door to the shipping dock.

Chet felt sufficiently comfortable with me to walk into my office one day, rapping gently on the door frame. "Do you have a minute?"

"For you, of course," I replied.

He began, "I want to tell you that this sustainability stuff is really working. I haven't seen such excitement and enthusiasm in any place I've ever worked. Everyone I work with is constantly thinking about new ideas, even while at home, and during the weekends. I've never seen anything like it. But it's pretty confusing right now. Will it always be like this?"

"Chet, I've never been through this either, but I think things will settle down in a while. Part of the reason for the confusion is that we're trying to do as much as we can as fast as we can, because of the pressure to lower our costs immediately."

"We all understand that," Chet said as he shook his head. "Anyhow, I just thought you'd like to know that we're really glad we're working here now. We never ever thought work could be this much fun."

"Me too, Chet; thanks for telling me."

"You're welcome. I gotta get back now," he said, and he left as quickly as he came.

I suddenly remembered I needed to talk with Tom, so I walked over to accounting.

"Tom, how are you doing with the non-financial metrics you've been working on?" I asked, and he motioned for me to take a seat opposite his desk.

"You know, I tried using those Lean accounting approaches a couple of years ago. While they seemed really logical and simple on the surface, they were so different from everything I had ever been taught and used, that I just couldn't bring myself to start using them. But at least they were somewhat defined. Now this sustainability stuff—these metrics aren't even defined! We're at the beginning of the sustainability movement, and it takes the accounting profession years to agree on anything this radical. Decades, if it's something major like this. So we're just going to have to invent our own. I've never done anything like that, and to be honest with you, I don't know how to do it. I can't believe I just said that—here I am, the accounting professional, and I just admitted I don't know how to do the kind of accounting we need."

"Relax, Tom," I said calmly. "After we're up and running for a little while, you can write articles and give speeches about sustainability accounting. Who knows? Maybe you'll write the textbook about it." The look of utter disbelief on his face was priceless—where's my camera when I need it? "Well, think about it. Somebody has to write one, why not you?"

"Hmmm . . . why not me?" he said. Now I was the one shocked. But then again, why not Tom? Really, why couldn't he write that book? I remembered meeting my Uncle Brad a few years back, after he had written a book on information technology for manufacturers. He said he had been sitting with two other certification instructors at a monthly dinner meeting of the Detroit chapter of APICS, the professional society for materials managers. One of them complained that the book they were using was outdated. Then another one said, "Somebody should write a new book." Then my uncle blurted out, "Why not us?" and they all looked at each other, knowing they were suddenly committing to write a book. So they wrote it, because it needed to be done. One more example of inner fire and public voice, I guess. I was starting to wonder how to keep the fire in our employees and our teams burning. Could it be sustained, long-term, at its present level? I suspected not. So what level could it be sustained at, and how could we measure that and know where we were?

"Adam?" Tom was looking at me quizzically.

"Huh? Oh, I'm sorry. My mind drifted for a bit," I said as I returned to Earth. (If he only knew...but I didn't want to tell him right now. I wanted our focus to stay on the current topic—sustainability metrics.) "I know I'm not an accountant, but as long as we can report our finances to the bank using their standard format, do you think it will bother them how we make our decisions in management and on the floor?"

"No, it won't," Tom replied.

"Then could we ask each team to select two metrics for each category: profit, people, and planet? This way the teams will choose what will work best for their areas, and these will be what they will be measured against. We'd need to approve them, of course."

"That might work. It's pretty unconventional," Tom replied.

I started laughing, "We stopped being conventional Friday night at the off-site and I don't think we'll be back there again for a long, long time. Do you?"

"Not really," he agreed.

I sat back in my chair and stretched my arms behind my head. "When I was talking about the teams, I was thinking more about the plant. But we have teams in the office too, don't we?" Tom nodded. I continued, "Engineering has one, customer service has one, and accounting has one. Is that right?" He nodded again. "Are there any others?" I asked.

"That's all there are," Tom replied.

I thought for a minute and then asked, "Maybe the executive staff should become a team as well?"

"We already meet weekly and do a fair amount of thinking, so maybe we've been one for years and didn't know it.

Besides, we shouldn't be doing the kind of detailed analysis the shop teams do. We don't have the time," Tom said as he looked down at his calendar.

"Yeah, I guess you're right," I said. After a few moments of silence, I continued, "Tom, what do you think of the idea of having us invited to a team meeting when the team is trying to decide on the metrics it will use?"

Tom chuckled, "Sounds good to me; if nothing else, it ought to be great entertainment."

"Do you mean they will entertain us, or our ignorance will entertain them?" I quipped.

"Yes," he grinned.

So that afternoon, Tom and I sat in the back of the team meeting room while the assembly team met. Annie, the current team leader, was skilled at her role. The scribe, however, seemed to be having difficulty. I noted that teams, in and of themselves, are quite important on the people side of sustainability. Employing teams allows people to try new roles, to accept more responsibility . . . in other words, to grow. And from the reports I'd been getting, several of the team leaders were sufficiently good at leading that I knew they'd be well-qualified for entry-level leadership positions in the company when they opened up. I focused back on the meeting . . . and what I saw was free-wheeling brainstorming. In other words, it was chaos. Then I remembered reading Margaret Wheatley's book, *Leadership and the New Science**,* in one of my senior psych classes. She wrote that if chaos were allowed to exist for a long enough period of time, it actually showed order. She also argued that any living being

---

* Wheatley, Margaret. 1999. *Leadership and the New Science: Discovering Order in a Chaotic World*, 2nd ed. San Francisco: Berrett-Koehler Publishers.

required chaos, because complete order meant no growth, even no movement. So a living being, whether a human, a team, or a company, needed to not only allow, but encourage chaos to thrive and survive. Given what I was seeing, if chaos could help a company survive, we'd be thriving very soon.

The team had no consensus on the metrics for any of the three sustainability bottom lines. There was no consensus whatsoever. Annie was trying—and she was doing an admirable job of leading—but the team didn't want to be led to any conclusions anywhere. After the meeting was over, I walked up to the front of the room. Annie looked drained.

"Annie, you did very well. That was a tough meeting. The team wasn't ready to create a consensus, was it?" I asked, trying to help her feel good about herself.

"No, it wasn't. I've never had them act like that," Annie said disappointedly. "It's almost like they were two-year-olds, acting up because their grandfather was visiting." And she looked up at me and started grinning. "I don't care if most of them are over 40; I'll bet that's part of what was going on, wasn't it?"

"I'm guessing that was part of it. But I suspect there were other factors too," I said smiling.

"Oh?" she asked, looking puzzled.

"Yes. They don't know how to choose, and they don't know how to achieve consensus easily. I think you did a great job; I'm really proud of you."

"Thanks, Adam."

"You're welcome," I said and left for my office.

Do you know how when you're in the middle of a situation you can't see something that is completely obvious to anyone else? Well, that's where I was with this sustainability implementation. As I was driving home, I kept having the nagging feeling I was missing something obvious. So I called Dennis and described the situation to him.

He responded, "That's a pretty common experience of companies when they first start on their sustainability journey, especially if they're in a hurry. What's my suggestion? They've got too many choices. Let each team choose one project, total, not one project from each of the three bottom lines. But look at its impact on all three bottom lines. Make sure the project can be completed rather quickly, and that it is guaranteed to succeed. That's important, because you want the momentum to continue. If early projects fail, it really hurts the momentum, and can actually kill the whole initiative.

"While they're doing that, your executive staff needs to define the sustainability metrics for your company. If you want to include others in that process, you could bring together the entire group that met off-site. But I don't think that will be necessary. You should probably include your sustainability director, though. That's Carl, right?"

"Yes, that's Carl. And that makes a lot of sense. I'll get the staff together tomorrow morning and get started on that," I said.

Dennis continued, "You should choose no more than two strategic metrics from each of the three bottom lines. That alone adds up to six, which can be too many. Then ensure that your tactical metrics directly support your strategy and explain how it works to everyone. In turn, each department should have tactical metrics from all three bottom lines to help in the day-to-day decision-making. I'll e-mail you a three-page set of potential sustainability metrics." (These are included in Appendix A.)

Tuesday morning I called a special staff meeting and included Carl. I made sure he told his team leaders to *not* try to define metrics yet.

We started with the three-page sheet Dennis furnished in his e-mail. After a couple of hours of animated discussion, we finally achieved reasonable consensus on our initial strategic metrics and some supporting tactical metrics.

Financial:

- Sales revenues.
- Operating profits as a percentage of revenue.
  - Reduced material costs.

Environmental:

- Reduced environmental impact.
  - Energy efficiency (total energy used per pound of product shipped).
  - Toxic free (total listed toxic pounds used).
  - Complete compliance with all regulations (no findings).
- Redesigned products for take-back.

Social:

- Ranked in *Fortune* magazine's "100 Best Companies to Work For."
- Community outreach.
  - Teaching the community about sustainability.

Each person agreed to take these metrics back to their departments, discuss it with employees, and bring us feedback. "These are cast in oatmeal at this point, not concrete," I told them.

I think it was Sam who asked the question that was obvious only *after* he said it, "Why don't we invite the EPA (Environmental Protection Agency) to help us with the environmental metrics?" We all looked at each other, and thought, "Why not?" So we did. Marie set the meeting up for the following week.

Sometimes sarcasm contains a seed of genius. Mary quipped, "Okay, then why don't we invite the Pope to help with the social metrics?" Everybody chuckled at that, but quieted down when I said, "You know, there might be something to that. The Pope is probably not available, but I've been meeting with Rev. Franklin every other Friday afternoon for the perspective he provides. It's helpful.

"I remember hearing about Tom and Kate Chappell, the founders of Tom's of Maine, the natural toothpaste company. Tom actually went to Harvard Divinity School to gain a better perspective on how to lead the company. They have been a leader in social activism and environmentalism for a while now. That idea might have some merit." The staff was almost as wide-eyed as when I first suggested sustainability. But they knew me well enough by now to not be as surprised when I came from left field or, in this case, a whole 'nother ball park. What they didn't hear was my next thought—maybe we should create a Board of Advisers, and ask Rev. Franklin to be on it, along with the bank president, a retired professor of marketing from the state university system, and others.

CHAPTER 12
On the Road Again

Wednesday morning found me at the airport at 6:30 a.m., half-asleep, waiting for my flight to Chicago, which would connect me to Boston and our third (and last) large customer—BayTech. I would fly back to Cleveland Wednesday night for a Thursday morning meeting with Lake Electronic Specialties. Then I would board a quick flight to Detroit Thursday afternoon to meet with Motor City Equipment. After that I would fly to Chicago for a Friday morning meeting with Illinois Electronic Machinery and finally leave for South Bend Friday afternoon—arriving at about the same time as Kelly. I actually didn't mind travelling, but if I had small children whom I wanted to see every evening, it would get old very quickly.

The trip Wednesday was actually rather interesting, at least the flight from Chicago to Boston. My seatmate, Liz Spinoza, was a writer for a business publication. She had heard a little bit about sustainability and was interested in finding out more. So we had a nice conversation. I was careful about what I was saying on the plane, knowing we had no privacy whatsoever. She understood and asked if she could call me and learn more about our journey; she thought there might be a feature article in our story.

My visit to BayTech, in Woburn, Massachusetts, was very cordial, as I anticipated. I met not only with the purchasing agent, Kim Vessella, but with the president, George O'Riley, as well. George had known my father for years; he was probably Dad's third customer. George had put in a good word for me, based on his relationship with Dad, when I was applying for my position in Boston five years earlier. He asked about Mom and how the company was doing.

I found out that Jeff had tried to entice him to switch to Electronic Specialties and had even intimated some rather uncomplimentary things about Brookings before he left our company. Nothing that could be used against him legally, of course; he was too slick for that. But he was clearly not the kind of representative we wanted as our face to the world. The more I learned about Jeff, the better off we were without him.

I felt comfortable enough with George that I asked if there were any additional products we could make for him. He promised to see what he could do. And then he completely surprised me—inviting me to join him for a late lunch at Woodman's in Essex, north of Boston. Woodman's was known to have one of the best clambakes in New England. Now a clambake features not only clams, but corn on the cob, lobster, and potatoes, and . . . I got hungry just thinking about it. The atmosphere at Woodman's was anything but elegant, but the food was delicious. Some sales calls are really fun, and this was close to the top of my all-time list. After lunch, I stopped by my condo and packed a few boxes of things I needed and took them over to a UPS drop station.

Then I went out for an early dinner with my old work buddies. It was really good to see them and catch up on what was happening. What I noticed as we were talking, though, was how much *I* had changed in the last three months. I felt like

I had moved to a different country, almost. They were talking about sports (how the Celtics were lousy again, and how the Sox were going to win it all this year), making sales quotas, their wives, husbands, girlfriends, and boyfriends. Carefree and happy, they weren't worried about a company closing its manufacturing facility and putting 200 people out of work. They didn't have bottom-line responsibility in a pressure cooker, and I did. I put on a happy face, of course, and it was good to be with them. But my world was different now, different enough that we no longer had very much in common.

And I'll have to admit—it felt a little weird flying into Logan and renting a car when I still had my own car sitting outside my condo. Some day in the near future I would need to take four days to fly to Boston, sort through my stuff, put the condo on the market, and either drive the car back or sell it. But right now I didn't have four days to spend doing that. Between the business and Kelly, I didn't have any free time at all.

I caught an 8 p.m. flight to Cleveland. Early Thursday morning I met with Lake Electronic Specialties, another of our long-time customers. Traci DeLaLonde, the purchasing agent, was as nice a person as one could ever meet. She brought in an engineer, Bob Miller, to meet me, because they wanted to talk with our engineering staff about some potential changes to the main product we were selling them. So I called Walter Chen on the speakerphone in Traci's office and Walter talked with Bob for nearly 20 minutes. I understood most of the conversation from a conceptual level.

After a quick flight to Detroit Metro, I arrived in time for my 3 p.m. meeting with Motor City Equipment in Southfield, Michigan. Again, it was a cordial meeting with another long-time customer. Then it was back to the airport for a quick hop to O'Hare. I was thinking I could give the pre-flight announcement in my sleep by now.

I called Dennis that evening. I updated him on the sales calls, then told him that I was dreading the one the next morning, because I figured they would be the most likely to jump ship. He helped me view things from a longer run, saying that most companies that embraced sustainability wound up weeding out the customers who didn't see the value of it, just like Lean companies had done. I agreed and understood that from an intellectual perspective, but I sure didn't like the potential impact from a cash flow and profitability perspective. The timing was definitely bad.

I then called Kelly (of course) and reconfirmed the time she would arrive at the South Bend airport Friday afternoon—3:30. Her parents were exited about seeing her again and looking forward to seeing me, too.

It was Friday morning, and time to visit Illinois Electronic Machinery. The company was one of our newer customers, doing business with us for about two years. Their primary relationship had always been with Jeff. So I was not terribly surprised when Jack Mears, the purchasing agent, said he had gotten a quote from Jeff and they were probably going to take it. I tried to talk with Jack about sustainability, and what it could mean to his company and his children, but he didn't seem interested in listening. He was cordial enough, just not receptive to sustainability. And the loss of the business would put us in the red until our sustainability initiatives lowered our costs or we found some more customers. It was time for Mom, Tom, and me to meet with our banker, and the sooner the better. We had talked this through with Tom before I left.

I arrived at the airport in South Bend at 3:00, just 30 minutes before Kelly. So I called the office and talked with Wayne and Tom, and then went over to her gate. Of course, her flight was late, half an hour to be precise. And when passengers started coming down the jet way, it seemed like everything stopped after the first five passengers. Two people in the front of the plane needed wheelchairs, and they were blocking the other passengers from deplaning. At last she came through the door. She saw me almost immediately and greeted me with open arms. After a few "hello, I missed you" kisses, I held her back a bit and just looked at her face—her eyes, her hair, her cheeks, her chin. She was so beautiful! There was an old Sergio Mendes tune, "The look of love is in your face . . ." It described her perfectly. And I know she saw the same in my eyes and on my face. I could feel my face glowing, just like when I have a sunburn.

When we walked through security, she dragged me by my hand, running with me to where her parents were waiting. She hugged and kissed both of her parents. Of course, she showed them her ring; they "oohed" and "ahhed" over it. We got our bags and headed for their house, a stately two-story brick surrounded by mature oaks and maples; it was not too far from the Notre Dame campus. Her dad carried her bag into her room; he told me I could leave my bag there too if I wanted! I know my face registered my surprise. "Adam, you don't get to be with each other very much. We understand. And we are ecstatic that you're finally engaged. We've known the two of you belonged together since your junior year, and were disappointed when you didn't get engaged before you graduated. Welcome to the family, son." With that, he gave me a big hug. And I suddenly realized that I had a father again. He wasn't the daddy who raised me when I was young, to be sure, but nonetheless he was a father who loved me and wanted the best for me, period. It felt good.

That evening over dinner Kelly's dad and mom asked about how things were going at Brookings. (Kelly had told them the basics.) They were interested in sustainability. Her father talked about Notre Dame's efforts in environmentalism. I was impressed; they were further along than I expected.

Saturday we talked about the wedding. They wanted family and friends to come celebrate, as did I. We all agreed on a date about six months into the future. While I understood why they wanted to have time to prepare for this celebration of their daughter's wedding, six months of seeing Kelly only every other weekend was already getting old after just four weeks! And getting together every weekend was just not possible—it would really damage both of our budgets and our professional lives.

So after Kelly and Connie talked through lots of ideas about the wedding, I got to spend some quality time with my best friend and wife-to-be. Too soon the weekend was over, even though we had decided to fly out Monday morning rather than Sunday night.

Shortly after I got to the plant, I went to the staff meeting. Tom had crunched the numbers over the weekend, and losing Illinois Electric was indeed going to put us in the red, about $300,000–400,000 per year. Not a large number based on our annual $50 million in sales, but Mom and I, as sole owners, would have to either fund that ourselves or find a source. Tom agreed that it was time for the three of us to talk with the bank.

The sustainability initiatives were moving forward. The Lean Green Team had decided to go dumpster diving. The team's goal was to eliminate the need for the dumpster in three months. What that required was for the team to find another use for everything that would have gone into the dumpster, or (better yet) to stop creating the waste to begin with. Wayne had told the team members that the project might be overly ambitious—they replied that it was basically a three-month kaizen blitz, and they were expecting support from management. In other words, they had challenged us to walk our talk.

Actually, the way they were doing it was pretty clever. They were going to put open containers in front of the dumpster and padlock the dumpster lid, starting immediately. Anything that would have been put in the dumpster was left beside it with a note telling where it came from, so the team could catalogue it. After the first few days, the team members created a Pareto diagram showing what was there and the process(es) that created it as waste. Their point was that we did not intentionally order and pay for waste to be delivered to our receiving dock. We ordered and paid for good stuff. So *we* made the waste. And therefore, *we* could stop making it. I really like it when teams get passionate! When that happens, I try to just stay out of the way and cheer them on.

A couple of our engineers were starting to get quite excited about redesigning our product so it could be returned and rebuilt to current standards. We'd have to think about whether this would have any effect on our marketing channels though. And, we would need to determine what it would do to income from new-unit sales and overall company profitability, because rebuilding would hopefully be less costly than building a new unit from scratch. The idea of leasing the functionality to our customers, rather than selling them individual units, was starting to sound halfway decent. We needed to talk with our customers, and we needed to do it now! Where could we find a real VP of sales and marketing when we needed one?!

Sam and one of the teams were starting to reduce our energy footprint. We had approved a small budget for them, even though money was tight and the return on investment was probably a couple of years. We needed the psychological impact of doing something visible. With the union's permission, six of our people from the shop floor were helping Sam, because there wasn't enough work on the floor to keep everyone busy. They were moving lights to be closer to the workplaces, removing fixtures where we didn't need them, and installing motion sensors that would automatically turn lights off. They were caulking, insulating, and generally tightening up our building, starting with the places identified by the energy audit they had requested. Sam was starting to talk about an eco-roof because our building was old enough that we were going to have to replace the roof in the near future. The staff really liked the idea, but it was expensive enough that we wanted to defer it until our cash flow improved; Sam and his team understood and supported that decision. Life is so much easier when people are aware of what's really going on. They knew we weren't BS'ing them about the finances.

We were quickly learning that with sustainability, just like Lean, there are very few actions without ramifications elsewhere. Everything is connected, and if we didn't think through the effects on the connections, we could make some pretty bad decisions. As one sage said, "Every problem we have today is a result of yesterday's solution to another problem." So we had to think in system terms, and not just mechanical systems, but also social and environmental systems. They (we) were all interconnected.

I called an all-hands-on-deck meeting Monday afternoon on the shipping dock to let everyone know that Illinois Electric was gone, and that we were now operating in the red. After my 10-minute speech, I got some surprising questions.

Someone asked, "If we're losing money, where does the money come from to keep paying all the bills?"

I replied, "The company borrows it from the bank or from its shareholders, which means Mom and me."

Another person asked, "Why would the bank loan you money if you're losing money?"

"Are you sure you're not a banker?" I laughed. "Seriously, that's an excellent question. That's the question Tom, Mom, and I have to answer for the bankers before they loan us any more. And the short answer is that we'll start making money again as we implement sustainability. As we all..." (and here, I slowly looked at the entire group) "implement sustainability."

Then someone remarked, "Why would Jeff sabotage us like that? He really hurt us bad."

I replied, "I don't know. But I wouldn't want to be in his shoes. Dad used to say, 'What goes around comes around.' I suspect he'll treat his new employer the same way. And sooner or later, it will catch up with him."

"What do we do if more customers stop buying from us?" Annie asked.

"Hang on until we can find more customers who will value who we are and what we do. When I'm meeting with our current customers, I'm asking them if we can make other products for them. And BayTech, in Massachusetts, is looking into it."

"Are you sure we'll make it?" someone along the back wall asked.

"I wish I could look you all straight in the eye and say 'yes.' But I can't. I am not *sure* that we'll make it. But I *think* we'll make it. And I hope and pray that we'll make it. I pledge that I will do everything humanly possible to help our company make it. The last thing I think about as I go to sleep at night is how to help our company thrive. The first thing I think about when I wake up is how to help our company thrive."

"What about Kelly?" (This one came from Annie.)

"Well, yes," I blushed. "I think about Kelly, too. For those who don't know, she is my fiancée. We got engaged recently."

"When's the wedding?" someone else asked.

"In about six months," I replied.

"Will she be moving here?" I began thinking silently, 'enough already with the personal questions!'

"Yes. She'll be moving here. There is no way I could move to Portland, Oregon, and leave the company in the shape we're in right now. I can't do that to my friends and neighbors, or my mom."

"Do you think other customers will leave us?" asked another individual.

On this one I thought a moment. Then I said, "I hope not, but I wouldn't be surprised if a couple more left. They won't hurt as bad, because they're smaller. The only way we can stay in business long-term is to get our price pretty close to our competition. I know it will be tough. But I also truly believe we can do it. And that it will make us the strongest and the best supplier in the industry.

"I'll relate a supposedly true story from several years ago. The Japanese yen was getting stronger. As it did, that made it more difficult for Japanese companies to export to the U.S., because it raised the selling price here in America. So every time the yen got stronger, the company president of one small manufacturer called the entire company together, just like this. He told them the latest foreign exchange rate, and then told them they had to somehow lower their costs another one or two or three percent. And somehow, they did; they cut their costs 50% over a one-year period.

"I will meet with you each time there is important news, good or bad. And in the interim, we all need each other to reduce all the waste we can find—reduce it and eliminate it. You all know that waste, as defined in Lean companies, is anything that does not add value to the customer. So I am delighted that one of our teams has decided to go dumpster diving. Those team members taught me something earlier today. They asked me how much garbage we bought—how much came in through the receiving dock. I said, 'none, of course.' Then they pointed out that anything we throw away as waste is something *we* turned into waste, except for packaging. I got it. We pay good money for good stuff, then we do things to the good stuff to make it bad stuff, and then we throw it away and pay somebody to take it to the dump. Would the Lean Green Team please come up here?"

The team came up front, looking a little nervous. "Ladies and gentlemen, please give this team a huge round of applause. They showed me what teams and sustainability are all about." And I started clapping. So did everyone else, with cheering and a little foot-stomping. The team members just started grinning at each other, then at the rest of the employees. They looked a little embarrassed, but mighty proud.

On impulse, I wanted to give them something to show how much their attitude meant. So I pulled my favorite pen, my Cross Townsend® titanium roller ball, from my pocket. "This is my favorite pen. My fiancée gave it to me when I graduated from college. I am giving it to you now, and I'm ordering one for each of you, just to show you how important you are to this company. Thank you!" And the crowd cheered and whistled. I made a mental note to have Marie buy a bunch of them and get the quantity discount; I had a feeling we'd be giving many of these pens away in the next year or two.

Just as I was leaving the plant Monday evening, Jessica Gomez from SVE, our largest customer, called. "Adam, it was difficult, but we'll be able to stay with you as long as you can grant the 10% reduction immediately, and another 10% in a year."

"Thank you so much, Jessica. That's great news, and we really needed that now. Do you want it on official Brookings letterhead?"

"Yes, when you can. I trust you, Adam." There it was again—trust—relationship.

After we hung up, I just sat in my chair, totally drained. I was beginning to fully understand why executives have heart attacks and strokes. I had never understood, and never would have believed even if Dad had told me, the amount of pressure that sits on a CEO's shoulders.

Tuesday I had a normal morning at the company—walking the floor, talking with people, and being available for questions. I deliberately complimented people for taking risks and trying new things. I made it a point to go out to the shipping area where the Lean Green Team worked and thank everyone again for their insights and commitment. I stopped by Sam's office to congratulate him on the progress he and his team were making. I could see changes, mostly small changes, but changes nonetheless. And I could feel the morale—it was higher than I had ever felt before. I had been concerned that telling everyone about losing Illinois Electric and going into the red would hurt morale. Amazingly, it seemed to work the other way!

I had Tom call Ron Meeker, our banker who had participated in the off-site, to schedule a meeting so we could discuss our financial situation and anticipated credit requirements. We wanted to meet with Ron first, then have him set up a meeting with the president, who would in turn set up a meeting with the appropriate board members. We were anxious to have the meetings as soon as possible, but understood that protocol required each person to be informed in turn, allowing him to elevate the request to the next level once he agreed with our request. Any other approach would have slighted at least one of the executives, which is not a good idea in any relationship. We kept reminding ourselves that relationships require a large investment of time.

Tom had e-mailed Ron the projected financials after the staff meeting in which we reviewed them so he would have a chance to prepare his questions before our meeting. One of the reasons we enjoyed working with Ron was that he was a true business banker in the best sense of the word. He was dedicated to helping his customers' businesses succeed, rather than being caught up in the power plays that characterize some people.

The EPA regional director, Paula Opdyke, and two of her staff arrived promptly at 2:00 that afternoon. I had the staff in the conference room waiting for them. We all introduced ourselves and I opened the conversation, "Paula, John, Brenda, thanks for coming. We'd like to ask your help. Are you familiar with the concept of sustainability?"

Paula responded, "Yes, we've heard of it."

I continued, "Good, that makes this conversation a little easier. We're starting to implement sustainability and are having difficulty creating metrics for the social and environmental bottom lines. We would like your assistance in defining metrics for the environmental bottom line."

I could still see some skepticism on Paula's face; her staff people were watching her.

"Let me show you what we've done so far," I said, showing them the metrics the staff created. "The 'no finding' metric is actually mild—the goal we made at our off-site vision session is to be a poster child for the EPA. We want to be so good you'll want to bring other companies by so they can tour our facilities and get inspired."

I only wish I had a camera. They got it, even though they didn't believe it. Finally, Paula spoke, "You have no idea how often we want to hear a company say that and mean it. I'm putting my career on the line by trusting that you mean it, even though I've been played for a patsy by one or two other companies in the past. Assuming you're serious, we'd love to help you. When would you like us to start?"

I replied, "Paula, thanks for trusting us. I realize trust and relationship are the foundation of business, and life. I also understand how trust can be difficult if you've been stabbed in the back. I just learned that the hard way, myself. So yes, we want to earn your trust."

"Can we start right now?" quipped Tom. "And that was only half in jest. We're facing tremendous price pressure from our two competitors, both of whom have outsourced their manufacturing to China. We're using sustainability as our way to stay in business, and every day counts."

"Okay, then," responded Paula. "Let's see what we can do to help."

They told us about their Lean and Environmental Tool Kit.* Then we started discussing the various possible environmental metrics and chose the ones we would use. We defined what they meant, where the data would come from, the cost of data capture, and how various data elements could be compared, etc. When we had worked for about an hour and completed our discussion, we were amazed when Paula said, "It looks as if the

---

* Environmental Protection Agency. Lean and Environmental Tool Kit. Available online at http://www.epa.gov/lean/toolkit/index.htm.

metrics you chose are about as good as any to start with." It was good to hear her affirmation.

So we thanked them for coming and invited them to come back any time, and to call or e-mail us any additional ideas. And they did. My opinion of government agencies improved several degrees through that encounter. What they were trying to do was protect the environment from people who didn't care about it or, worse, those who claimed to care and then betrayed that trust. When they realized we were serious, they bent over backwards to help us.

On Wednesday I got in my car and drove to various smaller customers in the upper Midwest to meet them in person. Right now, we didn't want to lose a single one; they were each vital to our survival. The trip was successful. Most of them had not even been approached by Jeff the turncoat. I don't know if he thought they were too small to bother with or if he just hadn't gotten to them yet. Without saying anything bad about Jeff, I got each of them to commit to staying with us for a year based on our commitment to sustainability and our long-term relationships.

Wednesday evening I called Dennis to update him on the week's events. He started cheering when I told him about the Lean Green Team and their attitude. "You've made it, Adam, you've made it!" he yelled into the phone.

"Huh?" I said, my mouth falling open.

Dennis exclaimed, "When you've got a team acting like that, you've won! It's all over but the shouting."

"Really?" I said doubtfully.

"Yes. It's all about relationship and attitude," he said. "With that attitude in the plant, and the relationships that will be created with others in the plant, how can you lose?"

"Now that you put it that way, I guess you're right. We can't lose." My brain agreed with him, but my gut still wasn't convinced.

I got back just in time for my 4:00 with Rev. Franklin Friday afternoon. He met me at the door.

"You know," I started, "I can't tell you why, but I am almost confident that we'll make it."

"Interesting you should say that," he replied. "I'm preaching about 'faith' on Sunday, and it sounds like you're finding some yourself."

"If you're talking about faith that the company will thrive in the future, yes, I have that. I think where it came from is that others have bought into this sustainability vision, and they are really giving everything they've got at work." I told him about the Lean Green Team and the locked dumpster. And, most importantly, what they had taught me about waste.

"Adam, you're wise beyond your years, and you don't even see it. That's a gift, both to you, and it's one you give your people at work."

"Huh?" (I love it when my eloquence totally confounds my listener.)

"Yes. What you just told me—a group of hourly employees from the shipping department had this insight, right?" he asked.

"Yes, and?"

"And they felt comfortable enough with you to explain that you were seeing things wrong," he said.

I frowned. "I guess they did, didn't they?"

"And how did you react?" he asked.

"I thanked them."

Rev. Franklin added, "And they knew you meant it. You were really happy that they'd done this."

"Oh, yeah—I wouldn't even want to try to BS the guys on the floor; they'd see through me in 10 seconds flat."

"How do you think the president of a typical company would have reacted to people from the floor telling him he was wrong?" he asked.

"He would have been threatened, and clammed up, or cut them down, or something like that," I replied, shaking my head.

"That's been my experience," he said, adding, "Okay then, how do you think your dad would have reacted?"

"Neutrally to somewhat positively—he would have wanted to think about it, and then he would have talked to Tom or Wayne or Mom."

"Do you see the difference?" he asked. "It's all about relationship. You helped them feel really good about themselves, recognizing their importance and creativity. They now feel powerful and needed. And when you gave them the pen Kelly had given you, in front of everyone, they must have felt 10 feet tall! You, Adam, are a natural leader. You really are a better leader than your dad."

"Thanks, John. I am still somewhat unsure of myself; I'm just doing what seems to be the right thing at the time."

"Keep doing it, Adam. Your parents were a living example of great values, and you have learned well. I've been reading a book by Margaret Benefiel, *Soul at Work*[†]. She talks about Reell Precision Manufacturing in St. Paul, Minnesota.

---

† Benefiel, Margaret. 2005. *Soul at Work*. New York: Seabury Books.

Here, I printed off their values from their web site[‡]." He handed a printed piece of paper to me and remarked, "Notice the first one: 'We are committed to do what is right even when it does not seem to be profitable, expedient, or conventional.' And the third, 'treat others as we would like to be treated.'"

"Sounds interesting, could I borrow the book when you're done?" I asked.

"Sure; you can have it for a week or two right now if you'd like," he said, reaching for it on the corner of his desk.

"I'd like that. Thanks."

As I drove home that night, I could not keep from thinking about my prior Friday evening with Kelly. Yes, I know, her parents were there too. But I was with Kelly, and that's all that really mattered. I found myself starting to count the days until next Friday when I would fly out to Portland again. Two weeks was becoming longer and longer each time. I was suddenly having much greater empathy for road warriors, and servicemen and women who were gone from their families weeks, months, or even years at a time. And I found myself thinking that maybe part of what sustainability is all about is recognizing the common elements of humanity in each of us—we share the same basic dreams and pains.

In his sermon Sunday, Rev. Franklin said that faith draws us to realize our ideals, walk our talk, and act in accordance with what we know to be true.[§] That sounded exactly like what we were trying to do inside our company. And I was starting to like Rev. Franklin enough that I wanted to ask Kelly if he could officiate at our wedding.

[‡] Reell Precision Manufacturing web site. May 2, 2006. http://www.reell.com/belief.htm.

[§] Anderson, Linda. http://www.uucckingston.org/Sermons/faith.html.

CHAPTER 13

You Can Take It to the Bank

We invited Carl to the staff meeting Monday morning to brief us on the status of the various sustainability projects. They were doing pretty well—but to the outsider, it still might have appeared like semi-controlled chaos. That was okay though. Some teams were still deciding which project to work on. Others had already started on their first projects. We had no major results yet, of course, but things were clearly underway, and morale was sky-high.

That afternoon, Tom, Mom and I were making sure we were prepared for the meeting with Ron the next day. Tom started, "Because my projections are just that, projections, we should probably ask for a larger credit line just in case. We obviously won't draw it down unless we need it, but having it will save us from going back to the well if the real numbers are worse than my forecasts."

I said, "We need to have a worst-case scenario plan too, in case some of our smaller customers defect before we get our costs down."

Tom replied, "Already got it done, Adam."

I smiled. "Thanks, Tom. I keep forgetting just how good you really are."

Mom nodded in agreement with me, then said, "I was at the off-site, as was Ron, but you two will have to handle the discussion on how sustainability will reduce costs and make us more competitive. I know the theory, but not the details."

I replied, "We already expected to do that."

So we met with Ron at the bank. As expected, he was not terribly surprised, because we had already told him Jeff had gone to the competition, and he knew our cost disadvantage. Ron actually surprised us when he said, "You know, I'm very pleasantly surprised that you've kept as many customers as you have as long as you have, in spite of your cost disadvantage. Especially when Jeff, who knows all your weak points, went to the competition and is now doing everything he can to poach your customers. In a perverse sort of way, that speaks volumes for your long-term competitive advantage as long as you can get your costs in line. I know the theory of sustainability from 30,000 feet. What are your detailed plans, and how much can they realistically be expected to contribute?"

So we went over the first set of initiatives, including the product redesign for rebuild, the dumpster diving, the energy conservation plan, and all the rest. Tom said, "We know these numbers are purely projections. The only way to find out how real they are is to wait and see what really happens. But they're the best numbers we can get at this point."

"I understand that, Tom. But how sure are you of the assumptions behind these projections?" asked Ron. "What happens if more customers go to the competition?"

"We thought you might ask that," answered Tom. "Here's what we think are worst-case projections," and he gave Ron the spreadsheets.

"Hmmm . . . do you have best-case projections as well?" asked Ron as he thumbed through the pages.

"No, but if things go better than we planned, we will use less of the credit line," Tom replied.

"Of course," Ron said and he studied the spreadsheets for a while. "You know the bank's policy on requests like this. I'll take these to Jim (Jim Stearns, the president of the bank) and ask him to meet with you. I'll recommend approval, but he'll want to ask his own questions. And if he likes what he hears, then he'll need to take it to the board."

"We know that, Ron," replied Mom. "When can we meet with Jim?"

"Let me ask him right now." He rose and left the room.

Ron returned, "How about this Friday at 2:00 in the afternoon?"

"Can we make it at 10:00 in the morning instead? I have a 1:00 flight," I replied. There was no way I wanted to miss even a minute with Kelly this weekend!

"Let me check," he said, and he left us again.

After a few minutes, Ron returned. "We can do that. I don't think you need to change anything or add anything to what you already gave me. With your permission, I'll give it to Jim so he can review it before the meeting."

"Sounds good," I replied. Tom and Mom nodded.

The next few days were a blur—it's really amazing how much work there is to do that does not directly cause product to go out the door. I talked with Barbara, Wayne, Tom, Walter, and Lorraine, all in separate meetings, to find out their opinions and ideas about the sustainability initiative thus far. The unanimous consensus was "so far, so good." They were holding their breath just like me hoping that sustainability would indeed prove to be a competitive advantage. They also truly believed that it would, which helped.

Mom and I had a serious discussion Wednesday evening about future ownership of the company. She was starting to think along the lines of selling some of her stock to employees, or even giving a few shares as a bonus for exemplary performance. I was starting to seriously consider having employees own a substantial share of the company, not just the 10% I had considered earlier. So we talked through the pros and cons. We didn't reach any solid conclusions though.

Thursday Lorraine got a phone call from one of our newest and smallest customers. They were switching suppliers. We weren't really sad to see them go; they had a one-track mind: price, not total cost of ownership, but price. From our experience with them, I would have guessed that they paid people to find reasons to reduce their vendor's price—damaged in shipment was one of their favorites. I remembered my dad joking once about paying the competition to lure away some of his customers. Now I was not so sure he was joking at all!

I talked with Dennis Thursday afternoon to tell him where we were with our projects. He said we were doing well, and also gave me some good advice on ownership issues.

Tom, Mom, and I were ushered into Jim's office by Ron precisely at 10:00 Friday morning. Lots of things have changed through the years, but punctuality remained highly valued at Farmers' and Merchants' Bank.

"Thanks for coming," Jim said. "I've looked over your numbers, and I have some serious concerns."

We three looked at each other; this didn't sound too good. We were expecting concerns, but not "serious" ones.

"And your concerns are?" I asked.

"Well, from what you gave me, your two major competitors are 20–25% lower in price on most of your products. The bank is in the business of lending money to companies who will be able to repay loans. I'm concerned that you might not be in business in a few years, thereby defaulting."

"We've started addressing the cost disparities . . ." I started to say.

Jim interrupted, "Yes, with this *sustainability* stuff. Although I like the way it sounds on the surface, I can't see how it will translate into profits. And if it doesn't, you stand an excellent chance of going broke. Is that correct?"

Damn! This guy doesn't pull any punches, does he? Maybe that's how he got to be president of the bank . . . I thought I might as well be as blunt as he was, "Not really. If our sustainability efforts fail, we'll be in serious trouble. At that point, we'd have to choose between shutting the company completely down or keeping design, sales, and accounting open here, while sending production to China like our competitors have done. Given the choice, we'd send production to China and keep the office open here. So as long as we can keep designing product and selling it, we won't go broke. Alternatively, we could just sell the company to another company or competitor, which would produce more than sufficient cash to pay off any loans."

"Okay, I just wanted to hear you say that. I appreciate your candor, just like I appreciated Chris'. We went through some interesting times together." He actually smiled a bit! Hmm, I wondered, what's next?

Jim turned, looked directly at Mom, and said, "Susan, this credit line request falls outside of our usual lending guidelines. Sufficiently far outside that I suspect the board will have considerable difficulty approving it. Nonetheless, because of how you and Chris ran the company for years, and how Adam is showing the talent to continue leading the company, I will recommend that they approve it. If they do, the amount might be less than you are requesting. Can you live with that?"

Huh? I thought to myself. Jim had gone from "I don't believe in this sustainability stuff" to "I'll recommend approval" in two minutes flat. I guess he was just testing me, and I passed.

Mom looked at me, then at Tom. We both nodded and I replied, "Yes, we can live with that. We would like to be at the meeting when the board considers this request."

"I'll be glad to arrange that," Jim said. "The board will be quite interested in hearing your reasoning. I'll send these materials to the members so they'll have time to review them before our next meeting, which is next Thursday. Can you be here at 6 p.m.?"

We looked at each other briefly and all nodded. "Certainly," Mom said.

The view of Mt. Hood was breathtaking as I flew into Portland Friday evening. I was on the left side of the plane, looking at a mountain off on the right (which I found out later was Mt. Adams). Then suddenly Mt. Hood appeared just off the left wing. I felt like rolling my window down, sticking my hand out, and scooping up some snow for a snowball. We seemed to be that close! I understood how Kelly fell in love with this place. Saturday, we drove up to Timberline Lodge and hopped on the Magic Mile chairlift up into the snow fields. I was speechless as I viewed the white-topped volcanic peaks toward the south, and the hundreds of square miles of hills covered with deep green conifers. A poet would have trouble describing that scene, and I'm certainly no poet. I took dozens of pictures of Kelly; she took dozens of pictures of me, and we asked several people to take pictures of the two of us. One, of Kelly standing on a rock with the snow-covered peak of Mt. Hood behind her, was good enough that I printed off and framed an 8 × 10 for my office and another for the house.

Sunday, we just stayed around her condo. I started missing her right after lunch, because I knew I'd be flying out on the red-eye that night. As much as I wanted to stay longer, I just couldn't justify missing a full day at the company. So we started talking about the possibility of her finding a job within commuting distance of the plant, so she could move back to the Midwest sooner. I knew what it would cost her, because I had completely fallen in love with Portland and Oregon too. And I hadn't even spent any time at the coast yet; Cannon Beach and Tillamook were next on our list of things to do on a Saturday. But being apart from one another hurt even worse, so I told her I'd start putting feelers out and asking others to do the same.

Then all too soon it was Sunday night and I had to get on the plane. I think our farewell kisses raised the temperature at the terminal by a couple of degrees. Amazingly enough I actually got some sleep on the way back. I fogged through O'Hare to catch my connection, and then slept a little more. I felt at least semi-human as I met with the staff. Tom updated them on our meeting with the bank, and then Carl discussed the status of the sustainability work. Other topics discussed by staff were outstanding customer invoices, product design work, etc., etc., etc. Our sustainability efforts were moving forward nicely. I could see that some of the projects would be providing tangible results soon.

The Lean Green Team made a special presentation to the executive staff Monday afternoon. The team showed how we could eliminate over 60% of what we were currently throwing away. The plan was to sell 30% of it, redesign processes to not make the waste to begin with, which accounted for another 15%, and have suppliers reduce packaging for most of the rest. I was so pleased! Their pens had arrived the prior Friday, so I presented each person with one, name engraved. (I made sure I got my own pen back; after all, it had been a special gift from my fiancée.)

I called Dennis Wednesday afternoon and talked to him about the upcoming meeting with the bank's board of directors. I was worried about what I would say to convince them to give us the larger credit line. He was quite Socratic in his approach.

Dennis began, "How many employees would lose their jobs if you outsourced production to China? About 200, right?"

"Yes," I replied, not at all sure where he was going with his questioning.

And he continued, "How much does your average worker make in take-home pay?"

"About $18 per hour," I answered.

"Would people have to find jobs elsewhere and move away?" he asked.

"Yes," I replied.

"So how much money would disappear from the local economy if those employees were laid off?" he prodded.

I quickly calculated—"$18 per hour × 2,000 hours per year is $36,000 per year per employee × 200 employees is . . . more than $7 million per year."

"And what impact would losing $7 million per year have on the merchants in the community, and on the value of housing in the community?"

I replied, "I'm not sure, but it wouldn't be good."

"And what impact would that have on the bank?" he asked.

"I got it! Oh my . . . thanks, Dennis!"

Given the fact that I was trying to be both the CEO (and a new one at that, which required more time and attention) *and* VP sales and marketing, it was no wonder the week just disappeared out from under me before I knew it. Suddenly it was Thursday, late in the afternoon, and time to prepare for meeting with the bank's board of directors. I was surprised at my modest degree of nervousness. I hoped that they would increase our credit line; if they didn't, I didn't know what else we'd do. But somehow I was pretty calm over the whole thing. Again, I noticed how much I'd grown professionally and personally; three months ago I would have been a nail-biting, stammering fool. But I had met with enough customers so I felt solid in my statements about our customer base. I'd seen the plant in action. The Lean Green Team was my favorite. I know, I'm not supposed to have favorites. But damn it, they were. They pushed the envelope farther than we had even dreamed possible, and they were delivering! So I was confident, and that confidence was grounded in my experience and in data I could cite if necessary.

The meeting with the bank started cordially enough, but it was soon clear the board was seriously concerned about our current financial and competitive situation, and highly skeptical of our plans. Board members pushed, poked, and prodded at the numbers and the reasoning behind them. Finally, the proverbial brown stuff hit the fan.

Zeke Williams, the chairman of the board and the city's leading attorney, led the charge. "Adam, I normally don't say this. But I don't have any reason to believe these projections about increases in sales or profitability due to your sustainability program. I wish I could support this request, but I can't. Why should I believe any of this?"

"Zeke, you should believe it because companies that have done it have succeeded. First, from a purely financial standpoint, check out the Dow Jones Sustainability Index compared to the NASDAQ or S&P, or the Dow Jones Industrial average. Check out the return to shareholders of the publicly traded companies on *Fortune* magazine's '100 Best Companies to Work For,' compared to the broader market indices—it is at least 50% higher. Check out what's happened with Timberland, or Wal-Mart, or DuPont, or GE. Let go of your preconceptions and look at the data. That's all we ask."

I continued, "From a qualitative standpoint, I've visited all our major and medium customers and many of the smaller ones. Virtually all of them are with us for the long term. I know that words aren't worth much in this day and age. But relationships are how we got where we are, and relationships are how we'll not only survive, but thrive, in the future. And I'll ask Tom to tell you what has happened in the plant, because I was not around when they implemented Lean. Tom?"

Tom picked up the conversation, "Zeke, you know me. I'm a numbers man. If I can't see it in a number, it isn't real, right?" Zeke nodded. "So listen carefully, because I'm about to say something that doesn't have numbers to back me up. I'm completely out of my comfort zone on this one, but I would testify in court that it is just as true as any number I have ever seen. The fact is I have worked at Brookings for more than two decades. I was there when we started on Lean about five years ago. And I saw people becoming excited, and the teams doing some pretty amazing things. But it didn't come close, not even close, to what I've seen in this last month. When we started that weekend at the off-site, I was as skeptical as you, maybe even more. But since then, I've been watching what's been going on in the company. Our inside sales force is on fire. On fire, I tell you. I have never seen them so focused. The Lean Green Team basically told Wayne, our plant manager, to stand aside while they did the impossible. And I think they're going to do it! What are they doing? They're intending to completely lock up the dumpster—permanently! I have never seen people on the shop floor have that much chutzpah. Never! I saw their presentation Monday afternoon, and they're turning our trash into income and reducing costs.

"When we first started our Lean journey five years ago, one of our consultants told me that the intangible results were worth at least as much as the tangible results. I thought he was completely full of it when he told me that. But it turned out he was correct. We started making more money than ever before, and I couldn't tell you exactly what caused it. But the money was completely real, because it was in our checking account in this bank. I'm here to tell you, sustainability is even more powerful, and we're just starting. When Adam told all the employees that Illinois Electronics was going to buy from Electronic Products instead of us, I was worried it would kill morale. It has done the opposite. I can't show you the numbers to prove it, but I am completely confident Brookings Manufacturing will be prosperous within a year, and for many years thereafter. I'm willing to stake my professional reputation on it."

The room was dead silent for a while. Then I decided it was time to drop the bomb. "Let's look at this purely selfishly, from the standpoint of Farmers' and Merchants' Bank. Let's assume that you refuse the requested increase in our line of credit, and we struggle and finally fail due to lack of capital. For the record, I am completely convinced that if we have enough capital, we will succeed. But let's assume that we fail due to lack of capital. Our fallback position is to outsource production to China. Brookings Manufacturing would still survive; our revenues would be about the same.

So this is no big deal, right? Not true at all. Somewhere around 200 jobs, manufacturing jobs, which net an average of $18 per hour, would be lost in this community. How many other manufacturing companies are still here? None. That's how many. None. And where else could these 200 people find jobs that would pay them as well? Nowhere within commuting distance. There *are* no others. So they would either have to go on unemployment and early retirement, or sell their houses and leave town. How many would wind up defaulting on their mortgages? You know what has happened to property values since manufacturers started closing their doors. Our city would lose $7 million in income per year. That's $7 million that gets spent in our local economy. What would happen to the merchants who depend on that cash flow? Many of them are weak already, because of the other plant closings. To get very personal, how healthy would your bank be? Brookings Manufacturing, or at least its shell, would still be here. But would you? Or would you have to sell out to a big city bank and become just another remote branch?"

Well, it was a bomb, all right. They sat there, stunned, mouths slightly open and eyes wide, Jim and Ron included. I hadn't warned them that I might say this, because I didn't want them to inadvertently spoil the impact. When Zeke finally recovered sufficiently, he said, "We'll talk things over; Ron will get back to you tomorrow to let you know what we decide."

"Thank you for your time," Mom said. "We know the way out." So we left.

When we got outside, I told Tom, "You were amazing! The way you put your reputation on the line—I am speechless. If we get this, it's because of you."

Tom blushed and replied, "Partially because of me, but you were masterful, Adam. I saw your dad in action lots of times, but he was never that powerful or persuasive." He turned to Mom, "Susan, I didn't mean any disrespect." Then he looked at me, "Maybe you should take up law; you'd have the jury eating out of your hands."

In the car on the way home, Mom turned to me, "Adam, you were superb. I am so proud of you! I really think we'll get it, because they won't vote against their own selfish best interest, and they won't vote to hurt the town if they can help it."

That night I called Kelly. It was great to hear her voice—instantly I felt the stress of the day just melt away. I told her about the meeting with the bank. She was ecstatic about the way we handled it and was confident we would get the credit extension. I also asked her about having Rev. Franklin co-officiate at our wedding. She was all for it. I told her I would ask him the next time we met.

Jim called me Friday morning. "Adam, I was impressed last night. So was the board. They voted to extend the full credit line, even though it falls well outside our usual guidelines. You really shook some people up. But you've got the full credit line. Congratulations!"

So I called Mom and asked her to come over Friday afternoon for an all-employee meeting at 3:00. She was there as I told our company the good news. And I told them how Tom had staked his personal reputation on our ability to deliver. Then Tom told them what I had told the board. They went wild—cheering, whistling, and clapping. Yeah, it felt really good. We were going to make it.

Later that afternoon I met with John again and asked him to co-officiate at our wedding. He was delighted to be asked, checked his calendar, and agreed. I told him about the experience with the bankers. The look on his face turned to wonder as I described the conversation during the board meeting, about Tom putting his reputation on the line, and my laying it on the line about the bank staying in business.

"Adam, I have to say something. It's hard to believe that you're the same Adam who first came into this study just a few weeks ago. Where do you think you found your courage and your voice, your inner fire, as it were?"

"I think it was because I had nothing to lose, in one respect, and because I believe so completely in what we're doing. I *know* we're going to make it. I basically knew it when we had the meeting with the bank. So I just let that show. I used to hide it, because I didn't want to scare people."

"Adam, one of the roots of powerful, effective leadership is authenticity. You were being authentic, and it showed. You were speaking honestly, from your heart *and* from your head, and it showed. You truly are a gifted and talented leader; Brookings is lucky to have you as their CEO."

"Really?" I said.

"Yes, really," John replied. "Now, tell me more about the wedding."

After I left John, I went home to a long weekend, one without Kelly (unless you count two or three hours per day on the phone as being with someone).

CHAPTER 14
It was the Best of Times, It was the Worst of Times

Monday, Monday, except it's changed. I don't fear Mondays anymore. Our staff meetings are interesting and productive; they no longer feel like a funeral in progress. During Carl's sustainability report, we learned that the insulation and motion sensors were now installed. Next, his team was going to be plotting the electric load caused by each major device to see where we could save, starting with reducing the demand load. Other teams had come up with ways to use less material, inspired by the dumpster divers, the Lean Green Team. The team was actually thinking of changing its name to the "Dumpster Divers." I hoped the team decided to do so; it really fit. That's what everybody was calling it anyhow.

The teams were starting to look for new challenges. We hadn't focused much on the social side of sustainability and only partially on the environmental side. I was glad Dennis was coming in for the day Tuesday. It had been a little more than four weeks, but I had touched base with him by phone almost on a weekly basis.

Dennis flew in Monday night; he had been with another client in the Chicago area that day. I picked him up at his hotel near the airport for breakfast Tuesday morning; this and the drive to the plant would give the two of us some quality time to talk. He was, of course, delighted to hear about the results of the meeting with the board of directors at the bank. And I thanked him for helping me create the viewpoint that persuaded them. "That's why I'm here, Adam, that's why I'm here. It frequently takes an outsider to see things from a completely different viewpoint."

"So what do we do about the social and environmental aspects of sustainability? How do we guide the teams?" I asked and then the waitress arrived with coffee and we placed our orders.

"Great question, Adam. And you're right. Teams need to be guided, not managed. Tell me again your main strategic points for each axis of sustainability?"

I had printed them out Monday night and had two copies with me. Dennis studied the information momentarily.

Financial:

- Sales revenues.
- Operating profits as a percentage of revenue.
  - Reduced material costs.

Environmental:

- Reduced environmental impact.
  - Energy efficiency (total energy used per pound of product shipped).
  - Toxic free (total listed toxic pounds used).
  - Complete compliance with all regulations (no findings).
- Redesigned products for take-back.

Social:

- Ranked in *Fortune* magazine's "100 Best Companies to Work For."

- Community outreach.
  - Teaching the community about sustainability.

He then added some cream to his coffee. "So how much work have you done on each?" he asked and took a sip.

"On the financial axis, we are working on reducing material and operating costs. Sales revenues are down at this point, rather than up. We're currently operating in the red due to the loss of three customers. On the environmental axis, we're looking at energy efficiency from two fronts: general use, like what it takes to heat our buildings, and production use, like the electricity it takes to run manufacturing machinery. We haven't looked hard at toxics at all yet, and we've met with the EPA once. We're starting to redesign our products for take back, and one of our people is looking to use recycled material rather than virgin resin for the cases for our product. On the social side, morale is higher than it's ever been, but we haven't started community outreach."

"Okay. Do you remember anything about appreciative inquiry?" Dennis asked.

"Yes, it's basically where the boss or consultant appreciates the things a person or company has done right, rather than just focusing on where they've screwed up," I replied.

"Uh huh," he said. "So let's do some appreciative inquiry on what's been happening at Brookings.

"First, you realize you're slowly going down the toilet—death by inches. Second, you have the courage to have an off-site and bring in a consultant you've only met on the phone for an hour, because your best friend (now your fiancée) recommends him. He suggests some off-the-wall stuff that sounds like new age woo-woo, not real hard-headed business strategy. The group adopts it anyhow, even though they have no clue where they're headed or how they'll do it. Third, your

VP of sales and marketing stiffs you and jumps ship for the competition, obviously trying to take customers with him. Your largest customer wavers and almost goes with him. To keep them, you have to sell at a loss. Fourth, one of your medium customers goes to the competition. At that point, you're barely breaking even. Fifth, on your second road trip, you lose another customer to the competition, so now you're under water. Sixth, your ideas about how to lead the teams got a team and its leader all confused so that they just floundered around.

"So what do you do? What would any self-respecting, prudent, intelligent business person do in this situation? Throw in the towel and try to sell the company, right? There's no way the company can survive. But you, Adam, obviously don't have an M.B.A., because you didn't know you were dead. Instead, you:

- Started sharing financial information with employees for the first time ever.

- Went on the road to convince customers to stay with you and deepened relationships. You were astonishingly successful, incidentally, considering that your company has a 25% price handicap.

- Empowered your teams to start thinking out of the box and swinging for the fences. And when one of them really did that, and told your VP of operations to take a hike, you backed the team up, instead of telling the team to obey the VP.

- When you told everyone about the second customer that jumped ship, they didn't cry or die. They just got more creative and determined, and miracles started happening.

- You called for advice when the team floundered, and you stopped other teams from following the same path.

Then you created guidelines so the teams could succeed.

- You met with a group of highly skeptical bankers, invited them to do the unthinkable as far as their lending guidelines, and showed them how it was in their best interest, and the community's best interest for them to do it. And your CFO put his personal credibility on the line.

- While all this was going on, you got engaged to your best friend and persuaded her to leave Portland, Oregon, which she loves, and move here to be with you, because you won't abandon your company or your friends or your home town."

I just sat there, stunned. It's like when you're climbing a mountain, and you're maybe halfway up, and all you can see is a lot more mountain to climb. Then somebody says, "Look over there!" And you look, and you can see fields, streams, and trees, and you can see how far you've come and you didn't even know it. That's how I felt just then. We *had* come a long way!

After a few moments, Dennis continued, "Every consulting engagement starts with the consultant leading the client up a hill. The client comes along with some misgivings and resistance. Somewhere along the line the client gets it, catches on fire, and really takes off. Suddenly the consultant has to run like hell to keep up. Instead of pulling and leading the client, the consultant is now shouting advice in the leader's ear to help him or her lead as effectively as possible. Adam, that's what has happened in your company. That happened when the Dumpster Divers told Wayne to pound sand and then went off and did their miracle. So now your leadership style needs to be facilitative—create a safe set of boundaries and parameters, and let your teams loose. At this stage of the game, some of the teams probably still need to be led, but I'll bet you most of them will soon be relatively independent. It's highly unusual for it to happen this quickly. That speaks very well of your leadership style, and of your teams and the experiences they've had before.

"One more thought," he added, "There isn't a well-defined road map for sustainability, as you well know. It is not nearly as well-defined as Lean. So, in one sense, it doesn't matter nearly as much exactly which projects a team looks at first or second, or even third. What matters is how the team is functioning, and how the company supports the teams, and whether the team can see tangible success at the end of the project. That was important in Lean; it is absolutely the most essential thing in sustainability. Without the enthusiasm and creativity of people in teams, sustainability would be impossible."

He continued, "So, now to your question. If you were the consultant, what would you suggest Adam do about the environmental and social bottom lines?"

I replied, "That's easy. Just ask the teams to start including the previously untouched areas in their list of potential projects."

"Got it in one!" grinned Dennis. "I wish I had more clients like you. But then my company wouldn't eat nearly as well, either. Do you think I could observe a team meeting or two today?"

"Yes. I'll ask Annie, and tell her it was you who told me how to keep the other teams from falling in the same quicksand. She's a natural team leader. I'm really proud of her."

"Great!" he said, "I have one more idea I'd like to run by you." I nodded for him to go on. "The Zero Waste Alliance, a non-profit in Portland, Oregon, has a sustainability scorecard, which can help a company quickly compare itself to a very high standard in each major functional area. It's called SCORE.* It would only take about two hours of your staff time to discuss it and gather the data. Then I'd have it scored and e-mail you the results. There's a small cost for using the instrument and having it scored."

"Sounds good; let's do it," I replied. "Let's head for the plant and get started."

Annie asked her team, the Waste Busters, to meet at 10:00 that morning. It was not their normal time, but they were excited about having Dennis observe. I had the first five minutes at the start of the meeting.

I began, "The last time I observed your meeting, the ideas I asked Annie to run with caused you to flounder. I'm sorry and I apologize. I'm new to this, too. And now you know, beyond the shadow of any doubt, that it's okay to make mistakes as long as they don't hurt somebody or seriously hurt the company. That's the only way we'll learn and grow.

"What we were trying to do was develop non-financial metrics so each team could look at improving all three of the bottom lines: people, planet, and profit.

"So let's look first at the environmental side. I have printed out the Lean and Environmental Tool Kit from the EPA's web site.† It has a list of basic environmental measures:‡

---

* Zero Waste Alliance. Sustainability scorecard. Information available online at http://www.zerowaste.org/score/index.htm.

† Environmental Protection Agency website http://www.epa.gov/lean/.

‡ Environmental Protection Agency (EPA). 2006. *The Lean and Environment Tool Kit, Version 1.0.* Information available online at http://www.epa.gov/lean/toolkit/lean_environment_toolkit2.pdf, pp. 78-89.

Input measures:

- Energy use.
- Land use.
- Materials use.
- Toxic/hazardous chemicals use.
- Water use.

Non-product output measures:

- Air emissions.
- Water pollution.
- Solid waste.

Downstream product measures:

- Product impacts.

Other measures:

- Money saved.
- Qualitative measures."

I asked the team, "Which of these would you like to investigate? Which might provide the best opportunity for improvements?"

The team members seemed a bit self-conscious because Dennis and I were there, but they soon got into the meeting. After some discussion, they decided to look at toxic/hazardous chemicals, because Sam's team had already done a lot on energy, and the Dumpster Divers (yes, they had changed their name) were focusing on solid waste outputs and materials use.

Dennis asked, "May I offer an idea?"

"Sure," replied Annie.

"Back where I come from in Oregon, there's a non-profit called the Zero Waste Alliance. They have a process called

CARS—Chemical Assessment and Ranking System[§], which helps you identify and rank the dangerous chemicals contained in the products you're using, then see possible alternatives and prioritize your actions. I brought along a brochure[**] for you to keep if you'd like."

"Let me take the lead on that," George Simonek, a 20-year veteran, said as he reached for the brochure. "I've wanted to do this for years. I know we try to be as safe as possible, but I would be a lot more comfortable if we could eliminate the toxic chemicals we currently use. So I'll start looking to see what we use and create a priority list for phase-out."

I acclaimed, "That's wonderful, George. I think you already know this, but I'll say it anyhow. Like the Dumpster Divers, this will require you and your team to work with other departments, like engineering and who knows who all else. And I'll make sure we provide the resources and support you need."

George asked, "Dennis, do you have any idea how the Zero Waste Alliance works and how much it will cost?"

"It's quite reasonable," he said. "I think the minimum is two meetings with some work in between to do the basic ranking. And I know they can help you find alternatives within a couple more meetings. But you need to talk with them directly to find out for sure."

"I'll be calling or e-mailing them to get things started this afternoon; I figure I can start on the toxic chemicals now, and cue the ZWA up for phase two," George said.

---

§   Zero Waste Alliance. Chemical Assessment and Ranking System. Information available online at http://www.zerowaste.org/cars/index.html.

**   http://www.zerowaste.org/cars/CARSBrochure.pdf.

Annie said, "Thanks, George. We hope you'll have lots of information by our next meeting so we can get started."

I called a special staff meeting at 11:00 so we could talk with Dennis about our progress, our problems, and our concerns. I expanded the meeting to include everyone who was at the off-site.

As the meeting started, I asked Dennis to explain SCORE to the group. Everyone was excited about the idea, so they readily agreed to meet for two hours so Dennis could help us fill out the SCORE data. I had each person briefly state what they'd been doing with respect to sustainability since the off-site. When we finished, Dennis said, "I am really impressed. You have done an amazing amount in a short time . . . Do you have any questions you'd like to ask? I can't promise I'll be able to answer them, but I'll try."

Tom started, "Dennis, I'm still having trouble creating metrics for the non-financial areas."

"I know it is a small consolation, Tom, but most companies have the same issue. As we agreed before, each company needs to define its own metrics from a rather large list of possibilities. The solution lies with which metrics are the most important to Brookings Manufacturing. You'll develop those over time. And if you try some and they don't work, nothing bad will happen to the company. You don't have to be perfect and have all the right answers here at the start. Can you give yourself permission to learn by trying, like everyone else?"

Looking more than a little uncomfortable, Tom replied, "I guess so. I'm so used to being precise and having everything well-defined. This is really difficult."

Wayne remarked, "Dennis, my teams are going gangbusters. I assume it's not realistic to expect them to be this creative for several years. How do I keep them motivated and focused over the long run?"

"I'm not really sure," he said. "I know you're not used to a consultant telling you this, but we really don't know yet because most companies have not been on a sustainability journey long enough for people to get tired of it. What we do know is this: because sustainability explicitly includes both social and environmental bottom lines, people are engaged at a deeper level than they were with Lean, which focused solely on the financial bottom line. They get to do things that directly benefit their children and the community. So we expect their enthusiasm to last longer. In a few years if their enthusiasm wanes, you can seek potential next steps."

Nancy, our purchasing agent, was next. "I'm trying to start buying from sustainable suppliers. How do I find them?"

Dennis replied, "There are two ways. You can grow your own, by helping your current suppliers become sustainable, or you can find suppliers who are already sustainable. Oregon has a Sustainable Supplier Initiative through the state government; there might be similar initiatives here in the Midwest. I know you make industrial electronics rather than consumer electronics, but you might check out the Green Electronics Council[††]. Or start asking at your local ISM[‡‡] chapter. There's also a Green Suppliers' Network[§§], but it doesn't focus on electronics manufacturing. Remember, you're on a journey. You just keep on doing the right things and moving toward your ultimate objectives, day in and day out."

[††] http://www.greenelectronicscouncil.org/.

[‡‡] ISM (Institute for Supply Management), formerly the National Association of Purchasing Management. http://www.ism.ws/.

[§§] http://www.greensuppliers.gov/gsn/home.gsn.

Mary, our VP of materials and logistics, asked, "What can I do to reduce transportation costs? How can I keep them from continuing to climb due to increasing fuel prices?"

"You're already starting to switch to local suppliers where possible," Dennis said. "That's the best approach. You could look at developing one or two more local suppliers if that's possible. Most importantly, start questioning the assumption that fuel prices will level off. They might not, at least for the foreseeable future. In fact, given the long-term economic pressures of supply and demand, I suspect fuel prices and transportation costs will keep going upward for a long time. So you can't keep them from climbing; all you can do is mitigate the impact on your company while you watch your competitors get hurt worse."

Walter, our VP of engineering, was next. "Dennis, we're starting to design products to be shipped back here and rebuilt. While that sounds wonderful in theory, in practice I'm not sure if it will be cost-effective. By the time we finish refurbishing a unit, it might cost us more than building a new one because we might have to replace some of the expensive stuff, and we'll have the added cost of disassembly and testing. Plus there is the added cost of getting it back here, including transportation, physical handling, and paperwork."

"Walter, I can't say for sure that rebuilding will save money, at least in the short run. But I'm glad you're looking into it. One other possibility is to design your products so they can be easily separated into their components for recycling, but refurbishing seems more sustainable from a theoretical standpoint. Please understand that some people are purists, and others are more practical. Sometimes the more practical answer, at least for the short term, falls short of the purist's answer to the same question. I keep reminding my clients that they do need to make a profit so they can stay in business. I'll be very interested to learn just how that refurbishing idea works."

Barbara asked, "When do we get started with the social side? We've focused on the financial side, and I agree that had to be our first priority. The environmental side is starting now, which is wonderful. But when do we start the social bottom line?"

Dennis replied, "Barbara, could I attend another team meeting with a team that might be particularly interested in the social side? I agree. I think it's time to get a team or two started on that."

"Sure. I have two teams in mind—the customer service team that normally meets at 3:00 p.m. today, and the subassembly team that meets on Thursdays. We could call a special meeting for them at 4:00," Barbara said.

"Let's do it. I'd like Adam to be with me in both meetings, if that's okay," replied Dennis.

"I'll check with the teams, but I don't anticipate any problems," she said.

Then Dennis led us through the SCORE introduction. He explained that it was broken into functional sections, such as purchasing, HR, senior management, and the like. He said, "When a company is first starting, it will normally get a lot of zeros; a one means substantial improvement. What does it take to get the highest score, which is a nine? Well, that's what we all have to shoot for long-term. A nine is possible, but difficult to achieve. But it's really instructive to see where you need to go. Given what I've heard so far, I'd guess you've earned a few ones, and maybe some twos or threes, but most of your scores will still probably be zeros." He helped us as a group fill out the leadership section. He was right. We got ones on a few of the leadership questions, threes on a couple, and zeros on the rest. Then we had people respond to the sections they were familiar with and gave all the responses to Dennis to get tabulated.

"You're doing great—look at all the ones you have that you wouldn't have had even a month ago!" effused Dennis.

But some of us were not as enthusiastic. "Does anybody get a nine on anything?" moaned Beth.

"There are a few . . . not many, but a few," replied Dennis, a bit concerned about the morale of the group.

"Like who?" challenged Beth.

"Let me give you two examples," he said. "There's a hamburger chain named Burgerville in the Portland metro area. The company signed up to have 100% renewable energy for all its facilities in August, 2005. Since then it has been reducing energy usage across the board. So the company got a nine on the energy row in the facilities section. And in March, 2000, Shaklee Corporation was the first company in the world to be certified climate-neutral by totally offsetting all its carbon emissions. Not only for the company's plants and offices, but also for the fleet cars leased to its distributor force, and for the plane trips awarded distributors. Its staff followed the spirit as well as the letter of the goal. So they earn a nine on the energy row in the internal office operations section."

"So nines really are possible then?" Wayne asked.

"Yes, possible, but not easy," replied Dennis.

"Not easy, the man says," chuckled Tom. Then he started laughing. "Not easy. Are you sure you're not British?" Dennis looked puzzled. "That was as classic a British understatement as I've ever heard," said Tom, trying to contain himself. And then he completely lost it—he laughed so hard we all started laughing, too. Finally, the laughter subsided.

Dennis was glad for the outburst; the humor had taken the edge off slightly. He added, "Try not to get discouraged. No company has nines across the board. We are all so far away from sustainability that it hurts when we stop to think about it. But we have to work to get there. Right now, at this point in history, you should consider anything that is a three or above a cause for celebration. But let's not kid ourselves how far we have to go as a society."

I agreed, "Yeah, it's so bad, sometimes you just have to laugh. But I'm committed to lead us there."

Tom interjected, "Before we finish, I want to present Dennis with his final check for the off-site. Dennis was too modest to tell you about the guarantee he gave Adam before the off-site. He said we should only pay him half his fees, plus his expenses, when the off-site was complete, and pay him the other half in a month if we felt the off-site was worth it. Dennis, it was more than worth it. The off-site was one of the best investments this company has made in the last 20 years. It gives me great pleasure as CFO to present you with your check. You have earned it." And with a huge grin, Tom gave Dennis the check. We all stood and started clapping.

That afternoon we met with the "Serve-Us" Team, which was comprised of our five customer service representatives. Everyone was a little nervous at having Dennis and me there. After initial introductions, I asked their leader, Gloria White, for permission to speak to the group. The group nodded their heads and she agreed.

"The initial education we provided team members explained the Triple Bottom Line—financial, environmental, and social. We concentrated on the financial to start with because we needed to, and still need to, reduce the cost difference between us and our competition. Some teams have also been addressing the environmental bottom line, like the team that has insulated the plant and reduced our lighting bills, and the Dumpster Divers who have dramatically reduced the solid waste that goes to the landfill. However, we haven't done much with the social bottom line, aside from participation in the teams themselves and increased sharing of the company's financial information. While they are a good start, they are not enough. Barbara suggested you would be an excellent team to start working on the social bottom line. We think this is so important that I brought Dennis with me; he's the consultant who has helped us create all the chaos starting with the off-site meeting." I smiled at Dennis; he was comfortable with my attempt at humor. "So I'd like to encourage you to start thinking about the social bottom line. My only request is that until our cash flow improves, please think really hard before asking for more than $100,000 per project, okay?"

So we started talking about the social bottom line. In the end, we decided that it had several components, all of which were focused on people:

- The employees of the company.
- The immediate surrounding community.
- The immediate families of the employees.
- The larger community, including the cities, towns, and townships where we all live.
- The people who actually use our products.
- The people who supply us with products and services.
- Future generations—this was the most difficult to discuss because the impact of our decisions on future generations would be open to considerable debate.

I passed out copies of the three-page sustainability metrics list Dennis had e-mailed me. The social metrics generated considerable discussion. In the end, the team decided to focus on internal training and the internal suggestion program. The team also volunteered to write to *Fortune* magazine to find out how to apply to become one of its "100 Best Employers to Work For," and to the state for the same information. It was also suggested that I have lunch in the cafeteria one day each week with specifically selected people. The plan was that each employee would have lunch with me at least once a year. The team volunteered to create the list of people with Barbara's help. I was delighted at that idea and told them so. Before we left, I asked the team to present its ideas to the staff and predicted that we would approve them with no problem.

Dennis and I had a repeat performance with the team of subassemblers, who called themselves "Classy Assy." We told them what Serve Us decided to do with the hope that they would focus on additional areas. The team was comprised of people who had young children, and for some team members English was not their primary language.

Jose, who was originally from Mexico, started the conversation, "Mr. Adam, my English is not so good, and I know that. I would really like a class to improve my English. Could the company have a class like that after my shift finishes?"

Tran, who was Vietnamese, seconded the idea. "I'd like that too. And if it would be possible, could we invite family members to that class as well? My wife just came here to America last year and she doesn't know hardly any English at all."

There were several other team members nodding their heads vigorously.

I eagerly replied, "We can do that. I'll have Barbara contact the high school and the community college to see who they'd recommend to teach it."

Nikita was next, "This will be a real stretch for me to ask, but if work gets really slow here and you don't have much for us to do, could we volunteer a half a day at a time to a community charity, like the local women's shelter, or helping at a grade school, or driving senior citizens to appointments?"

"Nikita, that's an excellent idea," I said. "I really like it, so let's see how we can make it work without hurting our ability to keep our customers happy. After your team has worked through the idea, I would like you to present it to the executive staff, okay?"

"I couldn't do that! I'm just an assembler!" she exclaimed.

"Nikita, trust me," I said as reassuringly as I could. "The staff will like your idea. And it gives them a chance to meet you. I know you'll be nervous, but it will be fine. I promise."

She was wringing her hands nervously, "Okay, if you say so. But I'm so scared." Maria reached over and patted her shoulder.

Jose raised his hand almost timidly, and said, "Mr. Adam, I am truly grateful for everything you have done for us already, and everything you have promised us this afternoon. Please do not think I am greedy, because I am not. But would it be possible to also have classes on money and credit cards? I do not understand what the credit card companies are telling me, and neither does my wife. We get confused when we write checks and when we get our checks back from the bank. Would that be possible?"

My heart really went out to him. "Jose, it will be an honor to have such classes. We will do that. I will ask your team to work with Barbara on this too, and to make a presentation to the executive staff. We have already agreed to do this, Jose, so don't worry. And our banker has already volunteered to lead that class. You could also ask for these classes to be open to family members, if there is enough room. We will say 'yes' to that also."

Then I turned to the entire team, and said, "The reason I want you to present to the executive staff is because I want everyone to see who you are and recognize your wonderful creativity and contributions. If I tell them the ideas, they do not see you. They will approve these ideas, because they are good ones. There is also another reason—when you present to the staff, you will learn about how to make presentations. I know you will be scared. I am scared too when I present to groups. That's okay. This will help you grow. And that's what Brookings is all about—growing our employees."

That closed the meeting. I was really proud of "my" people.

As I took Dennis to the airport, I asked, "So what do you think?"

"Adam, as I told the staff, I am truly impressed. You have done so much in such a short time, and with so few resources. And your answers during the team meetings were wonderful. You truly affirmed the worth of each individual and helped them not be afraid of being told 'no.'"

I dropped him off for his flight, and called Kelly as I was driving home. I was really missing her.

The next morning as I was walking the plant floor, Chet and Annie walked up to me at the same time, looking very concerned. My heart sank. Either of them could tell me just about anything, and they knew it. But when it took both of them, it couldn't be good. And it wasn't.

"Adam, we want to make a presentation to the executive staff," Chet said as he looked over at Annie. "Here's what we've found. Our process uses a chemical that is still legal, but is probably very, very bad. Best guess is it hurts humans two ways, through increased cancer rates and damaged reproductive capabilities. We try to follow the safety guidelines when using it, you know, in a well-ventilated area and not breathing the fumes, but that's not possible. So we want to replace it with an entirely different process. That will require capital investment and probably some significant engineering time as well. We're sorry, but this is what we have learned."

Damn! Just when things were stretched as tight as we could possibly handle . . . I thought and paused for a moment. "Chet, Annie, thanks for telling me. Yes, I'll call the staff meeting. And yes, I'll probably recommend we make the change, even though now is a very difficult time." What else could I say? I trusted them enough that if there were any other reasonable alternatives, they would have found them and recommended them. And if we put financial profitability before the health and safety of our workers and their children, even given our current financial status, what would that say about our values and the commitments we made during the off-site?

So we met that afternoon, the staff plus Annie and Chet. They presented their research and findings. The rest of the staff seemed to be thinking the same things I was—as much as we couldn't possibly do this right now, we couldn't afford *not* to do it even more, if that makes any sense. Tom, being our resident skeptic, suggested that Walter appoint an engineer to work with Annie and Chet to review their processes and look for any alternatives they might have missed, plus any holes in their logic. We would hear the engineer's report and make a final decision at our staff meeting a week from Monday. And, in the spirit of transparency, we would invite Chet and Annie to that part of the staff meeting.

Friday afternoon Kelly flew in and we spent the weekend at Mom's house, just being together. We were trying to figure out what kind of work she could do within decent commuting distance. Our wedding was still almost six months away, and those six months were looking longer every day.

CHAPTER 15

What's Good for the Goose . . .

After Nancy's questions about finding sustainable suppliers, it was time for me to hit the road again. This time I would be talking with our major suppliers to encourage them to start implementing sustainability themselves. So I had Nancy and Mary work up a presentation that explained what sustainability is, how it works, why they might be interested in trying it, and how they could get started. In the last section, I had them include Dennis' contact information as well as ours. We were committed to helping our suppliers succeed, just like we were committed to growing our employees. That's what relationship is all about. Nancy and I would be on this trip together; I would be meeting suppliers for the first time, and she would be talking to them about sustainability.

Since our travel would take us into the Boston area, I decided I would finish my trip there and take a couple of days to pack up the things I wanted from my condo, give the rest to the Salvation Army, and drive my car home. Dad's Chrysler 300m was a fine car, but I really preferred my Saab.

We set up an appointment with the VP of sales at each of the smaller suppliers, asking for the CEO to be there if at all possible. For the larger suppliers, we set it up with the person who managed our account, asking that the VP of sales and/or the CEO be there if at all possible. We left adequate time between appointments so we could present again to a more senior officer if the first person liked what they heard and the senior person was not in the initial meeting.

Nancy drove Kelly and me to the airport early Monday morning. We had the same flight to Chicago, where Kelly changed planes. Nancy and I deplaned, rented a car, and drove to meet our first supplier.

The first presentation, at PCBs Midwest, the supplier of our printed circuit boards, went reasonably well. (PCB in our industry stands for printed circuit board, a part used in many electronics products. In environmental circles, however, it stands for polychlorinated biphenyls, which are toxic chemicals. Context is everything with three-letter acronyms.) Beth, the VP of sales, and Stan, our account manager, met with us; the CEO was unavailable.

After the introductions and "thanks for coming," Nancy got right to the point. "Beth, Stan, my company is at a 25% cost disadvantage compared to our competition. We are trying to keep production in the U.S. instead of sending it to China. We started our Lean journey five years ago or we wouldn't be here today, but that's no longer enough. We have started implementing sustainability as a way to increase our competitiveness, and we need your help. We know we have a contract with pricing in place, and that it's good for another six months. However, we urgently request a 10% price reduction now, followed by another 10% in a year. We're willing to work with you to help you achieve that; we want you to keep your production here and remain profitable, too. Let me show you what we're doing, how we're doing it, and why we're doing it." She set up her laptop and projector while they brought us a second cup of coffee. Then she began the presentation.

Their reaction was almost predictable. It had basically the same acceptance pattern as our off-site, but in a very compressed time frame. First, they were polite, but listening. Then they were increasingly skeptical. Then their questions and uncertainties were vocalized.

"Why do you think this will work?"

"Business is all about making a profit—nothing else matters."

"It will cost too much."

"Our customers won't see any additional value."

"Our employees will try to run our business."

"That just isn't how our business operates."

"We've never done that before."

"Our accounting system won't permit this."

Etc., etc., etc.

Nancy nodded to me to help answer the questions. I had learned enough to use the Socratic approach to help them answer their questions on their own. After a while, they started doing it without my guidance. The more they poked, prodded, and probed, the more they convinced themselves to try it. Finally, they asked if we had a few minutes to meet with the CEO before we left. So we did. I briefed him on what my company had done and why, the results we had gotten so far, and what we were hoping to get. I told him what we had requested as far as price reductions. Then I encouraged him to listen to his VP and account manager. If they wanted, Nancy could come back in a couple of weeks to explain the concept of sustainability to their entire executive staff. We talked some more, and then he surprised me. "Adam, I'd like to invite you back to talk with the entire executive staff in two weeks, but I insist on at least paying your expenses. If this is half as good as you believe, we should be doing a lot more than that for you."

"We'll be glad to do that. But if you want to continue be-yond that, you should probably bring in Dennis and Karen or someone similar. We're not professional consultants; they are."

So that's how we left it.

We had a late afternoon appointment with our resin sup-plier in Des Plaines, right near the airport. They were polite but clearly uninterested. Maybe we shouldn't have been sur-prised—they were the industrial supply division of a gargan-tuan international oil company, one that was not at all interested in sustainability or the environment. Furthermore, our total annual sales revenue was less than their daily net profit, maybe even their *hourly* net profit! That night, Nancy e-mailed Mary the results of both meetings, saying that we would start looking for a resin supplier who was more cus-tomer-focused and sustainability-oriented. I remembered that BP (formerly known as British Petroleum) had broken ranks with the rest of the oil industry in 1997, pledging to reduce its greenhouse gas emissions.* Subsequently, the company started investing in alternative energy sources. Even if they couldn't give us a price break, they were making steps to-ward doing the right thing. So I encouraged Nancy to in-clude BP on her list of potential suppliers to call.

Monday night I had an e-mail from Dennis with our SCORE results attached. I replied that I would be out of town the rest of the week, and asked if he could talk us through the results by phone the following Tuesday at 11:00 our time. He replied that he could, so I had Marie set it up.

Tuesday, Wednesday, and Thursday went about the same way. About two thirds of our suppliers were interested and

---

* Arena, Christine. 2004. *Cause for Success: 10 Companies that Put Profits Second and Came in First.* Novato, CA: New World Library, p. 19.

supportive; the rest were merely polite. One thing surprised me: it wasn't the size of the supplier that mattered. It was purely their attitude toward new ideas. We got a very warm welcome from a supplier who was at least 20 times our size; not only did we get to see the senior VP of sales and marketing there, but the CEO himself spent 20 minutes with us; he seemed very interested in what we were saying. Nancy e-mailed Mary each evening with an assessment of the suppliers we had met with that day. Of course, I called Kelly every night as well.

When we flew into Boston Thursday evening I took a cab to my condo while Nancy grabbed a limo for a motel in Natick, close to our customer. It was good to get back, but it was no longer home. I had changed permanently, and I didn't want to go back to who I was before. The first thing I did was start my Saab and drive it through a car wash to remove four months of accumulated urban grime. When I got back, I started sorting stuff until I crashed for the night. Nancy and I completed our last appointment on Friday at noon. I drove her to the airport and then headed back to my condo to finish sorting and start packing.

Through my network of friends in Boston I had already selected a realtor to list my condo as soon as it was empty and presentable. So I met with her Friday night, signed the listing agreement, and gave her a key, which she put in the lockbox. I called the Salvation Army and the moving company; both were to be there Saturday morning. There was surprisingly little I actually wanted to move; the rest I was just happy to give to the Salvation Army so somebody else could use it. By 5 p.m. Saturday my condo was empty. I locked the door for the last time and drove over to Kevin's house.

My good friend Kevin Blount had invited me to crash at his place Saturday night. We went to Harvard Square then hit a night club or two. This was one more reminder of how much I had changed in the last four months. When I last lived in Boston, such a night would have been wonderful, the best. But now, with Brookings in the back of my mind all the time and Kelly at the forefront, all the entertainment, the music, street vendors, and everything else just seemed like noisy meaningless distractions. We left Harvard Square about 10 o'clock when it was just getting into its full rhythm, because I didn't feel like staying any longer. I wanted to get a good night's sleep and get up early so I could make it back home in one very long day.

I was up at 5:00 a.m., wide awake. Quickly showering and shaving, I was ready to leave at 5:30. I drove through the first toll booth on the Mass Pike with my Fast Lane transponder. I chose the New York Thruway on the advice of some friends—they said it would be easier than taking I-80 through Pennsylvania. I only stopped for food and gas or for five minutes at a rest stop when I needed to stretch. I called Marie at home Sunday afternoon when I crossed the Pennsylvania-Ohio border to let her know I would be at work Monday morning and asked her to tell Wayne and Tom. I got home late Sunday evening, surprising Mom because she did not expect me until the following morning.

I sensed something was up when I walked into the office Monday morning. Then I learned that Wayne, Tom, and Carl had scheduled a special staff meeting for 2:00 that afternoon to listen to four team presentations.

The Fixer-Upper Team (maintenance) presented the results of plugging the leaks in the compressed air system. Doing so allowed them to take our oldest electric motor off-line permanently, which was a nice reduction in electrical usage. The team members also worked with the other teams to stagger the start-up time for each of the pieces of equipment that drew major amounts of electricity to reduce our demand bill. Finally, the team explained how they insulated the plant and reduced the lighting—nice numbers! The financial payback on their total investment was three months; plugging the leaks and staggering start-up times basically paid for the insulation. My only question was why we didn't do this a few years earlier.

The Waste Busters presented a plan to start reducing our use of toxic chemicals. We unanimously approved the plan and asked them to keep moving forward as rapidly as possible. They also had a proposal to bring in the Zero Waste Alliance to identify products that included toxic chemicals. We approved that as well.

Serve Us presented a schedule for "The Boss Buys You Lunch." As an incentive for employees to meet with me, I would pay for their lunches. That was fine with me. They designated every Friday for those lunches, with six employees attending each Friday. My only concern was what would happen if I was on the road, because that's where I was starting to spend about half my time. When I mentioned that, Barbara had an interesting response, "Don't worry; we'll think of something."

Finally, the Classy Assy Team members presented their plans. They had busted their tails putting together a proposal for classes on English as a second language and personal finance. Wearing a suit and tie, Jose presented his team's proposal. Barbara had helped him contact the local community college and high schools. The cost was much less than I would have guessed. Barbara found a government program that would pay for most of the ESL instructor's time, and Ron Meeker had already volunteered to teach personal finance. Therefore, our cost was only for the workbooks for the participants. We enthusiastically approved the proposal;

he was beaming, and his team-mates, who were sitting around the edge of the room, burst into thunderous applause. Nikita presented her idea about volunteering in the local community. She and the team had thought things through very carefully, and designed the program so it would not impact our deliveries to our customers. Again, it was approved unanimously. She beamed! I swear she almost danced as she left the front of the room to go sit down.

Then came the meeting with Chet, Annie, and Beth, the engineer Walter assigned to look at the dangerous chemical. Beth said, "I'm glad I had a chance to review Chet and Annie's work. I was really impressed; they did a very thorough job. I couldn't find any holes in their logic, nor could I find any alternatives that would work. So, I have strong mixed emotions about this. On the one hand, I am proud and privileged to be working with such great people. On the other hand, this will cost well over $50,000 to implement, and I know how tight our cash flow is right now." She, Chet, and Annie looked at the rest of us expectantly.

Mary spoke first, "During the off-site, we all committed to doing the right thing, even when it hurt. Could we look at ourselves in the mirror if we turned this down now? Could we be proud of ourselves as a company? Could we ever dream big again? As much as I don't know how we'll do this financially, I think we have to. How can we tell our workers that they're important, and that their health and safety is important, if we don't start addressing this immediately?"

"The major reason we need to do this now is it's the right thing to do," echoed Tom. "There's one other consideration. I'm no lawyer, but I suspect that if we don't act on this now, we are opening ourselves up to potential liability if someone has a health issue in the future. I'm with Mary. All I ask is one week to work on the financing."

With that, the decision was basically made. We took a vote just for the record. It was unanimous. Chet walked around the room, shook each person's hand, and thanked them. Annie gave us each a big hug—hey, she was Annie, and that's just how she was. When she got to me, she said, "Thanks, Adam. This means more to me than you'll ever know."

As we were leaving the conference room, Barbara took me aside, and said, "I know we haven't been actively looking for a new VP of sales and marketing, but I recently became aware of a highly qualified candidate whom I think you should meet."

"That good, huh?" I said.

"Yes. Could you see her tomorrow morning at 10:00?" (I knew Barbara had already checked my schedule with Marie, so she knew I had the time available. She was just being her normal considerate self.)

"Sure. What's her name?" I asked.

"Oh, you'll find out at 10:00 tomorrow," and she smiled enigmatically.

Later in the afternoon I worked out the logistics for my West Coast supplier visits. I planned to leave Wednesday afternoon so I would be fresh for my first meeting in the LA area Thursday morning. We had three suppliers in southern California, and four more in the Bay Area. So I could fly to Portland early Friday afternoon and spend the weekend with Kelly.

Although I was dog tired, I had a little difficulty getting to sleep that night, wondering about the identity of the mystery candidate.

Precisely at 10:00 Tuesday morning, Marie came to my office door, and announced, "Your 10:00 is here."

I got up, walked around my desk, and then stopped and stared as Melanie Holland walked in. "Melanie!" I croaked.

"Yes, Adam, it's me."

"But why . . . what . . ." I was speechless. "I thought you'd moved to California with Jeff."

Smiling, Marie quietly closed the door as she left.

"I did, for a month. I couldn't take his dishonesty and back-stabbing anymore. So I started divorce proceedings and came back home; I'm living with my parents right now until I can find a job and a place of my own."

"But why are you applying to work here? Surely Jeff has told you all about us?"

"That's *exactly* why I'm applying to work at Brookings! It's because of what Jeff told me. I knew he was double-timing you for the last month or two before he left. It hurt me to watch, because Brookings had always treated him, and everyone else, very fairly. You know that he was doing everything he could to take as many of your customers with him. He bragged about losing requests for quotations, and even changing due dates on orders to cause customers to leave you. The more he talked about what he was doing, the worse I felt. And when he came home each night of that off-site, and started spouting about 'airy-fairy' management, and how soft you were as a CEO, and about how your 'woo-woo' consultants couldn't have run a 'real' business, I knew this was the type of company I wanted to work for. After he started with Electronic Products, he didn't get nearly as many customers to jump ship as he had told them he would. He was getting more and more angry; he couldn't understand how a customer could be loyal to Brookings when he could undercut your prices by 25%. After a month, I couldn't stand being around him anymore. So I called my parents, packed my things, and drove back. I filed for a divorce; he agreed to not contest it after I told him I knew a few things that would look very bad if they ever came out in court.

"I resigned from my old job when we moved to California, and they have already promoted an internal person to fill my position, so I don't have a job there to go back to. Given the choice, I'd rather work at Brookings anyhow. You're the best employer within a hundred-mile radius as I see it. Even before I left, you were the model employer in the area. And now that I've returned I've been having trouble believing what I've been hearing about what's going on here. You see, Barbara works out at the same health club, so I see her from time to time. When I got back two weeks ago, I happened to bump into her at the club, and she asked if I'd be interested in talking with you. I said something like, 'Are you kidding? I'd love to work there!' So she arranged this meeting. Adam, I want very much to work here. I want to work at Brookings, and nowhere else. Do you have any positions open? I'll even start in the factory or cafeteria if that's what's available."

"Melanie, we don't have any openings in the plant or cafeteria right now. But we do happen to have an opening for a highly qualified and experienced person in our sales and marketing department. Would you be interested?"

"Yes, I would. What do we do next?"

"I want to talk with Barbara and then with my staff. Since you trusted me enough to be completely honest with me, I want to be completely honest with you. The few times I met you I regretted that we hired Jeff and not you. I will be delighted to have you be part of our team here at Brookings."

"Thank you, Adam. You have no idea how much this means to me."

"You're welcome, Melanie. But I should be thanking you. It took courage to walk away from Jeff, and even more courage to meet with me this morning and tell me what you have told me. Give me your phone number; I'll be calling you within a day or so."

After she left, I just sat in my chair for several moments, letting the conversation soak in. I asked Marie to call a special staff meeting at 2:00 that afternoon; I could hear her smiling as she responded. I called Barbara and asked her to come see me. We worked out the details of what I hoped would be an attractive offer to Melanie. Then I called Mom and told her I wanted to meet her for lunch. It turns out she was already aware of Melanie's return and her discussions with Barbara. I'm beginning to suspect that part of a CEO's real job description reads: "The last person to find out what's really going on!"

I was still lost in thought when Marie reminded me, "Remember your 11:00 phone call with Dennis about SCORE?"

I swear, the title CEO should be renamed "CMO" (chief meeting officer) to conform to truth-in-labeling laws.

As the team arrived in the conference room I could sense their anticipation. Marie had passed out the printed copies of the report the previous day so people could review it and start formulating their questions. I had her tell each person to not talk about it to anyone until after the meeting, because if people misunderstood it, our sustainability implementation could be hurt.

Promptly at 11:00 we called Dennis. "Dennis, we're all here," I said.

"Good," he said. "Let's start. Let me talk you through the basic report first, then open up for questions."

What I didn't know until later is that Marie and Barbara had been working with Dennis for 15 minutes prior to the meeting, so he could use his computer in Oregon to project onto the screen in our conference room. It turns out having it set up that way really helped.

"In this chart (see Figure 15-1)," Dennis said, "Brookings is the lighter line on top; the benchmark of all companies who have used SCORE thus far is the dark line. Remember, two months ago you had zeros on almost all of these metrics. So you're making great progress. A one, by definition, means you're getting started, so that's what you would hope to achieve in many categories. So what do you notice about this data?"

Marie volunteered, "It looks like our two strongest areas are executive leadership, thanks to Adam, and also the sustainability coordinator position."

Tom chimed in, "Yeah, but it looks like my area is one of the worst."

Dennis nodded, "That's true, but that's not at all unusual. Changes often filter slowly into the formal management systems. When I look at the results, the one that pops out at me as a place to look is office operations. Often, there's low-hanging fruit to be picked there. Also, office practices often present low-risk opportunities to learn about how sustainable decision-making works in real life and the results are usually visible to everyone."

I jumped in, "I know top management got a pretty good score, but I still want to know what we need to do next to move us forward."

Dennis clicked forward in the presentation (see Figure 15-2). "Then let's review the Top Management group in detail, so we can look at the individual scores for each practice. What do you notice from this data?"

"Well," I said as I touched my chin, analyzing the chart. "We're strongest in Vision. But we got zeros on Transparency and Reporting. What were those again?"

Dennis pointed to the SCORE assessment. "Let's go back to the actual items associated with those two areas." He

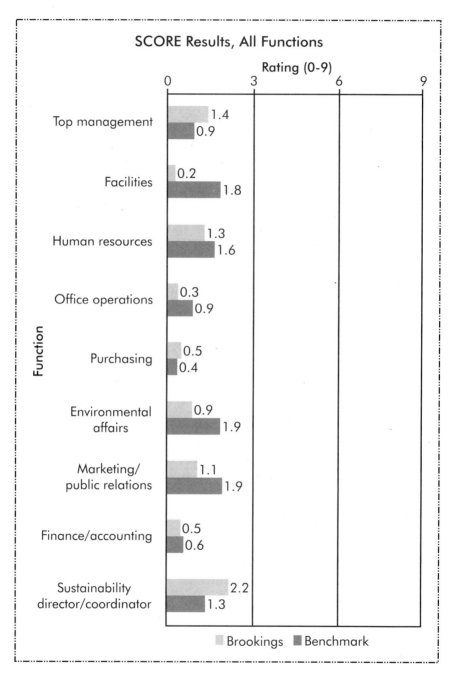

Figure 15-1.

The Squeeze

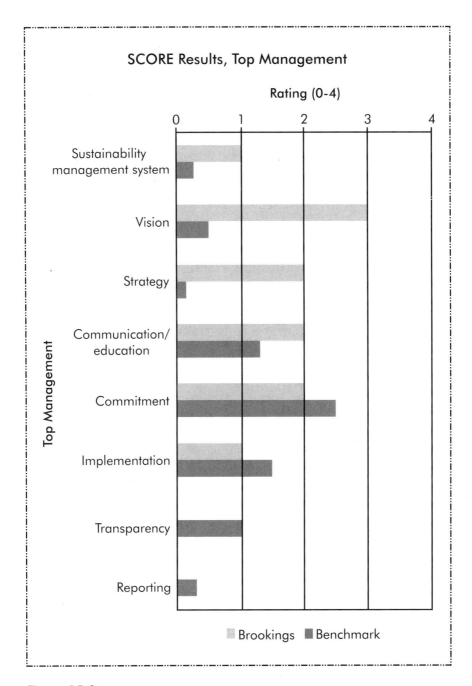

Figure 15-2.

fiddled with the computer until the chart shown in Table 15-1 came up.

He continued, "So to earn a one for Sustainability Reporting, you'd need to produce an internal report, which implies you have established goals, projects, and metrics."

"That sounds doable," I said, nodding my head.

"Notice, too," Dennis added, "that at the Initiative level, you'd make that information public and, eventually, to get a nine, have it consistent with international standards."

"What I love about this too," I commented, "is that it not only lets me know where we are now, but it gives us a great sense of what fully sustainable, or something close to it, looks like."

After we discussed the other categories, Dennis praised our progress. "You've made remarkable progress in a short time. My only concern is that you might try too much and burn yourselves out. Sustainability is a journey. Its pace

Table 15-1. Transparency and Reporting SCORE

Points	Practice	Incubator 1 Point	Initiative 3 Points	Integrated 9 Points
	Sustainability reporting: annually produce and review a sustainability report reflecting goals and progress.	Produce an internal document used by managers and employees that reports on goals, projects, and sustainability metrics.	Produce reports available to the public.	Produce reports that meet standards such as the Global Reporting Initiative or the Greenhouse Gas Protocol.

should be that of a marathon; it's not the 100-yard dash. Please slow down, smell the roses, and think of this as a long-term commitment."

After a quick lunch and some schmoozing with the people I saw in the cafeteria, it was time for the staff meeting to discuss hiring Melanie. Our fair city is small enough that the staff had each met Melanie at least once, and they had formed an overwhelmingly positive impression of her. I learned later that several of them secretly had the same thought as I— wishing that Melanie was our VP of sales and marketing, rather than Jeff. We knew she would need to learn about our products and capabilities. Our big concern was how she would handle competing directly against her former husband. So we decided to invite her to meet with all of us the next morning to talk that out and let her ask any questions she might want to ask.

When I called to ask her to meet with us, I said, "Melanie, we are in unanimous agreement that we would like you to be part of our team. But we need to talk through some issues that won't be particularly easy, and we thought you might have a few tough questions to ask us as well."

"Adam, that sounds wonderful," she said. "I appreciate your openness; I promise the same."

At 9:00 Wednesday morning, Marie brought Melanie into the conference room where we were waiting. I introduced everyone, because she hadn't met Carl before. I began, "Melanie, everyone in this room has said they would like you to be part of our team. So this is not a 'job interview,' per se. What we want to do today is creatively work through some potentially sticky issues. Are you okay with that?"

"Yes." She turned and slowly met each person's eyes for a moment. "As I told Adam yesterday, Brookings is the company I want to work for, no matter what position is available. And I promise to be totally open and honest in my answers."

I continued, "We have three major questions, and I'm sure we'll have some others as well. They are:

- How quickly can you come up to speed with our product line and our competitive capabilities? And, how quickly can you learn enough about our competitors' products to be able to sell our products and services effectively?

- How can you help us tighten our relationships with our existing customers?

- This one is the tough one. Will you be able to sell effectively and professionally against Jeff, who now works for our strongest competitor, and who knows and fully exploits every one of our weaknesses?"

Melanie responded, "Those are excellent questions. And I also have three questions. My biggest question is this: Will Brookings survive? My second is, can sustainability provide sufficient competitive advantage? My third question is, where is the leverage point for me to make the largest difference possible?"

And so we started. An hour later, we were all pretty wrung out, but we had reached consensus. Melanie would be starting the next Monday and would spend the first month learning our products and services (including spending a day or two on the plant floor watching products being made), interviewing several customers by phone and meeting our most important ones (all the large and medium customers, plus some small ones) face to face. We agreed it might make things easier if she reverted to her maiden name; that should avoid potential initial discomfort by customers. So her business cards would read "Melanie Fenstermacher." We assumed

Jeff would not want to tell our customers she was his former wife, because then he'd have to explain why she chose to leave him and start working for us. We couldn't think of any way he could use the separation from Melanie to his advantage; there was just no way for him to look good if the topic was brought up.

The meetings in LA followed the same pattern as the ones with Midwestern suppliers; two suppliers were interested, one was polite. Then I flew to Portland for the weekend, arriving at 3:30 p.m. Friday to Kelly's open arms. We went out to the Blue Moon on Northwest 21st for dinner and a brew or two, then down the street a couple of blocks to a pub that had live entertainment. I couldn't help contrasting this Friday night with the previous Saturday night in Harvard Square. Yes, Boston (and Cambridge) is a great place for young professionals. But Portland had Kelly, and that made all the difference in the world.

The weather for the weekend was forecast to be decent, so we drove to the coast Saturday morning. I couldn't believe the miles of broad sandy beach, almost completely empty. Cannon Beach was a quirky touristy town with interesting artists. We stopped at a couple of state parks and walked to the headlands—breathtaking! We stayed overnight in a motel at the ocean's edge. We kept the sliding door open so we could hear the surf. When we woke up Sunday, Kelly seemed pensive and withdrawn.

"What's wrong, Kelly?" I asked.

"Nothing . . ." she replied quietly, pursing her lips.

I didn't buy that, but decided not to press it. But her exuberance was gone, and by the time we got back to her condo early Sunday evening I had to ask again. "What's wrong, Kelly?"

"I can't do this," she replied, almost whispering.

I felt dread seeping into my bloodstream, but forced myself to remain calm. Fearing that she might want to call off our engagement, I asked, "Can't do what?"

"Oh, Adam!" and she turned and flung herself into my arms, sobbing. "I want to marry you so much. But the thought of leaving Oregon hurts so much!" She started crying softly into my shoulder. Finally, she got control of herself and said quietly, "This is where my soul sings. I need to be here."

Ahh, there was the rub. And I couldn't blame her. It wasn't just her friends, because she could make those anywhere. It was Oregon itself—the mountains, the coast, the lush Willamette Valley, the gentle weather, the extraordinarily polite people. I couldn't blame her at all. So I wasn't completely surprised when my mouth opened and I heard myself say, "Kelly, my love, just give me five years to get Brookings where it needs to be, then we'll move back here. Okay?" Brookings was important, and my mom was important, but my wife must come first.

The look she gave me would have won an Academy Award. Her eyes, filled with heart-wrenching sorrow, slowly became hopeful. "Really? You really mean that?" she said, sniffling.

"Yes. I can see why you love Oregon. I want to live here too. But I can't abandon Brookings right now."

"Ohh, Adam! I'm so glad!"

Each parting was becoming more difficult. Kelly and I truly belonged together. After I kissed her goodbye at the curb and got onto my flight to San Jose, I started thinking about who I might talk to back home about finding her a position. Halfway through the flight, I had an interesting idea. Since an internal person had been promoted in the marketing department to take Melanie's old position when she left, I wondered if that person's position was now available. So Monday noon I called Melanie to ask. I felt a little guilty asking her to help my fiancée move to be with me, considering she had just broken up with her husband. She promised to look into it soon; I think she heard in my voice how much I needed to have Kelly with me.

Two days, four supplier visits, and then I was on the red-eye back home. This time I couldn't take the extra time to spend with Kelly. When I got to the office Wednesday morning, I made the rounds and found Melanie wearing jeans and a t-shirt, working in the final assembly area. She seemed to be doing okay; Annie was grinning ear to ear as she watched. "She picked it up pretty quick," Annie said as she waved to Melanie. "She only watched for an hour or so, and then asked if she could help. So we let her. Good choice, Adam."

I sought out Chet to get his opinion about what was happening with people and their attitudes. "Adam, I wouldn't ever want to work anywhere else. Neither would anyone else. That's a fact. You have no idea how much we appreciate what you've done for us. Any time you need any of us for anything, and I mean *anything,* let me know. We'll be there," he said sincerely.

"Thanks, Chet. That's really good to hear. I'll take you up on that." Little did I know . . .

I had lunch with the employees on Thursday as a makeup for the previous Friday. The team had done a good job of mixing people from various areas. I dined with Val from accounting, Chet (the plant steward who worked in final assembly), Sara from engineering, Keith from the stockroom, Jim from quality, and Nora from injection molding. They seemed nervous; I was glad Chet was there because he wasn't afraid of me. He broke the ice, making the others feel easier. Then I asked them how things were going in their areas, and to tell me a little about themselves. The more I get to know people, the more impressed I am with their courage and love of children and family. I think that's why sustainability is so powerful.

Friday was basically a repeat of the Thursday lunch experience. That group opened up a little faster. I guess the word had gotten out that I was relatively harmless. Besides, what's not to like about a free lunch?

Friday afternoon I met with John again at his office. I don't remember what we talked about. All I know is I valued his perspective, because his primary motivation was for humans to develop as fully and completely as possible, rather than maximizing profits for some company. When I have two minutes to rub together, I want to talk with Mom about creating a board of advisers and I want him to be on it.

CHAPTER 16
First Glimmer of Hope

"Brookings—Miracle or Mirage?" was the headline of the front page feature article, by Liz Spinoza, in the business section of the Sunday *Chicago Tribune*. I had met Liz on my flight to Boston a few weeks earlier. She called and interviewed me on the phone. I gave her permission to talk with other employees, and she came out to the plant and talked with several people, both management and hourly. Her article told the Brookings story up to the present, including our current fight for survival given the price differential between our products and the competition. She had even called our largest customers and a couple of our key suppliers. She tried talking to our bank, but they would say nothing except to confirm they had a long-standing banking relationship with us. The article highlighted the off-site as a potential turning point, citing the new attitudes and programs arising from it.

When Liz asked to interview me, and then the staff, I had discussed it with the staff. Their questions surprised me; I was expecting questions like "Will this help us or hurt us competitively?" And, to be honest, those questions eventually did get asked and discussed. But the staff's initial questions made me feel selfish. They asked, "Will this encourage other companies to start adopting sustainability? Will this help make the world a better place for our grandchildren, and their grandchildren, to live?" As the staff started asking their questions, I knew the "right" answer to her request for interviews—the article would probably help make the world a better place for our grandchildren. It would probably encourage other companies to consider moving toward greater sustainability. So how could we decline?

Unexpectedly, the article started a small firestorm. I guess news was slow on that Sunday (not enough murders or burning buildings), because the Chicago CBS affiliate picked it up for the 11 o'clock news. CNN didn't want to be caught napping, so they started mentioning it. Our phone started ringing Monday morning at 7:00 (even though our office doesn't open until 8:00) with reporters requesting interviews, politicians trying to make political hay, professors wanting to talk, job-hunters looking for jobs . . . We had suddenly become a three-ring circus! Needless to say, all this hoopla was the major topic of conversation during our staff meeting that morning.

We selected the three reporters who seemed the most appropriate to grant interviews to. They were from the *Wall Street Journal,* CBS, and *Business Week.* We arranged for the interviews and gave them access to our plant for pictures of people (with the right to review all photos before publication to insure no proprietary information was visible). Melanie was in her element—creating press kits, and organizing tours and interviews.

But somehow, somewhere in the process of the CBS interviews, one of our people made an off-hand comment about our prior VP of sales and marketing, who was now working for the competition, and how Melanie was his ex-wife. CBS smelled a much more interesting story, so they called Jeff to interview him. In his defense, he didn't know why they were interested in him until he had a camera trained on his face and a mike stuck under his nose. When they asked him about his former wife working for Brookings, he lost it. What he called his former wife had to be bleeped by the censor, and what he said about us was perfect—a screed of half-truths and misinformation that couldn't stand up to the facts and interviews presented in the rest of the story. There was poetic justice seeing the "real" Jeff show his true colors on national TV. He had indeed fallen on his sword; his credibility in our industry was completely gone.

Kelly came out for the weekend again. I was disappointed when Melanie told me her former employer had no openings in the marketing department. They were eliminating one mid-level position instead of replacing the person who had moved into her slot. I told Kelly what I tried to do. She was glad I tried and said, "Something will work out. It always does."

The notoriety slowly dissipated. The good news from all the publicity was our existing customers were more solidly behind us, and other potential customers were starting to call us rather than waiting for us to call them. Understandably, our suppliers were quite pleased with the free publicity, all of it positive.

While we were working on reducing the toxic chemicals we used, the consultants from the Zero Waste Alliance held the first two meetings to identify products we purchased that contained toxics. Our list was larger, much larger, than I ever thought possible. Others were equally surprised. We encouraged the Fixer-Upper Team (maintenance) and the We Have Designs On You Team (engineering) to methodically reduce the use, and even the presence, of those products as quickly as they could. George had already categorized the chemicals we used as benign, marginal, and dangerous, and created a plan to start eliminating the most dangerous ones. That went well with what we had already seen from Chet and Annie. George even created a progress chart for the cafeteria, with three color-coded columns: green, yellow, and red. Each chemical in the red column had a brief explanation about where it was used and how we were trying to eliminate it.

The knowledge of persistent, bio-accumulative toxics (PBTs) kept haunting me. I wanted to have children with Kelly, and I wanted our children to be healthy. Call me selfish or call me sentimental, if you want. Every pound of toxics we quit using would be a pound of toxics that would not be manufactured, and that would not wind up in the environment where it could poison somebody. I was looking forward to completely ridding our plant of all toxics. I had shocked the staff once again when I said I wanted to be able to drink the water, or any liquid that we used, at any place in our facility. And I wanted to be able to breathe the air everywhere, without having to worry about poisoning myself. When we talked about that during our off-site, they thought I was making a point. Now they were beginning to think I might be serious. I was glad they were starting to think I was serious, because I was dead serious.

It was a Wednesday morning when Bob Moorehead, the purchasing agent at CME, our second largest customer, called. "Adam, do you have a couple of minutes to talk?"

"Bob, I'll always have time for you," I replied.

He began, "Before I get to the real reason I am calling, I want to say thanks again for the publicity. Our business has increased due to those articles, and we really appreciate it."

"You're very welcome. Ours is starting to pick up a little too, but when the articles mentioned the 25% cost difference, that didn't help us too much."

"Well, your business might be picking up a bit more, effective immediately," Bob said. "We're starting to design a new product line and would like you to be a major supplier for it. Could you spare your best designer for a few weeks to work on it with us?"

I was totally silent. I just sat there and looked at my wall. This was the kind of call I had dreamt about ever since I came back to Brookings. And here it was!

"Adam? Adam, are you there?" I finally heard Bob's voice in the handset.

"Yes, I'm here," I said excitedly. "That is such good news! I was a bit out of it for a moment. I'm back now. Of course we can have our best designer work with you, for as long as it takes."

"There's one catch, however. We want this to be a technological breakthrough, so we want exclusive rights to all the products you develop for us for the next five years," Bob added.

"That sounds okay, but I'll want to check with my executive staff," I said as I picked up a pen to write myself a note.

"I figured you would. When can you get me an answer?" he asked.

"By tomorrow morning, if not sooner," I said, putting down my pen.

"I'm looking forward to working together with you, Adam."

"Me too, Bob."

Ten minutes later I assembled the staff in the conference room. The mood swung from disbelieving to ecstatic and back. We talked through the exclusive rights request, and decided to counter with an offer of three years. But if they insisted on five, we could live with it. Walter said that either he or Beth should work with CME. Then he suggested that we send Beth, because she was plenty good enough to do what they needed, and it would give her an excellent chance to develop her design skills on cutting-edge technology. Yet another decision made to intentionally help an employee grow.

I called an all-plant meeting for that afternoon to tell everyone the good news. And I guess once good things start, they seem to multiply, at least for a while. One week later we received a second request, almost identical, from BayTech in Massachusetts. But I'm getting ahead of myself.

Thursday afternoon, the day after the CME call, Melanie walked into my office and closed the door. "Adam, you're aware that Christine, my right-hand marketing person, is in her eighth month of her pregnancy, right?"

"Uh huh," I said.

She elaborated, "This is their first child. She has told me several times she wants to stay at home and raise the baby full-time. After the first few months, she might be available for special projects, but nothing more; she wants to stay at home with her child for the next few years."

"Uh huh," I said again. (Did I sound brilliant or what?)

"I want to hire a replacement for her," Melanie continued.

"Sounds good," I replied without hesitation. "Talk to Barbara and let's see who she can find."

"I already did. We have a promising candidate coming in tomorrow. Could you meet with her at about 2 p.m.?" I was pleased with Melanie's leadership. After all, she was still a new employee and just learning the ropes.

"Sure. Do I know her?" I asked. Melanie was already standing up and headed out the door without answering me. She must not have heard my question.

I didn't think anything more about it until Melanie knocked on my door the next afternoon at 2:00 sharp. I rose and started walking to the door to see the candidate, and then just stopped and stared. It was Kelly. She started walking toward me, faster and faster. She then launched herself into my arms. Melanie cleared her throat after far too short a kiss. "I take it you have already met the candidate, then?" she asked with a huge smile on her face.

"Yes, we've met before," I answered, as I held Kelly some more. "Melanie, can you stay and talk about this?"

"Yes, I'd be happy to," she said.

"Marie," I called through the door, "please call Barbara and have her come to my office."

"Yes, Adam," replied Marie. I could hear her smile in her voice.

When Barbara arrived, we sat down at the conference table in my office. I blurted out, "As much as this would be a dream come true, I don't know if we can do this." I could see everyone's mouth drop.

"Why not?" asked Barbara.

"Because Kelly and I are engaged, and in four months we will be married. Doesn't the company have a policy against this?"

"No," said Barbara. "In fact, we have a married couple working here. Remember Ramon and Maria—he is in shipping and she works in assembly."

"You're right. I'd forgotten." I was deep in thought for a moment.

Finally I said, "Wouldn't this cause people to be worried about favoritism? Melanie, could you manage Kelly effectively? Could you give her honest criticism and constructive feedback when required, without worrying how it might affect your own job?"

"Yes, Adam," Melanie replied. "First off, I know Kelly is a consummate professional. She would not come to you if I criticized her; we would work it out between us. Second, you are too fair, and too honest, to let that happen for long. The fact you're even thinking about it says there is only a small risk, and we can live with that."

Melanie added, "And I've talked with her for a few weeks now trying to help her move here ever since you asked if my old company had a position open. She is well qualified for the position, more so than any of the other candidates I've seen. So it comes down to this. If she weren't your fiancée, would we be hiring her? As the hiring manager, I say, absolutely 'yes!'"

"As HR director, I say absolutely 'yes!'" added Barbara.

"I guess we need to do the right thing, then, and ask if she'll start working here two weeks from Monday," I said, smiling at Kelly all the while. She leaned over and kissed me to seal the deal.

Barbara smiled, "I think our candidate has said 'yes,' Melanie. Let's leave so we can finish getting the paperwork ready." Then, looking at us impishly, she asked, "Adam, do you know where we might be able to reach the candidate this weekend to give her our official offer letter?" And she started laughing as she got up and walked out the door, Melanie following close behind her.

When we finally came up for air, Kelly called her boss and gave her two weeks notice.

The weekend was glorious. We talked about her move and agreed she would have movers pack her things and move them into storage here. She could live at Mom's house until we found a place. She wanted to keep her Miata, so she was going to drive it from Portland, leaving on Friday afternoon in two weeks, and arriving as soon as she could. Somehow, the idea of a road trip with my fiancée sounded appealing, so I said I'd be glad to fly to Portland and drive out with her. She liked the idea. Kissing her goodbye at the airport wasn't nearly as difficult, because I knew that in two weeks we would be together for good.

The future of Brookings was looking brighter—the financial situation had stabilized and actually improved to breakeven. And, we hadn't needed to use as much of the credit line as we had expected. Of course, we still prepared the monthly reports for the bank.

Our teams were cranking. They settled back into more of a marathon pace compared to the sprint they were on the first couple of weeks. The English and financial planning classes started; they were both hugely successful. Equally important, we were improving on most metrics across the board. Raw resource usage was dropping—the amount of purchased materials, water, and electricity, were all less than ever before when measured against units of output.

Mom and I had several more long conversations about ownership. We agreed to our earlier design that she would keep her 51% of the shares for the time being; I would keep 39% and give 10% of my shares to a pool that would be disbursed throughout the year as bonuses for exceptional merit. I also suggested we consider slowly moving toward having the employees own the majority of the voting shares in the company over a five- or ten-year period. She agreed. We discussed the fact that after she started selling her shares to employees, she would no longer own a majority of the shares. Therefore, in the event she and I disagreed, the employee-owned shares would be the swing vote. Taking this into consideration, we decided to keep her the majority shareholder for the next year at least.

The EPA visited again to see how we were progressing. The representatives were impressed and said they'd like to visit on a quarterly basis as appreciators, not as auditors. We liked the sound of that phrase.

At our Monday staff meeting a week after Kelly's surprise visit, we decided to review where we were against our original metrics.

Financial:

- Sales revenues were improving slowly with a ways to go.
- Operating profits, as a percentage of revenue were increasing; we were back in the black.
  - Material costs were reducing with a ways to go.

Environmental:

- We were reducing environmental impact.
  - Energy efficiency: total energy used per pound of product shipped had been reduced by 10% with still more to go.
  - Toxic free: total listed (toxic) pounds used—we were moving in the right direction with phasing out toxic chemicals and with CARS, but there was still a long way to go.
  - We were in complete compliance with all regulations: no findings—the EPA wanted to appreciate us rather than audit us—a big win!
- Redesigned products for take-back—this project had started nicely. Customers wanted us to help them design their products; we were including take-back ideas with their designs, too.

Social:

- To be ranked in *Fortune* magazine's "100 Best Companies to Work For"—we would apply for this next year, and to our state's "100 Best Companies to Work For" too.
- Community outreach—teaching the community about sustainability—still needed to do this.
  - We were offering additional classes for employees and the community to improve their lives—a huge success.

Wayne suggested that we post the metrics and our achievements to date in the cafeteria. Of course!—sometimes the obvious is so obvious we can't see it. We also made sure each team would have a small area to post its goals and progress so everyone could see them.

Life was getting better all the time. I ate lunch with a group of employees again on Thursday, because Friday morning I was flying out to drive back with Kelly as she moved here permanently (until we move to Oregon in five years).

I was at the airport in plenty of time for my 6:00 a.m. flight to Chicago, with connection to Portland. Given the time changes, I would be in Portland at about 10:00 a.m.

Kelly had decided to retain ownership of her condo and lease it. She already had a tenant signed. When she finished packing Thursday night, she left a key with her best friend so the movers could come on Saturday and pick everything up. She had already shipped four boxes of clothes to my house a week earlier, so she would have enough to wear until the movers arrived.

Since this was Kelly's last day of work, we weren't sure what time she'd be leaving her company. It turned out that her co-workers wanted to take her to lunch; they even invited me along!

Right after lunch, she said her final goodbyes, then we headed east on I-84, up through the Columbia Gorge. We took the extra time to drive up to Crown Point and take pictures, then to Multnomah Falls to do the same. The pictures would have to hold us over until we could return. Then we just cut loose. Friday night we were in Boise. We made Cheyenne the next evening after 12 more hours. I loved her Miata, but it seemed to be getting smaller as the trip progressed. We spent Sunday night in the Quad Cities on the Iowa side of the Mississippi River. We arrived at Mom's house Monday at 3:00 p.m. with our bottoms quivering from the constant vibration of the car. We had made it; we were together at last.

During the trip I learned the depth of her understanding and commitment to sustainability. She had been reading a lot in the prior months. To minimize our footprint, she wanted us to have a house that used zero net energy, minimal water, etc. She wanted us to use a car as little as possible. And she wanted us to use organic products wherever we could. She wanted us to educate others and encourage them to do the same. And she wanted to start a sustainability book discussion group at work, and maybe another one at church.

Tuesday morning we were at the office at 8:00. It felt odd, but so right, walking into work with Kelly's arm around mine. The staff had postponed the weekly staff meeting until Tuesday morning. Tuesday I took Kelly out to lunch, just because we could do that. It was so nice having her here and being with her all the time. I was rapidly getting used to this, and I was enjoying every minute.

And then things changed . . .

CHAPTER 17
All's Fair in Love and War

On Thursday Melanie got a terse e-mail from SVE, our largest customer (the one who had finally agreed to the 10% reduction this year and 10% next year, instead of 20% immediately). It stated that Jessica Gomez had been transferred; another purchasing agent named Hector Lopez was going to be our point of contact.

Friday we got an e-mail from Hector with the ultimatum to match Electronic Products' price immediately (which was now 25% lower than our 10% lower), or they would change suppliers. Melanie tried to call him, but he was not available. I tried to call him, but he was not available. Things looked bad.

We called a quick staff meeting, but we couldn't take an additional 25% off just like that, so we e-mailed him back that we would like to talk with him. There was no response.

Friday afternoon I met with John. "What do I do?" I asked him after I briefed him on the situation.

"Are you having trouble believing that things will work out well?" he asked with a concerned look.

"Yes," I replied.

"Let's remember what has happened since I first met you. The first time we met, you had no idea how to keep the company going. You could only see the death spiral you were in, and you needed a miracle. Is that correct?"

"Yes," I said again, slowly nodding.

"You got your first miracle during the weekend off-site. Have there been others?" he asked, already knowing my answer.

"Yes." Again, I felt like I was being led . . .

"What were they?" he persisted gently.

"Getting engaged to Kelly, who I thought I was losing as a friend. Melanie showing up on our doorstep—and her hiring Kelly so we didn't have to be apart any longer. The phone call I received from Bob Moorehead, who asked us to partner with them in a cutting-edge new product, and then receiving a similar call from BayTech. The level of creativity and excitement sustainability has caused, which permeates our entire company. The article published in the *Chicago Tribune*, which caused coverage in the *Wall Street Journal*, CBS, and *Business Week*."

"So if you were looking at these last few months completely objectively, how would you define them?" John asked, trying to stifle a grin that was twitching in the corners of his mouth.

"As one miracle after another," I said, looking back at him with awe. "Thanks, I needed that."

"So what would be the highest and best way to continue from here? What would you be proud of as an outcome?" he asked.

"Continue to treat others with respect. Hold them to the highest standards of conduct," I said, thinking out loud.

"Yes . . . absolutely," he affirmed.

"So the Golden Rule doesn't mean I have to be a doormat, does it?" I said, as the implications of that comment sank in.

"It doesn't mean that at all. Loving someone does not mean you have to let them treat you poorly. In fact, it sometimes means the opposite—that you have to hold them to a higher standard than they hold themselves to. That's one way of helping somebody grow. Loving other people is the underlying element in all faith traditions. And one working definition of love is helping the other person live up to their potential. This implies helping them learn to love others as well, to help them in the same way."

"Thanks. I'll see you Sunday," I said with a broad smile as I got up to leave.

"See you then," John replied cheerfully.

Saturday, Kelly and I met with Madeleine, the realtor I had called Tuesday morning. We talked about our hopes and dreams, and looked through various listings, discussing resale values, school districts, and the like. Here I was, not even married, and I was starting to get interested in school districts. Hmmmm.

Sunday Kelly sat beside me in church, with Mom on her other side. She looked so comfortable between us. Kelly knew she belonged right where she was. Sunday afternoon Madeleine showed us some houses. As we drove around, Kelly mused, "They just don't get it, do they?"

"Get what, Kelly?" asked Madeleine.

"Look at these houses. They're not designed to minimize energy use. In Portland, there are houses that use zero net electricity per year with no other heat source. The way these houses here are designed assumes energy will remain plentiful and cheap."

"I'd never thought of that, Kelly," Madeleine responded.

"Adam," Kelly said. "Let's quit looking at conventional homes to buy. Let's either rent for a year or stay with your mom and build a home that is truly energy-efficient and environmentally sensitive. I'll bet anything that when we decide to sell it, it will be worth a lot more than any conventional home costing the same today, because it will use a lot less energy."

I replied with a smile, "Sounds good to me. Madeleine, instead of looking at houses, let's start looking at building lots." So we made an appointment to do that the next weekend.

Monday at noon we got an e-mail from Hector stating that since we did not meet his conditions, we should not ship any more product, effective immediately. Something smelled rotten. I called the director of purchasing at SVE and got her voice mail. I called the CEO and got his voice mail.

I called an all-plant meeting and gave them a brief rundown on the situation. It felt like a wake; this had the potential to kill us financially, and it was already doing a number on our morale. I told everyone, "I know this hits us hard, just when we're starting to gain ground. I smell a rat, and I'm going to keep working on this until we know what's really going on. Keep doing your best; we'll overcome this just like we have overcome all the other obstacles. Remember where we were a few months ago—we didn't know how we were going to survive. Remember all the improvements we've made—the dumpster diving, the energy savings, the toxic chemicals reduction, the classes in English and personal finances, and sharing financial information. Remember the articles and TV coverage. Remember that CME and BayTech, our other two largest customers, have called on us to help design new parts. Remember how our suppliers and bank have supported us. We're going to make it through this, too.

We have too many people who want us to succeed." (And I silently thanked John Franklin for the meeting on Friday, which provided the foundation for what I was saying now.)

Tuesday morning when I got to work I had an e-mail from Jessica, from her home e-mail address. She asked me to call her at 7:00 that evening and gave me her home phone number.

I called her at 7:00 on the dot, her time, 10:00 mine. She seemed nervous when she answered. The first words she said were, "Adam, if anybody finds out I talked with you, I'll lose my job."

"You have my word, Jessica. You're safe. I know it's nothing you could do anything about, but what's going on?"

"I disliked Jeff before, but now I despise him!" she said vehemently. "He is a back-stabbing, arrogant, self-centered bully! He kept putting pressure on me to dump you and switch to Electronic Products. I refused. He threatened my job. I told him to try, that I wasn't worried. Then I got demoted; I'm now in the lowest position possible in our purchasing department. I'd always gotten excellent performance reviews, now this. Jeff's last words to me were, 'Be thankful that I'm a nice guy; you still have your job.' Jeff said something once about being tied in with a member of the board of directors of our parent company, Advanced Electronics Holdings, in New York. I don't know how he's tied in, though."

"Jessica, I am so sorry Jeff has dragged you through this. I take it that Hector is following Jeff's orders?" I said with a slight sigh.

"Yeah, Jeff made sure everyone in the purchasing department knew he had the director's ear," she said disconcertedly.

"What about the CEO?" I asked.

"I don't know—the director is a very powerful man. Whatever he says goes in our company." I could sense the resignation in her voice.

"Can you give me the director's name?" I asked persistently.

"The one I think Jeff is tied to is George VanderMoelen. Jeff mentioned George a couple of times while he was threatening me. But be careful, Adam."

"Jessica, thanks for risking your neck for us. I'll make sure nobody ever hears about this phone call until Jeff is neutralized and George is gone."

Oh, boy! Now what? I told Kelly what I learned and we talked about it. I realized I needed to talk to our friendly bankers (about the fact that we would be using more of our line of credit, and why) and our attorney, not necessarily in that order.

Wednesday morning I called Harvey Smith, our company attorney, and asked to meet with him as quickly as possible. He could make some time available at 3:00 that afternoon, so I made the appointment. I called Ron at the bank and asked to speak with him and Jim at 2:30, since the bank was only a couple of blocks from Harvey's office.

I thanked Ron and Jim for meeting with me on such short notice. I began, "The short version is, we're being shafted by the guy who used to be our VP of sales and marketing, Jeff Holland. Here's what I know so far . . ." and then I briefed them on what I had learned from Melanie and Jessica. "I'm meeting with our attorney at 3:00, but I wanted you to know that we'll be needing more of that line of credit than we were anticipating. I'm glad it's there."

Jim replied, "Adam, we have complete faith in you and your company. We'll help you any way we can. Go talk to

Harvey and figure out how to nail Jeff's small family attributes to the wall."

The conversation with Harvey was interesting, to say the least. We talked about bringing the district attorney in, but chose not to start with that. Our initial salvo would be a letter from Harvey to the president of SVE stating that our contract could not be unilaterally cancelled, and that we would continue to ship product per the terms of the contract until it was completed. That would give us six months. "I'm still worried, though," I said.

"Why?" Harvey asked.

"Because they'll figure out some way to nullify the contract anyway, or to hurt us in other ways if we keep shipping. For example, they could claim that our products fall outside specifications. We all know that we meet specifications, but they could claim otherwise and cost us lots of time and money to prove that we're within them."

"I know, but I still think this is the best way to start. It tells them that you're not going to let them walk all over you."

"Okay, but what will we do about that corrupt director? How do we get to Jeff?" I asked.

"Let me work on that; I'll get back to you after I consult one of my friends in California. I have a couple of ideas, but I need to clarify how things work out there. Eventually, we will go after Jeff, probably by suing Electronic Products for the actions he has taken while in their employment. I want to let everyone know what a scumbag he is, so that no reputable company will hire him. That will leave him working for the kind of company he deserves," he said with a feral grin. "Remember how he looked on national TV a couple of weeks ago? He's already dug his own grave."

"In the interim," he warned, "be a little extra cautious—you, Kelly, Melanie, and your mom, too. Somebody as hateful and unprincipled as he seems to be might also try something else, including physical violence."

"Damn. I hadn't even thought of that. Thanks."

So when I got back to the plant I found Chet. "You know your offer to help me, any way, any time, any place?" I asked.

"Yes, and I meant it, too," he replied.

"Well, here's the deal. Jeff Holland is trying to ruin our company by doing illegal things with our largest customer. He got the purchasing agent demoted and they're trying to cancel our contract, effective immediately. They can't do that legally, of course, but they're trying. Anyhow, I'm just a little concerned that he might hire somebody to try some physical intimidation or actual violence against me, Melanie, Kelly, or my mom. Can you put the word out to your friends to let you know if they hear of anything? And I'd appreciate it if you and your friends would sort of watch our comings and goings, just in case somebody tries something."

"Adam, we'll do that. You can count on us to watch your back," he assured me.

"Thanks, Chet." I felt better. Yes, business really is all about relationship. If we were in it just for the money, could I have asked this favor to keep me and my loved ones safe? Probably not. And he wouldn't have even made the original offer of helping me any time, any place, any way.

Thursday I was talking to Carl about our sustainability journey. He said that one of the teams had come up with an idea for a visual presentation of our overall sustainability status. They wanted to use a spider diagram. He showed me a rough sketch of it (see Figure 17-1).

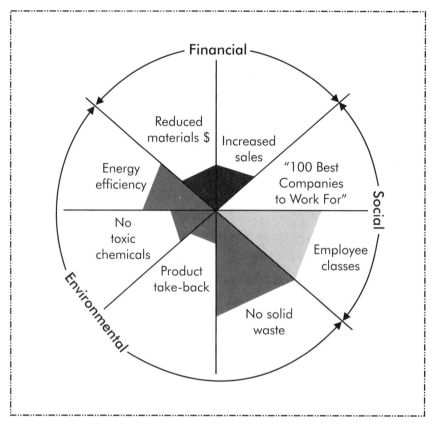

Figure 17-1.

Thursday afternoon I called Dennis to let him know about SVE. He promised to use his network to help find out what was going on with VanderMoelen. Then he asked another Socratic question, "He's on the board of the corporate parent, right? Do they have an ethics committee? Wouldn't their auditors be interested in this type of behavior?" Given the recent lapses of ethics in corporate America, there is no way an auditor could walk away from investigating something like this. Ahh, leverage, sweet leverage . . .

The following Monday at our staff meeting, Carl asked if Nancy could join us. When she arrived, she announced, "A couple of our key suppliers are now starting their own sustainability programs. We expect more to start in the near future. They're grateful to you, Adam, for visiting them and talking to them about it. The first two are asking if they can visit our plant and talk with some of the people on our teams." The staff's agreement was instantaneous and unanimous.

I suggested, "If more than one wants to visit on the same day, and as long as they're not competing with one other, perhaps we all can use it as a learning experience. Should we have a 'supplier sustainability day' once a quarter?"

Nancy replied, "Hmm, we could present our progress, disappointments, and current challenges in the morning session, conduct a plant tour just before lunch, and then have open discussion on whatever people want to talk about in the afternoon, like reducing packaging, or redesigning for take-back, or finding federal or state programs to help fund sustainability initiatives. And we could make sure suppliers can talk directly with whomever they want inside our company."

"Sounds good," said Wayne.

"Could you put the first one together for a month from now?" asked Mary, our VP of materials and logistics.

"I think that should give me enough time. I'll start on it today and let you know," Nancy replied.

The rest of the week was routine . . . not uneventful, but routine. Until Thursday morning, that is, when Chet came into my office. He had a somewhat grim look on his face. "I have some friends who heard that a person from out of town was looking to have you 'learn a lesson in humility,' as they so politely put it."

"Yes, and?" I asked.

"My friends passed the word back that anybody who tried to do that would find themselves very unwelcome around here, or anywhere else. We also said that if anyone wanted to teach you a lesson, they would have to teach us first. We told them what you're trying to do here and how much we appreciate it. Our message will reach the proper ears; you shouldn't have to worry anymore."

"Chet, I owe you one, a huge one . . ."

"No, you don't, Adam. We're just glad to have a chance to help you after all you've done for us, and our company, and the community. Understood?"

"Understood, Chet," I acknowledged and he left.

I received an e-mail from Herbert Walker, the CEO of SVE, Friday morning, requesting to talk with me on the phone at 2:00 that afternoon. The conversation was rather interesting. After the initial greeting, Herbert got right to the point.

"I understand you received some e-mails recently from Hector Lopez insisting that you reduce your price by 25%, and when you did not, he tried to unilaterally terminate your contract. Is that correct?"

"Yes, that's correct," I replied.

"This is after you voluntarily gave us back 10% a couple of months ago, even when you had a valid contract. Correct?"

"Yes, that's correct," I said again.

"And your contract runs for six more months?" he asked.

"Yes, your company signed a one-year contract with Brookings approximately six months ago."

"Adam, I apologize," Herbert said sincerely. "I was not aware at the time, but one of your competitors started pulling levers inside my company. We have taken care of that situation. Jessica Lopez has been reinstated as your purchasing agent. Your contract will continue as it always has. We have started an internal investigation to find out how this occurred so it will not happen again. We have also informed that competitor that they are no longer welcome to be a supplier to us or to any of our sister companies under our corporate umbrella. Is this acceptable to you?"

"Thank you, Herbert. That's great news for us," I said with a silent sigh of relief.

"I would hope that news of this unfortunate incident would not become public knowledge," he requested.

"We have told as few people as possible on this end. I will make sure each person is informed of the fact that the matter is resolved to our complete satisfaction," I replied.

"Thank you. I understand you're trying to help companies become more competitive by using this sustainability stuff?" Herbert inquired.

"That's correct. Would you like to know more?" I offered.

"When you're in the area again, I'd like to invite you to make a presentation to my executive staff. As you know, this area is pretty environmentally and socially conscious anyway, and sustainability would fit the culture out here. I think it's time we started moving in that direction."

"I'd be delighted to," I said, smiling.

"Great. Any chance it will be within a month?" he asked.

"I'll make sure it is."

"Have a good day, Adam."

"You too, Herbert, thanks for the call. And thanks for making things right." I quietly returned the receiver to its cradle before joyfully jumping out of my chair—I couldn't contain my excitement—we had won! *YES*!!!

What a great way to start a weekend. I called a quick all-employee meeting to tell them the good news. Then I called Harvey, Jim, and Ron to tell them. Finally, I called John; I thought this news might brighten up his weekend as well.

CHAPTER 18
Pleasant Surprise

We spent the weekend in South Bend with Kelly's parents; she with her mom, focused on the wedding, and me with her dad, Michael, and her brother, Danny, who had come home for the weekend too. Danny lived in an apartment near Notre Dame, where he was completing his senior year in English. I told Michael and Danny of the most recent events at Brookings Manufacturing. While I was telling the story, I felt like I was reading part of the script of *The Godfather*. Danny concluded that English was sounding more and more interesting all the time. Michael was, of course, worried about Kelly and to some extent me. I assured him I thought we'd be fine from here on out.

Monday's staff meeting was upbeat to say the least. We were confident we had finally turned the corner. I started making plans to visit SVE in two weeks. I wanted Melanie along so she could establish face-to-face contact with the CEO and executive staff of our largest customer. I was also inviting Kelly along; we would pay for her plane fare out of our own pockets. I had always wanted to spend time with her in San Francisco because it is such a great place. So I was planning on flying out Thursday, meeting with SVE Friday morning and Quark Friday afternoon, then spending Saturday and Sunday sightseeing with Kelly, and flying back Monday. Melanie would go out earlier in the week to meet other customers face-to-face.

Tuesday morning we got a fax from the second largest electronics manufacturing firm in Europe. They had heard about us due to the article in the *Wall Street Journal*. The company's engineers were interested in talking with us about designing and building a substantial component for a new machine they were building so they could leapfrog the competition. They were selecting us because of our work on sustainability, which was more important in Europe than the U.S. I planned to fly to Europe with Walter to negotiate the deal. I invited Kelly along, at our own expense of course, to spend a couple of extra days sightseeing.

It was looking like we would have to hire another design engineer. Luckily, between Walter's connections, our leadership in sustainability, and our reputation for being a great place to work, we seemed to be having a much easier time enticing highly qualified candidates to come to work for Brookings. In the past, our location in a small city in the upper Midwest was a major drawback, and we hadn't had any powerful attractors to offset that.

Two weeks later, Melanie, Kelly, and I were flying to California to present the concepts and practices of sustainability to SVE's executive staff. I had Melanie lead the presentation so she would be seen by them as our primary contact. That's why we had hired her. She did a superb job. Not only highly professional, she was clearly enthusiastic about what sustainability meant to Brookings, to our community, to our customers and suppliers, and to her personally. She started, "Sustainability is about making decisions considering not only finances, but social and moral/ethical issues. Luckily, instead of being in conflict, these powerful forces are completely aligned. Ten years from now, companies that have not adopted sustainability will be relatively scarce, because most of those who resist doing so will be out of business. It is not only our duty to our shareholders, it is our duty to our communities, our families, and ourselves to implement sustainable practices as quickly as we possibly can.

"The opposite of sustainability is remorse; remorse that lasts for the rest of your life. It is looking in your son's or daughter's eyes 20 years from now, and trying to answer the question. 'Dad, didn't you know what was going on? Why didn't you *do* something about it when you could?'

"What is sustainability? We have lots of definitions, but the one that works for me is embracing the three Rs: respect, relationship, and responsibility. It is about respect for each other, respect for our earth, and respect for future generations. It is about relationships with one other, and relationship with future generations. And it is about responsibility—responsibility to do something. It is thinking of ourselves as stewards, in a long line of stewards. Each prior generation until now has tried to make life better for their children. How can we do any different?

"If we want to leave a decent world for our children to live in, how can we continue to create and use toxic chemicals, especially when we are now learning that they show up in our bodies? If we want to leave a decent world for our children to live in, how can we poison the air and water, and use up natural resources so that there are none left? If we want to leave a decent world for our children to live in, how can we throw away all those precious materials, to be mixed into landfills where they are rendered toxic and useless for future generations?"

Melanie started clicking through the slides. She showed the definitions slide, the dwindling resources/increasing demand slide, the financial rewards slide, and the toxics release inventory slide. Then the slide about breast milk appeared on the screen. She looked at each person slowly, and said softly, "I plan to have children in a few years. When I do, I will be poisoning my baby every time I feed her . . . poisoning my baby (and she cradled her imaginary baby in her arms, looking at her) . . . every time . . . I feed . . . her . . ." and she sat down, weeping silently. There was not a dry eye in the room.

After a little bit she stood up and said quietly, with intensity, "We're not asking you to stop being profitable. We're asking you to stop poisoning your children and ours, your grandchildren and ours. Is that too much to ask? And we're asking you to leave some resources for them to live on. Is that too much to ask?"

There was complete silence . . . stunned, uncomfortable silence.

Melanie looked around the room slowly and said, "That was not a rhetorical question. How many people in this room are willing to stop poisoning your children and mine? I need to see hands."

Hesitantly, one hand raised, then two, then more, until all hands were finally raised. "Look around you. This is your commitment to each other. Hands down now, and get ready for the second question. How many of you are willing to leave some resources for your children and their children, so they can have full, rich lives? I need to see hands again."

This time, all hands went up immediately.

Finally, she asked, "And how many of you are willing to treat other human beings with respect, including your employees, your communities, your customers, and your suppliers?"

Again, all hands went up.

"Good," she said. "You have just declared your intent to have your company become sustainable. Actually, sustainability is very simple. If something you're doing will harm people or the earth, find a way that won't. In practice, it can get a little more interesting, but it's not really that difficult, as long as you make decisions using the Triple Bottom Line: profits *and* people *and* planet.

"And I can tell you that at Brookings, as at most companies who implement sustainability, it has actually improved our financial bottom line. It turns out that as we looked at the environmental side, we found we were wasting energy and materials, even though we had been on our Lean journey for five years. As we reduced the waste, our costs started coming down.

"More importantly, the people in our company are now more creative, more passionate, and more committed to the company and each other than they ever were before, including when we started Lean. To get personal for a minute, after I heard what Brookings was doing, I walked into Adam's office and asked to be hired into any position they had available, including the assembly line or the kitchen. And now I wouldn't consider changing companies even for a large increase in pay. There is no way I could work for a company that is not moving rapidly toward sustainability. It's pretty easy to understand when you think about it.

"Let's consider two scenarios. In scenario one, employees are told to use all their creative energies so the owners can make lots of money, and to ignore the possible effects on the health of their own families and their workers and communities. In scenario two, employees are invited to use all their creative energies so their children and communities will be healthier and better places to live.

"At the risk of stating the obvious, which company will be more successful in engaging the creative energies of their workforce? *That* is the power behind sustainability. This has major ramifications for all businesses, because once companies start their sustainability journey, they want to partner with other companies that have the same values. So they will start eliminating suppliers, and even customers, who continue to operate in the traditional 'take-make-waste' mold. It won't happen overnight, but it will happen. In fact, in our strategic off-site where we embraced sustainability, we identified one customer and three suppliers whose values were antithetical to ours. We have stopped doing business with them.

"Wall Street has already figured this out. A company that is socially responsible carries a market premium over a conventional company, because conventional companies engender higher risk for the shareholders—risks of debilitating lawsuits over the environment, risks of executives cooking the books to make themselves wealthy, risks of being caught short when supplies of raw materials dwindle and the prices of raw materials rise.

"We recently got an inquiry from a very large European company whom we had never contacted. They singled us out to be a supplier because they found out about our stance on sustainability. We figure that customers who embrace sustainability are better customers; they'll stay in business longer, be more ethical, and be better business partners than customers who only talk about price and who will drop you for a nickel on a $1,000 part.

"That's the 30,000-foot view of what sustainability is, why we're implementing it as rapidly as we can, and why we're telling every company who will listen what it is all about. We ask you to do the same. This is not just about making money; this is about life. Now, since I only joined the company a few weeks after its commitment to sustainability, I brought along Adam to help answer questions, because he started it at Brookings. Do you have any questions?"

Herbert Walker, the CEO, asked, "I know this sounds completely cold and crass, and I don't mean it that way at all, but we have to justify investments to headquarters back in New York. How can I justify the investment?"

Melanie nodded to me, so I answered, "There isn't much investment required to start. Our largest single expenditure to begin with was bringing in two consultants for one weekend to facilitate our strategic planning off-site for my staff and other key people throughout the company. Thereafter, most decisions we've made have had sound economic justification."

"Which ones haven't had sound economic justification? Would you mind telling us about them?" he asked.

"The major one, and there has been only one of these, was when two of our leaders from our shop told me they had discovered that one of the chemicals we were using was very dangerous, potentially endangering the health of our workers and of their future children. Their team researched alternative processes and made a recommendation. They knew how tight cash was, and still they had the courage to ask for what was right. We had one of our senior engineers double-check their work—they were spot on. Our CFO spoke passionately in favor of making the change. His only request was that he needed one week to figure out how to make the money work. We did it because it was the right thing to do; if we had turned them down, all of us would have suffered.

"The other ones that come to mind are the classes for our employees and the community. For some of our workers, English is not their primary language. So we have brought in instructors to help them improve their English skills. They asked if they could bring family members as well, and we agreed. Our out-of-pocket cost is relatively small—it's for the books, plus the lights for the room. We found a grant to pay for the instructor. The classes are after hours and purely voluntary. They asked for a class on personal finances, so we have started that too, open to employees and their families. That instructor is our banker—he volunteered as a way to help the community. Both classes have been highly successful and have created loyalty and goodwill beyond measure."

"How have your suppliers reacted?" asked one of the executives.

I explained, "About two thirds of them are interested or very interested. We told them up front we needed price concessions equivalent to the ones we gave you—10% now, and 10% in a year. Perhaps that dampened their ardor a bit. But we needed those to be able to compete successfully against our competitors who are selling product manufactured offshore. And we're convinced that any supplier who implements sustainability reasonably well will do better than those numbers anyway."

"How do you know that it's working?" someone else asked.

"I can tell you, but I'd rather show you," I said. "Come visit our plant. We'll let you see the entire facility if you wish; you can speak with anybody you want, and ask any question you want. You'll very quickly see that the real success is in the enthusiasm and motivation of our workforce. I have no idea how that will manifest itself in the next five to ten years; all I can say is that we have unleashed the genie, and we don't want to put it back in the bottle. We, and our entire workforce, are having way too much fun!"

"You mentioned a consultant. Would you recommend them to a friend?" asked Herbert.

"Absolutely! I don't think we would have succeeded without Dennis and Karen," I replied. "Dennis is a former CEO; Karen also has years of corporate experience. They guided us through the initial visioning sessions, and then Dennis answered my questions weekly by phone during the first two months. The most difficult part of sustainability is the culture change—changing from single bottom line to triple bottom line, and empowering people at all levels to start making decisions that way. It is truly a revolution inside the factory walls. I wouldn't want to start that journey without an experienced guide, one who has your best interests at heart.

"Let me share this story. Tom, my CFO, was extremely skeptical when I first organized the off-site and said I was bringing Dennis and Karen in. Our financial situation at that time was so grim that he didn't relax until I said I'd pay for them out of my own pocket. At the end of the off-site, he stated publicly that he was proud to present the check to them, drawn on company funds, because they had delivered value far in excess of that check. You can call him and talk with him if you wish."

"If we want to do this, what do we tell our people?" Herbert asked.

"I would suggest holding a strategic planning meeting off-site as a good start before you tell your people much of anything. One difference, however, and this was one of Dennis' many excellent ideas. Don't just invite the executive staff to the off-site; involve key people from each department as well. We have eight people on my staff, including me. We had 18 at the off-site, which included our major shareholder, our banker, the shop steward, a person from quality, two people from the shop floor . . . you get the idea. It was a much more powerful planning session, and the primary deliverable at the end was that we knew where we were going and why. We had complete buy-in at all levels and a compelling vision to tell our people. I'll share something else, too. Because of the price differential between us and our competitors, we were slowly losing ground, so our workforce knew we were in trouble. They were suspicious of anything that might smell like a layoff, so we had that obstacle to overcome. In fact, Chet, our shop steward, was somewhat hostile the Friday night of our off-site. But when we cleared the air, he became one of our strongest supporters."

Herbert spoke again, "Melanie and Adam, I want to thank you for coming today. You have made a major difference here; I'll want to talk with people after you leave, but I think you've succeeded in having us examine our basic decision-making values. Two questions: 1) Would you be willing to supply additional products for us, and 2) Would you be willing to make the same presentation to the executive staff of our corporate parent in New York? We'd be honored to pay your expenses."

I nodded to Melanie, who replied, "We would be delighted to supply additional products, and we would likewise be honored to make the same presentation in New York. I only hope I don't lose my composure like I did here; this was the first time I presented that slide in public, and it got to me."

Herbert responded, "It got to us, too. It's okay to be human, even in a boardroom. We sometimes forget that and need to be reminded of it. So please don't hide it; you wouldn't be as powerful or authentic if you did. One final question: would you give me the contact information for your consultant?"

I replied, "Yes," pulled out my PDA, and wrote Dennis' information down for Herbert.

And with that, Herbert stood and the meeting was over. Once we got outside, I turned to Melanie, "Melanie, you were fantastic! Thank you, and thanks for allowing your humanity to show. That really got to me, too, you know, now that Kelly and I are engaged. I'm starting to think about being a father, and that slide rips me up inside."

Melanie and I went to Quark that afternoon for a similar presentation. Kelly was with us as we arrived at the Quark plant. When Kent learned that Kelly was now working for us, he insisted that we invite her in to the meeting as well. Melanie was just as powerful in her presentation that afternoon. She was becoming more important to our company every week; she was extremely effective at bonding with customers.

Then Kelly and I spent a wonderful weekend, far too short, in the city by the bay. We rode cable cars, went to Ghirardelli Square and Fisherman's Wharf, browsed through the shops, and just enjoyed each other's company.

The Thursday after we got home from California, Kelly and I took the short hop to Chicago with Walter to catch the United/Lufthansa non-stop to Frankfurt, then the connecting flight to our new customer. We decided to use the weekend to see some sights and get through our jet lag so we would be fresh and ready for the business meeting on Monday. So Kelly and I explored just a bit of Europe—the old castles, the sidewalk cafés, and the wine with each meal.

Our meeting with EU Electroniks, a German company, was a real eye-opener. I sort of knew that Europe was ahead of us on environmental issues, but I didn't realize just how far! For example, their Green Dot logo on a package means *everything* inside that package is *fully* recyclable. If it's on a skid, the skid itself is recyclable! Their precautionary principle, simply stated, is that "in cases of serious or irreversible threats to the health of humans or ecosystems, acknowledged scientific uncertainty should not be used as reason to postpone preventive measures."* When applied to chemicals, the position is that unless a chemical is proven to be benign, it is assumed to be dangerous. And only benign chemicals are allowed to be used in a wide variety of applications.

The U.S. grandfathered in tens of thousands of chemicals with our TOSCA legislation in 1979, most of which have still never been fully tested to determine their long-term effects on humans and the environment. Because of Europe's precautionary principle, cosmetics manufactured there are much safer than those made in the U.S. If the women here ever learned what they were putting on their faces everyday, there would be a revolt in the streets.

Then there's RoHS—Restriction of the use of Hazardous Substances. It restricts the amount of lead, cadmium, mercury, hexavalent chromium, PBB, and PBDE (two types of flame retardant) and became effective July 1, 2006 in the European Union.

EU Electroniks was cordial and open, and when we finished negotiating we had a signed contract for development and manufacture of a brand new product, one that would challenge our engineering staff. We really did need to hire some more engineers, and we needed them now! We gasped as we recognized the extent of their requirements; they would be by far our most demanding customer, because we had to fully meet all EU standards. Hey, that's one way to become the leader—meet the toughest standard worldwide. Now we

---

* Martuzzi, Marco and Joel Tickner. 2004. Fourth Ministerial Conference on Environment and Health. Budapest, Hungary, 2004. http://www.euro.who.int/document/EEHC/ebakdoc09.pdf, p. 7.

can start pushing for legislation in the U.S. to match European standards, and watch our competitors squirm.

A week later, Nancy's first-ever supplier sustainability day was a huge success. We didn't have two suppliers—we had ten! Our teams were proud as they acted as tour guides and answered questions about their accomplishments. Given the rave reviews from the suppliers on their rating sheets, this event will become a permanent fixture, at least for the foreseeable future. Several suppliers indicated they wanted to have some time to tell what was happening on their journey toward sustainability too. We might truly have unleashed a whirlwind! But I think that can only be a good thing. And while they were touring our plant and meeting our people, they started conversations. Several e-mails and phone calls later, those conversations resulted in some of our people, from engineering, quality, the shop, and materials management, visiting those suppliers.

In 26 weeks, we have gone from a company that had no future, to one that is vibrant, and filled with hope and creativity. We have gone from employee distrust to trust, so much that the shop steward saved me and my fiancée from physical harm by putting himself in harm's way. We are now attracting and retaining the best and brightest people. We are helping our community, and there are opportunities to do even more. And we are just starting!

Two weeks after the supplier sustainability day, SVE called and asked to visit our facility, which we were delighted to arrange. This was followed by invitations to BayTech and CME. We had these customers visit on different days, however, since they were essentially competitors. Thus we started the tradition of Fridays as "tour" day. I've moved my "Boss Buys Lunch" day to Monday. As customers toured our plant, they suggested that some of our people visit them. So they did, strengthening the bonds between our customers and us.

Our sustainability efforts just keep going. We are thoroughly committed to eliminating all toxic chemicals from our facility and processes, and encourage our suppliers to do the same. Our energy and water used per unit manufactured continue to decline.[†] We are starting to think about investments with a longer-term payoff, such as solar power and a living roof for our plant. While in Europe, we learned that Germany, of all places, had the highest percentage of solar power of any nation. This in spite of the fact that they are farther north than most of the U.S., and have the same amount of sunshine as Portland, Oregon, even in the winter!

The wedding was a wonderful event. And two years later, our first child, Christina, was born. As Kelly and I stood beside the crib and admired her, I realized that she was truly what sustainability was all about.

* * * * *

"Never doubt that a small group of thoughtful, committed citizens can change the world. Indeed, it is the only thing that ever has."—Margaret Mead

Good luck on your journey. I hope this book helps you. Your comments are welcome. Please feel free to contact me at glangenwalter@confluencepoint.com.

[†] For an example of improvements in energy and water use by a manufacturer, go to the Interface Sustainability web site: http://www.interfacesustainability.com/.

Sustainability Metrics*

The following outline is intended to be used as a springboard for a company's discussion on sustainability metrics. Each organization should develop metrics that are most meaningful for its unique situation.

I. Sustainable leadership, vision, and strategy

    A. Is there a written statement of sustainable vision and strategy? Y/N

    B. Is the sustainability vision incorporated into the overall organizational vision, business plan, and critical success factors? Y/N

    C. Is the sustainability statement available to the public? Y/N

II. Governance structure and management systems

    A. Is the strategic plan for the sustainability initiative in place? Y/N

    B. Do you have a sustainability position at the executive level, full time? Y/N

---

* Sustainability Metrics © ConfluencePoint. Used with permission.

C. Do performance reviews incorporate sustainability indicators? Y/N

D. Are there rewards for sustainability improvements and innovations? Y/N

E. Is there a structure throughout the organization to execute and maintain sustainability? Y/N

F. What is the percentage of locations that have an EMS (Environmental Management System) in place, such as ISO 14001?

G. What is the amount of sustainability expenditure as a percentage of the total budget?

H. Are there effective sustainability communications (web site, newsletter)? Y/N

III. Economic performance indicators—most companies have already defined their economic metrics and performance indicators, which usually include:

A. Earnings or operating profit, as a percentage of revenue

B. Net sales

C. RONA (return on net assets)

IV. Environmental performance indicators

A. Are materials and resources catalogued? Y/N

B. What is the ratio of total finished product (excluding packaging) shipped to total input materials?

C. What is the percentage of input material that is virgin material?

D. What is the percentage of the solid waste stream NOT going to landfill, by volume?

E. Energy use

   a. What is the total energy used?

   b. What is the renewable percentage of the total energy used?

    c. What is the energy used/output, or BTUs per unit of finished product shipped?

    d. What is the indirect energy use, e.g. employee commuting?

F. What percentage of raw materials is environmentally benign?

G. What percentage of finished goods is environmentally neutral, as used by the customer?

H. Water use

    a. What is the total metered water input/used?

    b. What is the total metered water input/used per unit of finished product shipped?

    c. What is the total recycling and reuse of water, as a percentage of that used?

I. Biodiversity

    a. As a percentage of total land owned, how much land is in green and biodiversity-rich habitats?

J. Uses, emissions, effluents, and waste

    a. What is the total quantity and volume of toxic substances used?

    b. Were there any significant spills of toxic substances in the last five years?

    c. What is the yearly volume of greenhouse gases being emitted to the atmosphere?

    d. What action has the company taken to offset emissions?

    e. What is the yearly volume of ozone-depleting substances (e.g. CFCs) emitted in pounds?

    f. What is the yearly volume of NOx, SOx and other significant emissions?

    g. What is the yearly total amount of waste committed to landfills?

    h. Were there any significant discharges of waste to the ground water?

K. Environmental impacts of products and services

    a. What is the percentage of product reclaimed at the end of its useful life?

L. Environmental compliance

    a. What is the number of adverse findings by environmental agencies?

    b. Is your company an environmental "poster child"? How many company tours are requested by environmental agencies per year?

V. Social equity performance indicators

A. Fiscal responsibility

    a. What percentage of the company's pension liability is funded?

    b. What is the ratio of the highest-paid employee's salary to the lowest-paid employee's salary?

    c. What is the percentage of the workforce earning a living wage in the community?

    d. What percentage of the workforce and their families are covered by a health plan?

B. Investment in people

    a. What is the dollar value of training per employee /year?

    b. What is the percentage of employees who have an individually designed growth plan?

    c. What is the annual employee turnover, as a percentage?

    d. What is the percentage of leadership positions filled from within?

    e. Does the company offer internship programs?

C. Workplace leadership

   a. Is there a climate of mutual trust and respect?

   b. Is there integrity throughout the organization?

   c. What is the percentage of time that middle- and top-level leaders spend developing their staff and others?

D. Employee creativity and continuous improvement

   a. What is the number of suggestions implemented per employee/year?

   b. Is knowledge sharing encouraged?

   c. Is the company ranked in the "Top 100 Employers to Work For" lists?

   d. Diversity: does the company reflect community demographics?

   e. What is the percentage of management meetings that start with a moment of silence?

E. Workplace safety

   a. What is the number of deaths due to on-the-job accidents?

   b. How much time is missed from work due to occupational accidents, injuries, and illnesses, per person, per year?

F. Product responsibility

   a. How many product recalls have there been in the last five years?

   b. Do products and services help society?

   c. Are your products and services truly sustainable?

G. Community relationships

   a. Has sustainability information been made available to the community?

   b. How many hours per employee are donated for community service?

      c. What is the amount donated to charities, as a percentage of gross revenue?

      d. What are you doing to improve the lives of people who live in your communities?

VI. Customer relationships

    A. Are the relationships based on mutual respect and trust?

    B. Have you helped your customers understand and implement sustainability?

VII. Supplier relationships

    A. Are the relationships based on mutual respect and trust?

    B. Have you helped your customers understand and implement sustainability?